VANGUARDS OF FAITH

VANGUARDS
OF
FAITH

Adrianne Asheburton

CFI Book Division
Gordonsville, Tennessee

Published by CFI Book Division
P.O. Box 159, Gordonsville, Tennessee 38563

ISBN: 979-8-9868765-9-7 Large Print Edition
ISBN: 978-1-7344387-8-9 Standard Print Edition

Typeset in 14/16.8 Minion Pro

Dedicated to Alexander de Neufville Snyman who was a theologian, excellent Bible teacher and my friend. He mentored and taught me about God's gift of righteousness through the faith of Jesus Christ, our Creator, Redeemer, Sustainer and giver of eternal life.

(1 Peter 1:18-21; Colossians 1:14-17;
Romans 5:6, 8, 18; etc.)

… And in this word "faith" I mean not a mere theoretical notion, but "faith" in its only true meaning of the *will submitted* to Him, the *heart yielded* to Him, and the *affections fixed* upon Him. This only is faith; and this itself by the grace and gift of God. And this faith, of the will submitted to God *through* Christ, of the heart yielded to God *in* Christ, and the affections fixed upon God *by* Christ—this is the faith of angels as truly as of men.

A.T. Jones

Table of Contents

1

Adam, Where Are You?

Let your imagination grasp what it would have been like, lying in your earth womb, feeling the warmth of the soft loamy soil beneath your back. After your lungs expanded to full capacity with the breath of life, your first experience as your eyes fluttered open was looking up into the loving face of your Creator. He might have said, "Hello, Adam. Welcome to My world; I created it, especially for you."

Looking around, you beheld a beautiful garden, lush with all manner of vegetation, with colorful flowers permeating the air with their sweet fragrance. A bright flash caught your attention as brilliantly plumed birds flitted through the bushes near you.

Sitting up as you heard a rustle in the vegetation, there came into your line of vision all types of different creatures. As these beasts, large and small and all different shapes paraded past, your Creator invited you to give each one a name. When you had finished naming them, you realized that the animals had been in pairs, male and female, but there was no other creature like you. A sense of loneliness filled your heart with yearning.

Lovingly, the Creator laid you down again in a deep, unconscious sleep, and while in that condition, He removed from you a rib and with it, fashioned a companion for you, bone of your bone and flesh of your flesh. From you came the first woman who would be the mother of all human beings.

You and your wife were created to know only a life filled with the joy of devoted companionship and other-centered love. Being of "one mind" and in perfect harmony with your Creator, your life as husband and wife would be contented and at peace. From you and the woman as "one flesh" would spring sons and daughters who would populate the entire Earth. Such was the Creator's intention for His human family that was created in His image.

How Sin Entered Our World

The Creator blessed Adam and Eve with the task of tending their Garden home. "And the LORD God took the man, and put him into the Garden of Eden to dress it and to keep it" (Genesis 2:15). As they worked, placing each stem and branch just so, lifting each blossom to inhale its sweet fragrance, they marveled at the glory and power of their Creator. The Creator's character was exhibited in every detail of the various shapes, sizes, and colors of the wide variety of animals and plants. The harmony and peace of nature spoke to them of the Creator's love for all His creation.

Everything their senses could perceive was created to make their existence delightful. Birds flitted and sang above them as Adam and Eve went quietly about their work. Nearby, animals of all sorts were attending to their own affairs, munching grass, building their nests, or basking in the sunshine. Occasionally, the man or his wife would speak to an animal that approached them. There was no fear in the Garden. No animal had any reason to fear the presence of man. All creatures existed in a harmonious and congenial environment. From the hand of God, everything He created was magnificently perfect, and He pronounced it "very good."

One day as Eve worked contentedly among the flowers, she noticed that she had wandered some distance from her husband. Looking up, she realized that she had arrived at the center of the Garden, at the tree God claimed as exclusively His own. God specifically instructed Adam that "of every tree in the garden [they] may freely eat," except this one tree.

There was nothing remarkably different about this tree except that God informed our first parents that there was some sort of danger in it and they should avoid it altogether. It was here only God permitted Satan to have his chance for testing Adam. Satan did not have unlimited access to innocent Adam and his wife. To protect Adam and Eve, God restricted Satan to this one forbidden tree.

God gave Adam and his wife an unambiguous command that they were not to eat the fruit found on it. The restriction imposed upon our first parents was not arbitrary or spiteful, but protective. A dire consequence awaited them if they chose not to believe what the Creator instructed them about this particular tree. The tree was not fenced off, no barricade stood between them and the restricted tree, no briars or thorns hindered touching it. But they were given a clear and specific warning. "Of the tree of knowledge of good and evil, thou shalt not eat of it: for in the day that thou eatest thereof thou shalt surely die" (Genesis 2:17). They had free choice whether to believe or reject the warning.

As she turned away to rejoin her husband, Eve heard a voice speaking to her from the forbidden tree. Looking up, she did not at first notice anyone who could have called out to her. So far as she knew, she and her husband were the only two persons in the Garden. Yes, shining angel visitors had talked with them about the goodness and love of their Creator, and every day their divine Maker came in the cool of the evening to hold delightful conversation with them. But Eve had never seen any other person, so who was speaking to her now?

Then she noticed a beautiful serpent gliding along a lower branch of the tree, slowly advancing toward her. From this snake, Eve heard a voice that made an astonishing statement. "Yea, has God said, 'Ye shall not eat of every tree in the garden'?" (Genesis 3:1). In his question, Satan attacked the integrity of God's word. In doing so, he undermined the veracity of the One who spoke those words. Satan's intention was to make God appear to be a liar and cause Eve to doubt.

Startled, Eve stepped back. What an extraordinary thing. Though she and Adam often spoke cheerily to the animals they encountered in the Garden, she had never heard an animal utter anything that sounded like her own language!

Recovering her composure, but without considering the danger of conversing with this creature, she answered, "We may eat of the fruit of the trees in the garden, but of the fruit of the tree which is in the midst of the garden, God has said, 'Ye shall not eat of it'" (Genesis 3:2, 3). A true statement, and if Eve had stopped there and retreated to safety she would have escaped all the trouble that soon came upon them. Eve knew the fruit on this tree was not hers; she could not eat it.

But Eve made a grave mistake, not just by continuing the conversation with this strange and bewitching snake that somehow had developed the power of speech, but she also decided to augment the word of God. "Neither shall ye touch it," she added, words God never spoke to her or Adam. Though it might have been a logical conclusion, her addition to God's word opened the door for Satan to infect her mind with doubt about God and His character. Once you find a person to be a liar, you doubt that you can ever trust the person again.

All the trouble the world has experienced began with this small addition to God's simple warning about sin. Taking advantage of Eve's willingness to converse with him, and her inaccuracy in quoting God's word, Satan boldly presented his challenge in the most beguiling manner. No hint of evil, malice, or trouble could be detected in Satan's smooth words surreptitiously uttered through the beautiful serpent in the tree. Hidden out of view and using the serpent as his spirit medium, Satan murmured soothingly, "Ye shall not surely die." Don't worry about what God told you. He didn't mean it *literally*.

Satan hurried on before Eve could respond to this bold-faced contradiction of God's word—the first lie ever spoken on this planet. "For God knows that when you eat of this tree, then your eyes will be opened and you will know all things, just as God knows all things, both good and evil." He exclaimed, "You will be like God!" (Genesis 3:4, 5). The lie appeared to be a forthright statement of a couple of simple facts previously unknown to Eve.

Satan tempted Eve with an especially appealing idea—eat the fruit and you *can be just like God!* What a wonderful prospect. Being like her Creator was surely something to be desired. God was kind, gentle, and loving. Who would not want to be like Him?

However, the evil innuendo was double-faced. The implied question, *Don't you want to be like God?* insinuated the more sinister idea that God was withholding His best from Eve and her husband. Satan's implication was that Eve was somehow *less than perfect*. But Adam and Eve had been created in the image of God, perfect in every way. Their physical, mental, and moral characters were aligned with the mind of God.

Satan then presented the devious idea that God had a dark side and was withholding His most desirable characteristic from His creatures by forbidding this one tree where they could obtain godhood by knowing both good *and evil*.

Deceived by the lie, Eve made a more detailed examination of the tree branching out above her. It was tall and beautiful and not very different from many others in the Garden from which she was permitted to "freely" eat. The serpent curling in its branches was not harmed by being in the tree. Contrary to her presumptuous addition to God's word, touching the tree did not seem to be a problem, at least not for the snake. Here Satan's deception was reinforced by her own misinterpretation of God's word.

Yes, Eve thought, "it was good for food and pleasant to the eyes," no harm in it at all. Surely, since it was a tree of knowledge and obtaining that knowledge would transform the partaker of its fruit into a god, it must be "a tree to be desired to make one wise" in all things. The snake had apparently learned how to talk by eating the fruit.

Eagerly, "she took the fruit thereof, and did eat." Running back to Adam, gushing with exhilaration about her discovery, "she gave also unto her husband with her; and he did eat" (Genesis 3:6).

Immediately, their eyes were opened, not to more excellent knowledge of good, but to the existence of sin and rebellion. In that one seemingly minor act, Adam and Eve partook of the mind of Satan and broke every one of God's Ten Commandments. They coveted and then stole what was not theirs, thus dishonoring their Father. The act of rebellion was spiritual adultery. Setting aside their "first love" for their Creator, they replaced that other-centered love with selfishness. By choosing to disobey, they placed their personal opinion above God's word, thus making of themselves gods in place of their Creator. Once she accepted Satan's lie, the fruit of that tree was an idol for Eve, to be obtained without compunction because it was "pleasant to the eye." Covetousness was born in Eve's heart.

When confronted with their sin, both Adam and his wife bore false witness against each other, blaming one another for the problems that faced them—nakedness, fear, and shame. Attempting to evade all complicity for their disloyalty, when their Maker asked them to explain what had happened, they laid the cause of their rebellion at God's feet. They blasphemed His holy character by implying that *He* had caused them to sin by placing the tree in their midst and creating the snake that enticed them. Adam said, The woman that *You* gave to me is the reason I sinned. It's *Your* fault for making her and giving her to be my wife.

From that day forward, the human family would know trouble, pain and sorrow. Only in the seventh-day Sabbath would they have rest.

The Sabbath provided a refuge from the cares of the doleful existence they would spend scratching the earth and wrestling with weeds to eke out their daily food. Toil and sweat six days a week, but on the seventh day, through confident faith in His love for them, the Sabbath brought God's personal presence into their lives as they communed with Him in quiet praise for His mercy and love. If they chose to reject this weekly rest and time of special fellowship with their Creator, Adam and Eve and their children would have no rest or peace, day or night.

This is always the plight of the wicked who seek to save themselves. "And the smoke of their torment ascendeth up for ever and ever: and they have no rest day nor night, who worship the beast and his image, and whosoever receiveth the mark of his name" (Revelation 14:11).

The worst of all these violations of God's commands was the crime of murdering the Son of God. The penalty for Adam's sin was death. "In the day that thou eateth thereof, thou shalt surely die." You may reply, "But obviously, Adam and Eve did not die that day; otherwise, we would not be here." It is true enough that if Adam and Eve, as the first parents of the whole human race, had suffered the punishment of their sin that day, the human race would have ceased to exist then and there, and we would not be engaged in this discussion.

Despite the insult and heart-pain inflicted upon their Creator, as soon as Adam sinned, the Saviour came searching for him in the Garden, extending His hand of mercy toward His erring children. He came searching for His children not because He wanted to punish them but because He loved them. "Adam, where are you?" *I am your best Friend. Why are you hiding from Me?* (see Genesis 3:9).

Of a certainty, God knew where Adam and his wife were hiding; knew of their rebellion and its resultant shame and nakedness. Adam's development of a righteous character included his being confronted with his sin.[1] Adam and Eve must be allowed an opportunity to confess and repent. However, instead of confession and repentance, Adam and Eve sank deeper into sin by blaming one another and ultimately accusing God Himself for the problem. Even though filled with shame for what they did, they accepted no responsibility for their sin. Shifting the blame to someone else, they would not admit that their iniquity

---

1. By enduring the trial and overcoming the temptation to rebel against God, they would have developed righteous characters.

had created a barrier between them, and between each of them and their loving Creator.

> Behold, the LORD's hand is not shortened, that it cannot save; neither His ear heavy, that it cannot hear: but your iniquities have separated between you and your God, and your sins have hid His face from you, that He will not hear (Isaiah 59:1, 2).

> For if we sin wilfully after that we have received the knowledge of the truth, there remaineth no more sacrifice for sins, but a certain fearful looking for of judgment and fiery indignation, which shall devour the adversaries (Hebrews 10:26, 27).

Through the deception he perpetrated against Eve, Satan secured the downfall of the whole human race that was yet unborn to our first parents. But our Almighty God was not to be outdone. Speaking directly to Satan and through him to the guilty pair standing nearby, aching with shame and trembling with fright before their Creator, God succinctly stated His everlasting covenant promise to save His people from sin. "I will put enmity [intense hatred] between you and the woman, and between your seed and her Seed: and He shall crush your head, and you will bruise His heel" (Genesis 3:15).

The curse was not against that particular serpent resting in the tree but upon the "*seed* of the serpent." The phrase symbolized Satan and all who would follow him. That seed would be Eve's children who chose to conform to Satan's evil mind and submit to his rule over them. On the opposing side in the conflict were "the seed of the woman," signifying in a corporate sense those individuals who chose to develop righteous characters through the Saviour's work in their lives.

But more importantly, this promise pointed forward to a particular Seed, a preeminent Seed who is Christ Jesus, the Son of God. Christ is *the Seed*, the one descendant of Eve toward whom the promise in Genesis 3:15 pointed. The apostle Paul declared, "Now to Abraham and his seed were the promises made. He saith not, And to seeds, as of many; but as of one, And to thy Seed, which is Christ" (Galatians 3:16). The original promise to Adam and Eve was a glimpse of the everlasting covenant plan of redemption.

When Adam chose to rebel against his Maker, in mercy, the penalty sin incurred was placed upon the head of the Saviour. Four thousand years would pass before the promise given in Eden was ratified. At Calvary, Jesus confirmed the Edenic promise through His own blood shed for the guilty race.

Nonetheless, as soon as the covenant was spoken by God it contained all the creative and sustaining power of the Godhead to preserve Adam's life. The instant Adam sinned, the Saviour stepped forward and the human family was placed on a second probation.[2] This is why Adam and Eve did not die the day they ate from the forbidden tree. God already had the solution for the sin problem and it was set in motion as soon as sin entered this world. Living each day sustained by faith in God's word, Adam and Eve looked down through the ages to the coming Saviour's first advent.

From the beginning, Adam and Eve had been forewarned of the dire consequences should they choose to eat of that special tree's fruit. Their decision to disobey was an active and deliberate choice. At the tree of knowledge of good and evil, Adam and Eve could have made the choice to love their heavenly Father above all things and to reveal their love in unwavering allegiance to their Creator by refusing to heed Satan's lie about God. Had they relied steadfastly on God's word, they would have brought honor and glory to their Maker by refusing Satan's sophistries. That was God's desire for His children, but He would not force them. When He created mankind with the power of free choice, He took a great risk, but His love demanded that risk.

God has declared good news to us. "For I know the thoughts that I think toward you, says the LORD, thoughts of peace and not of evil, to give you a future and a hope" (Jeremiah 29:11). Believe the good news that your iniquities are forgiven, and your warfare against God will be ended.

---

2. Probation allows an individual to be subjected to a period of testing and trial to ascertain fitness. From the day they were created Adam and Eve were on probation to determine if they would steadfastly believe God's word. However, after they sinned, the second probation gave them the opportunity to demonstrate their appreciation of God's graciousness and mercy by living in conformity to His will.

2

How War Entered Our World

After Satan secured the fall of mankind, there ensued a conflict that has embroiled all of humanity throughout the ages and will continue until the end of time. This war started in heaven before our world was created. It is impossible to understand how the war began in heaven, in a perfect environment where prior to the war there was total peace and harmony among all of the heavenly host. God had created a flawless community of angels whose love for one another was not marred by self-serving attitudes.

The highest angel was Lucifer, the "covering cherub" (Ezekiel 28:16), whose position was at the left side of the throne of God. Ezekiel 28:14 calls Lucifer the "anointed cherub." The Hebrew word translated "anointed" is *mashah* and describes an individual or object set aside especially for God's service. It is a position of honor and represents the increased responsibility conferred upon the individual. In the hierarchy of the angelic host this meant Lucifer served in a leadership role. No one was higher than him except the Son of God and (of course) the Father Himself.

The Bible describes Lucifer as a beautiful, perfect creature. His sinless purity allowed him to walk "in the midst of the stones of fire" that surround the throne of God (Ezekiel 28:14).

Thou hast been in Eden the garden of God; every precious stone was thy covering, the sardius, topaz, and the diamond, the beryl, the onyx, and the jasper, the sapphire, the emerald, and the carbuncle, and gold: the workmanship of thy tabrets and of thy pipes was prepared in thee in the day that thou wast created. (Ezekiel 28:13)

For some inexplicable reason, one day Lucifer decided he wanted more than he had been given by his Creator. He saw Michael, the Archangel who was seated on the right side of God's throne. He too was beautiful and majestic and served God the Father as the commander of the heavenly host. Lucifer noticed that Michael not only walked among the stones of fire but also entered into the fiery light that surrounded God, while he was excluded from Their personal counsels.

Jealousy and covetousness grew in his mind as he dwelt upon what he thought was unfair treatment. He became determined to possess what Michael had.

> For thou hast said in thine heart, I will ascend into heaven, I will exalt my throne above the stars of God: I will sit also upon the mount of the congregation, in the sides of the north. I will ascend above the heights of the clouds; I will be like the most High (Isaiah 14:13, 14).

Lucifer was not interested in being "like the most High" in character. He wanted all God possessed and more. He coveted God's full authority and power over all creation. Relying on the innocence and naiveté of his angelic family Lucifer began to circulate subtle lies designed to cause doubt concerning God's character.[1] Eventually, one third of the angelic host were so deeply deceived they followed Lucifer into open rebellion.

> And there was war in heaven: Michael and his angels fought against the dragon; and the dragon fought and his angels, and prevailed not; neither was their place found any more in heaven (Revelation 12:7, 8).

Genesis 3:15 is a declaration of unrelenting war. Arrayed on one side are Christ and those who freely choose to follow the Lamb wherever He leads them.

> And I looked, and, lo, a Lamb stood on the mount Sion, and with Him an hundred forty and four thousand, having His Father's

---

1. What could God do to vindicate His character? The entire Bible from Genesis 3:15 (with the first statement of the everlasting covenant) to Revelation 22:21, teaches us how God solved the problem of Satan's malignant attack on His personal integrity as a God of love. God gave Himself as the redeeming sacrifice for sin committed as a result of believing Satan's lie (John 3:16, 17).

name written in their foreheads. … These are they which follow the Lamb whithersoever He goeth. These were redeemed from among men, being the firstfruits unto God and to the Lamb. And in their mouth was found no guile: for they are without fault before the throne of God (Revelation 14:1, 4, 5).

On the other side of the war are Satan with his evil angels and all Satan's human agents who work with intensifying wickedness and blasphemy right up to the moment when Christ returns in clouds of glory. Our Saviour warned us:—

And ye shall hear of wars and rumours of wars: see that ye be not troubled: for all these things must come to pass, but the end is not yet. For nation shall rise against nation, and kingdom against kingdom: and there shall be famines, and pestilences, and earthquakes, in divers places. All these are the beginning of sorrows (Matthew 24:6-8).

Just before Christ's return, wickedness is found even in the church. As the world careening toward its destruction increasingly follows Satan, the church readily adopts ungodly attitudes and behaviors in the mistaken belief that compromise will yield greater acceptance of the church's tenets. We are to stay away from this dangerous situation.

This know also, that in the last days perilous times shall come. For men shall be lovers of their own selves, covetous, boasters, proud, blasphemers, disobedient to parents, unthankful, unholy, without natural affection, trucebreakers, false accusers, incontinent, fierce, despisers of those that are good, traitors, heady, highminded, lovers of pleasures more than lovers of God; having a form of godliness, but denying the power thereof: from such turn away (2 Timothy 3:1-5).

The war will reach its culmination when "that Wicked [shall] be revealed, whom the Lord shall consume with the spirit of His mouth, and shall destroy with the brightness of His coming" (2 Thessalonians 2:8). The entire world will witness the exposure of the impenitent apostate church under the control of the Deceiver.

And men were scorched with great heat, and blasphemed the name of God, which hath power over these plagues: and they repented not to give Him glory. And the fifth angel poured out his vial upon the seat of the beast; and his kingdom was full of darkness; and they gnawed their tongues for pain, and blasphemed the God of heaven because of their pains and their sores, and repented not of their deeds (Revelation 16:9-11).

The war blazes through each of us whenever we allow Satan to deceive us into thinking sin has no consequence. We continue the war when we believe the lie promoted by Satan that God is a selfish, vicious ogre who wants to torture us forever in a never-ending fire. We bring disgrace and great pain to our heavenly Father when we repeatedly sin, trampling upon the crucified Son of God who stands between us and that awful gaping chasm of eternal destruction that sin caused.

God has promised "liberty to the captives, and the opening of the prison to them that are bound" in Satan's chains of darkness.

The Spirit of the Lord GOD is upon Me [Jesus Christ]; because the LORD hath anointed Me to preach good tidings unto the meek; He hath sent Me to bind up the brokenhearted, to proclaim liberty to the captives, and the opening of the prison to them that are bound (Isaiah 61:1; cf. Luke 4:16-21).

God has declared good news to us.

For I know the thoughts that I think toward you, says the LORD, thoughts of peace and not of evil, to give you a future and a hope (Jeremiah 29:11). Believe the good news that your iniquities are already forgiven, and your warfare against God will be ended.

3

Sin's Remedy

The law of God demands the death of the transgressor; there is no other way. Sin means death to the perpetrator because sin has death wrapped up in it. "By one man sin entered into the world and death by sin" (Romans 5:12). "The sting of death is sin and the strength of sin is the law" (1 Corinthians 15:56). The Law of God is eternal, unchangeable, uncompromising, holy, just and good (Romans 7:12). Through the Law comes knowledge of what sin is. Therefore, it is not an enemy ("against us"); it is our "schoolmaster" to educate us about our need of a Saviour. But the Law cannot save us.

> So then, no human being can be found upright at the tribunal of God by keeping the Law; all that the Law does is to tell us what is sinful (Roman 3:20, NJB).

> What should we say, then? That the Law itself is sin? Out of the question! All the same, if it had not been for the Law, I should not have known what sin was; for instance, I should not have known what it meant to covet if the Law had not said: "You are not to covet" (Romans 7:7, NJB; cf. Exodus 20:17).

Death never would have come into this world if sin had not first been conceived in the heart of mankind, implanted there through Satan's evil insinuations against the character of God. Eve was infected with "the lust of the eyes" (1 John 2:16) as she indulged her curiosity and gazed upon the forbidden tree's fruit. "After desire [lust] has conceived, it gives birth to sin, and when sin is fully grown, it gives birth to death" (James 1:15, HCSB).

The broken law of God is immortal, insusceptible, and cannot extend forgiveness to the transgressor, "for the wages of sin is death" (Romans 6:23). "Every man shall be put to death for his own sin" (Deuteronomy 24:16). "The person who sins is the one who will die" (Ezekiel 18:20, HCSB). The Law stands impassive, immutable, and solid as granite, a silent witness to the pure, holy, and unchangeable character of its Source.

Why did God not carry out the death sentence when Adam sinned? Why did Adam not die that afternoon in Eden, as God said he would? Was the serpent, that old "dragon, which is the Devil" (Revelation 12:9), correct in what he told Eve?—"thou shalt *not surely die*." Was God's sentence of death a toothless scare tactic intended to coerce fearful obedience from His creatures?

The answer is profound and will be the study of the redeemed for all eternity. Christ, the Son of God, stood between the broken Law and the condemned sinner, taking the full penalty upon Himself. In that one act, the divine character of love (*agapé*) is revealed—God was willing to lay down His own life so the creatures He loved beyond measure could have a second chance. The purity and depth of His love is unfathomable by the human mind.

> For the love of Christ constraineth us; because we thus judge, that if one died for all, then were all dead: and that He died for all, that they which live should not henceforth live unto themselves, but unto Him which died for them, and rose again. ... And all things are of God, who hath reconciled us to Himself by Jesus Christ ... to wit, that God was in Christ, reconciling the world unto Himself, not imputing their trespasses unto them; and hath committed unto us the word of reconciliation. (2 Corinthians 5:14, 15, 18, 19).

Note the apostle Paul's repeated emphasis on the love of God for lost humanity. *One* died for all, not "some" predetermined "elect," but *all*. The Godhead gave themselves to reconcile the *world* and bring us back into the fold. God does not impute our sins to us because He placed all the sins of the world upon the Saviour (see Isaiah 53:4-6; John 1:29).

> For I am persuaded, that neither death, nor life, nor angels, nor principalities, nor powers, nor things present, nor things

to come, nor height, nor depth, nor any other creature, shall be able to separate us from the love of God, which is in Christ Jesus our Lord (Romans 8:38, 39).

Never assume that those events in the Garden of Eden surprised God. Nothing "surprises" the omniscient God who upholds the universe with the power of His word. He knows all things, even "declaring the end from the beginning" (Isaiah 46:10). When God created our world, everything in it was perfect and "very good."

Mankind was created in God's image to reflect our Maker's moral character. Included in that gift was the awesome power of freedom of choice. God did not create automatons who had no ability to reason logically from cause to effect. We are free moral agents with the right to choose to obey or rebel. Even though God knew the outcome of giving such freedom to Adam, He did not dictate his choice or demand specific action from him.

God was not caught by surprise when Adam sinned, so that He then had to devise an alternate plan for His creation's safety. No, God was prepared for the contingency of Adam's wrong decision. In keeping with the divine character of love, from before the foundation of the world, the Godhead covenanted together to redeem mankind if Adam should fall. Should Adam fail his test of allegiance, Christ was ready to step between His beloved child and the execution of the death penalty. *Before* there was sin, there was a Saviour. Before the defection of Adam occurred, the Son of God volunteered to surrender His precious life to save the human race from the penalty of sin, which is death and eternal destruction.

Christ is "the Lamb of God that takes away the sin of the *world*" (John 1:29). He is further described by the apostle John as "slain from the foundation of the world" (Revelation 13:8). The apostles Paul and Peter declared the same truth: Salvation was God's plan before there was sin in this world. As soon as Adam sinned, the plan of salvation went into operation and in Christ the whole human race was legally justified before the broken Law (emphases supplied in the following references).

Forasmuch as ye know that ye were not redeemed with corruptible things, as silver and gold, from your vain conversation received by tradition from your fathers; but with the precious blood of

Christ, as of a lamb without blemish and without spot: Who verily was *foreordained before the foundation of the world*, but was manifest in these last times for you (1 Peter 1:18-20).

For we which have believed do enter into rest, as He said, As I have sworn in My wrath, if they shall enter into My rest: although the works *were finished from the foundation of the world.* (Hebrews 4:3).

[God] Who hath saved us, and called us with an holy calling, not according to our works, but according to His own purpose and grace, which was given us in Christ Jesus *before the world began* (2 Timothy 1:9).

With the promise of His sacrifice, Christ effectually mitigated the death penalty for Adam and his posterity, placing the human race on a second probation.[1] Christ was ready when sin entered the world, with just as much power to save as when He died on Calvary's cross. And because of God's great love for mankind, the moment Adam sinned, his next breath and heartbeat were by the grace of God. His probation was renewed, mercifully allowing Adam another chance to prove his loyalty to his Creator and Redeemer.

The day Adam sinned, when Christ spoke the words of the everlasting covenant in the Garden, He knew that during His incarnation, Satan would "bruise His heel" by tempting and harassing Him throughout His thirty-three years on earth. How glad Satan was to learn his adversary was going to enter the earthly battleground in the same flesh and blood as every other human he would tempt into sin.

In His omniscience, Christ looked down through the ages and knew that four millennia after Adam's fall and rescue from the death penalty, Satan would inflict upon Him the torture, pain, and disgrace of death on a Roman cross. But by demonstrating on Calvary's hill His character of self-sacrificing love, Christ would "crush [Satan's] head."

The cross proved that Satan's ultimate desire was to kill God and steal His throne. "How art thou fallen from heaven, O Lucifer [Satan], son of the morning! … For thou hast said in thine heart, I will ascend

---

1. The first probation was the test of the tree in the center of the Garden. Adam and Eve were given the opportunity to exercise their free will at that tree. A faithful decision would have one outcome; a rebellious response quite another.

into heaven, I will exalt my throne above the stars of God ... I will be like the Most High (Isaiah 14:12-14). Satan's own desire was declared when he tempted Eve—"you will be like God!"

When Adam rebelled, he stood guilty and condemned before the violated Law, and legally, only he could pay the debt for his sin. There is no such thing as "vicarious" atonement. Vicarious means experienced in an imaginative way, as the work of a play actor. Christ's experience was not imaginative, but real. As the "Last Adam" (1 Corinthians 15:45), Christ took upon Himself real fallen flesh and blood and in that flesh, died as the human race, lost in sin—*not instead of us* but *as* us (2 Corinthians 5:14; 1 Peter 2:24; Romans 5:18). It is illegal and immoral for an innocent person to suffer the penalty instead of the guilty party. Therefore, Jesus assumed our guilt and died as us. Since legally only the guilty could pay for his crime, Adam would have died that afternoon in the Garden of Eden if a powerful and qualified Saviour had not been ready at hand.

The instant Adam yielded to the temptation of Satan, the Son of God presented Himself as the Surety for the entire human race. If not for the fact that Jesus is "the Lamb slain from the foundation of the world" (Revelation 13:8; cf. 1 Peter 1:18-20; 2 Timothy 1:8, 9; Hebrews 4:3), Adam would have ceased to exist that very afternoon, and "in Adam" the human race, yet unborn, would have died also.

But as soon as Adam sinned, the Son of God stepped forward in agreement with the Godhead's everlasting covenant promise and said: "My blood Father; My blood instead of Adam's. As We covenanted among Ourselves, We will give the human race another chance."

> For when God made promise to Abraham, because He could swear by no greater, He sware by Himself, saying, Surely blessing I will bless thee, and multiplying I will multiply thee. ... Wherein God, willing more abundantly to shew unto the heirs of promise the immutability of His counsel, confirmed it by an oath: that by two immutable things, in which it was impossible for God to lie, we might have a strong consolation, who have fled for refuge to lay hold upon the hope set before us" (Hebrews 6:13-18).[2]

2. The "two immutable things" are His promise that He would "save His people from sin," first given to Adam in Genesis 3:15, and His oath, confirmed through the demonstrated covenant shown to Abraham in Genesis 15:17. The "smoking furnace and burning lamp" were God the Father and His Son.

What astounding love is expressed in that one self-sacrificing act of mercy! Adam drew his next breath and felt his next heartbeat by the grace of God. All praise and glory be to God! As soon as there was sin, there was a Saviour *from* sin. Jesus is "Emanuel, God with us," for "He shall save His people *from* their sins" (Matthew 1:21, 23).

Adam continued to live by grace for 930 years, during which he witnessed the dreadful consequences of his faithless behavior. Many of his sons and daughters chose to exercise their inherited fallen natures in rebellion against God, filling their hearts with evil that grew in magnitude with each new generation until the whole world was populated with people whose hearts "were only evil continually" (Genesis 6:5).

Corporate Work of Christ

The everlasting covenant embodies the truth that the promised Messiah would be "the last Adam" and would stand as the Kinsman Redeemer for the lost race. He stood in Adam's place, corporately identified with Adam's lost race, and *as* fallen mankind (not *instead of*), Christ assumed the just punishment for sin. "Thus it is written, 'The first man Adam became a living being'; the last Adam became a life-giving spirit" (1 Corinthians 15:45, ESV). In this statement, the apostle Paul referred to Genesis 2:7. "And the LORD God formed man of the dust of the ground, and breathed into his nostrils the breath of life; and man became a living soul." [3]

Though in the English translation the "life" given to Adam appears in the singular grammatical form, the original Hebrew word *chayyim* is a plural noun. When God created Adam, He was creating corporate mankind. From that first man sprang every human who has ever existed on this planet. When Adam fell, and Christ rescued him from eternal nonexistence (true "death"), He was, in effect, rescuing the entire corporate human race that was in Adam's loins.

---

3. "Soul" literally means a living human being, self, or person, and is used when referring to the life-giving gift of God's breath, as in "her soul departed"— i.e. she "ceased to breathe." Adam did not *have* or *possess* a "soul." When he was created, Adam was not infused with a self-existing thing called a "soul." The Word of God says that Adam *became* a living soul (Genesis 2:7)—a living, breathing unity of flesh formed from the dust of the earth and the breath of life given by God. Without the breath of life, mankind is just a lump of dirt, "for dust thou art and to dust thou shalt return," (Genesis 3:19). "Thou takest away their breath, they die, and return to their dust" (Psalm 104:29).

As the "last Adam," Christ took humanity's place and assumed responsibility for the sin problem that, with Adam's one sin, infected the whole human race.

> Wherefore, as by one man sin entered into the world, and death by sin; and so death passed upon all men, for that all have sinned … Therefore as by the offence of one judgment came upon all men to condemnation; even so by the righteousness of One the free gift came upon all men unto justification of life. For as by one man's disobedience many were made sinners, so by the obedience of One shall many be made righteous (Romans 5:12, 18).

Christ assumed the position of corporate man and, as the "life-giving Spirit," He took upon Himself a human body and worked out the plan of salvation in Adam's fallen nature. By living a life of faith in His heavenly Father's power over sin and death, Christ lived and died as the corporate fallen human race. Anything short of this would have been legal shenanigans and a lie. God cannot break His own Law and remain the Sovereign LORD of the universe.

The Saviour had to assume the nature of Adam that needed redeeming in order to perfect salvation for fallen mankind. Unfallen Adam did not need saving, nor was he subject to the death penalty. If Christ was incarnated in unfallen flesh, He could not have accomplished the necessary work to save the sinner, which included being "touched with the feeling of our infirmities" and "in all points tempted like as we are, yet without sin" (Hebrews 4:15). If in any manner Christ had been exempt from "touching" fallen humanity, then we would not have a "complete Saviour."

If there were any limitations separating His human nature from "ordinary" human beings, then what Christ *could not* touch through His human nature, He *could not* have redeemed.[4] Therefore, in His incarnation, Jesus was compelled by His love for those whom He intended

---

4. "For that which He has not assumed He has not healed; but that which is united to His Godhead is also saved." "Within the sphere of the fallen human nature Jesus Christ lived a perfect life. That which He assumed was healed; in this was our redemption. It was in hallowing and redeeming of fallen nature that the Son of God showed Himself to be our Saviour." Harry Johnson, *The Humanity of the Saviour* (London; Epworth Press, 1962), pp. 129, 169.

to save and by the just demands of the broken law, to take upon His sinless nature the fallen nature of mankind that needed redeeming.

Jesus' human feet descended heaven's rescue ladder coming all the way down to the ground (see Genesis 28:10-16). He touched the very place where we stand condemned by our sin.

> Let this mind be in you, which was also in Christ Jesus: who, being in the form of God, thought it not robbery to be equal with God: but made Himself of no reputation, and took upon Himself the form of a servant, and was made in the likeness of men: and being found in fashion as a man, He humbled Himself, and became obedient unto death, even the death of the cross (Philippians 2:5-8).

> Forasmuch then as the children are partakers of flesh and blood, He also Himself likewise took part of the same; that through death He might destroy him that had the power of death, that is, the devil (Hebrews 2:14).

And in that fallen flesh and through faith in His Father's power over sin, Christ lived out a perfect, sinless life, proving Satan's accusation against God—that the law cannot be kept in fallen flesh—is a baseless lie.

The faith through which Jesus accomplished His mission is the same "measure of faith" that He gives "to every man" (Romans 12:3; cf. Galatians 2:20; 5:16, 17). His gift of faith was tested and proven sufficient to withstand all the "fiery darts" the devil can throw at us. Every person may overcome sin in their present life if they will choose to exercise that gift of faith. God did not perform some legal fiction that day in the Garden of Eden.

It is patently illegal in any judicial system for a person to be executed instead of, in place of, or for someone else.[5] No one, no matter how willing, can assume the role of a vicarious substitute and suffer the murderer's punishment for breaking the law.

---

5. Civil law does not permit substitution in the death penalty. Charles Dickens in his *Tale of Two Cities* (1859) attempted to demonstrate how a man could give his life in place of another, if the man was motivated by love. But Sydney Carton's good deed of selfless love for a woman and her condemned husband was, in fact, legal shenanigans and trickery. Carton did not *become* the man he was saving, but died under false representation. However, Christ corporately took upon Himself the burden of fallen humanity as a whole, becoming as mankind, just as Adam was the whole of humanity when he was created (see Romans 5:15-19)

Therefore, when Christ stepped forward into Adam's shoes, He *became* the new head of the fallen race, *assuming* the guilt and punishment that Adam should have suffered. And the human race continued from that day to the present because of Christ's one, merciful, selfless act. At the moment Adam sinned, all the human race was dead "in Adam," but the work of our Redeemer instantly intervened and extended probation and life for Adam and his posterity. "As one man's trespass [Adam's] led to condemnation for all men [the entire human race that was "in Adam"], so one Man's act of righteousness [Christ's] leads to acquittal[6] and life for all men" (Romans 5:18, RSV).

Christ's sacrifice, *as* the corporate human race, satisfied the just demands of the broken law, and legally justified all of humanity through His "one righteous act" (Romans 5:18, 19). We are not condemned for the sin of Adam, as the doctrine of "original sin" claims. We condemn ourselves when we refuse to believe God's good news, and throw away salvation so freely given to us.

> He that believeth on Him is not condemned: but he that believeth not is condemned already, because he hath not believed in the name of the Son of God. And this is the condemnation, that light is come into the world, and men loved darkness rather than light, because their deeds were evil. (John 3:18, 19).

If Christ had not intervened the moment our first parents sinned, we would not be here now. The world would not have a human population because all would have died "in Adam" at the dawn of creation six thousand years ago. A rational, sober acknowledgment of this fact will direct how we live our individual lives day by day. Our heart-appreciation of the gift of salvation from sin provides the most powerful motivation for our full and complete surrender to God. This results in willing obedience to all of His Commandments.

> For the love of Christ compels us, because we judge thus: that if One died for all, then all died; and He died for all, that those who live should live no longer for themselves, but for Him who died for them and rose again (2 Corinthians 5:14, 15, NKJV).

---

6. Acquittal means setting free from the charge of an offense by verdict, sentence, or other legal process. It is God's act of declaring sinners free from guilt, and makes us fit to stand before Him through the work of His Son, Jesus Christ.

The afternoon when Adam sinned, he learned that his sin caused the death of the Lamb of God. He realized he was a murderer. As he witnessed the shedding of the lamb's blood, spilled because he chose to disobey a simple command, Adam was heavy with the knowledge that because of his one sin, he caused the death, not only of that innocent lamb but of the promised Messiah prefigured in the animal sacrifice.

Notwithstanding his shame and guilt, with the covenant promise of God ringing in his ears, Adam found peace in the demonstration of God's commitment to save him. In the act of slaying the innocent lamb, Adam saw Christ's day prefigured and rejoiced that there was a Saviour who has the power to save from sin, and restore loving fellowship with the Creator.

God's everlasting covenant is an all-encompassing remedy for the sin problem. No greater love has ever been exhibited in this world than the love embodied in the Godhead's promise to save us from sin. The Godhead assumed full responsibility for the eradication of sin and its effects. God the Father

> … so loved the world that He gave His only begotten Son, that whosoever believeth in Him should not perish, but have everlasting life. For God sent not His Son into the world to condemn the world; but that the world through Him might be saved (John 3:16, 17).

When considering the Godhead, we often forget the Third Person, but He is as much involved in the saving of mankind as the Father and Son. The Holy Spirit is the "eyes of the LORD" running throughout the earth, ever seeking those who have willing and open hearts. It is the Godhead's greatest desire "to seek and to save" the lost (Luke 19:10). "For the eyes of the LORD run to and fro throughout the whole earth, to shew Himself strong in the behalf of them whose heart is perfect toward Him" (2 Chronicles 16:9).

The Holy Spirit has the power to convict us of our sin, to teach us righteousness, and to warn us of coming judgment. It is the Holy Spirit who gives to all men the gift of repentance (John 16:7–13; Acts 5:31). All three divine Persons gave unstintingly of Themselves to save mankind.

Yes, "we had the sentence of death in ourselves," but God's power over sin and death has "delivered us from so great a death, and does deliver" in our daily lives when we yield ourselves to Him. Therefore, "we trust that He will yet deliver us" from the power of our fallen flesh with its temptations, propensities, and sinful inclinations. Then, when Christ comes to claim all who have chosen to believe the good news, "in the twinkling of an eye, at the last trump," we shall be set free from our fallen human flesh (2 Corinthians 1:9, 10; 1 Corinthians 15:52, 53). Very soon, Christ will destroy the very presence of sin in the universe when He returns as "King of kings, and Lord of lords" (Revelation 19:16).

> Then I saw heaven opened, and there was a white horse. Its rider is called Faithful and True,[7] and He judges and makes war in righteousness. His eyes were like a fiery flame, and many crowns were on His head.[8] He had a name written that no one knows except Himself. He wore a robe stained with blood, and His name is the "Word of God." The armies that were in heaven followed Him on white horses, wearing pure white linen. A sharp sword came from His mouth, so that He might strike the nations with it. He will shepherd them with an iron scepter. He will also trample the winepress of the fierce anger of God, the Almighty. And He has a name written on His robe and on His thigh: KING OF KINGS and LORD OF LORDS (Revelation 19:11-16, HCSB).

7. Cf. Revelation 3:14.
8. Cf. Daniel 7:13, 14; 10:5, 6.

Notes

4

God's Everlasting Covenant

When Adam sinned, God came searching for him in the Garden, not with condemnation but with the solution to Adam's dire situation. Adam made a fig leaf garment to cover the nakedness of his sin, but his man-made solution was insufficient to atone for the crime committed.

The everlasting covenant spoken in Genesis 3:15 was to Adam the first lesson of his inability to save himself from the death penalty. That his sin demanded death was unequivocally demonstrated in the death of a lamb. The lamb's skin used to remove Adam's physical nakedness symbolized Christ's white robe of righteousness. Through faith in Christ's power over sin, His spotless garment of righteousness eliminated Adam's spiritual nakedness. Now, as our High Priest performing His cleansing work in the heavenly sanctuary, Christ is enrobing all His faithful followers in His own righteousness. He will then present us "without spot or wrinkle" before His Father's throne.

> I will greatly rejoice in the LORD, my soul shall be joyful in my God; for He hath clothed me with the garments of salvation, He hath covered me with the robe of righteousness, as a bridegroom decketh himself with ornaments, and as a bride adorneth herself with her jewels (Isaiah 61:10).

> Let us be glad and rejoice, and give honour to Him: for the marriage of the Lamb is come, and His wife hath made herself ready. And to her was granted that she should be arrayed in fine linen, clean and white: for the fine linen is the righteousness of saints (Revelation 19:7, 8).

Jesus admonished us, "Buy of Me … white raiment, that thou mayest be clothed, and that the shame of thy nakedness do not appear" (Revelation 3:18). We cannot "buy" righteousness with money or "good works." We can only purchase it with what we have, a life full of sin that we can surrender at the foot of the Saviour's cross. "Ho, every one that thirsteth, come ye to the waters, and he that hath no money; come ye, buy, and eat" (Isaiah 55:1).

"The LORD God [is] merciful and gracious, longsuffering, and abundant in goodness and truth" (Exodus 34:6). In keeping with the veracity and demands of His Law, the Son of God obliged Himself to take upon Him the life that had sinned and fulfill the just requirements of the broken Law.

Nothing could save Adam from the death penalty except the precious blood of God's own dear Son. No angel or any creature could atone for the traitorous behavior of Adam. "For it is not possible that the blood of bulls and of goats should take away sins" (Hebrews 10:4).

The penalty and power of sin were broken by the faith *of* Jesus Christ—*His* faith.[1] Our Saviour and Lord assumed the penalty for sin when He stepped between the broken Law and the spiritually "dead" Adam. He destroyed the power sin has over our lives, thus freeing us to say "no" to every besetting sin.

> For the grace of God that bringeth salvation hath appeared to all men, teaching us that, denying ungodliness and worldly lusts, we should live soberly, righteously, and godly, in this present world; looking for that blessed hope, and the glorious appearing of the great God and our Saviour Jesus Christ; who gave Himself for us, that He might redeem us from all iniquity, and purify unto Himself a peculiar people, zealous of good works (Titus 2:11-14).

> Knowing that a man is not justified by the works of the law, but by the faith *of Jesus Christ* … the life which I now live in the flesh I live by the faith *of the Son of God*, who loved me, and gave Himself for me (Galatians 2:16, 20, emphasis supplied).

---

1. It is not *our* faith (or "trust") "in" Jesus, which is weak and vacillating, but Jesus' own personal faith given to us as a gift (Romans 12:3). It is the tested and proven faith *of Jesus* "which works by love" in us to accomplish God's will in our lives (Galatians 5:6).

Forasmuch as ye know that ye were not redeemed with corruptible things, as silver and gold, from your vain conversation received by tradition from your fathers; but with the precious blood of Christ, as of a lamb without blemish and without spot: Who verily was foreordained before the foundation of the world, but was manifest in these last times for you (1 Peter 1:18–20).

Through the blood of the Lamb, Who was foreordained to meet the penalty for our sin, Adam received a second probation, another chance to prove his allegiance to the one merciful and ever-loving heavenly Father.

God's everlasting covenant unfolded before mankind the plan of deliverance through Christ alone. No additions, no substitutions. Through Christ alone is salvation from sin possible and eternal life secured. The only way to regain moral perfection is through faith in the Lamb given by God Himself, prefigured in that animal slain at the gates of Eden. We can obtain eternal life only by responding to Christ's work *for* us and *in* us. When we respond appropriately to the gift of salvation (Christ's legal acquittal before the broken law secured from the foundation of the world) His righteousness works out in our life. We are transformed by the creative power of God into a "new creature: old things are passed away; behold, all things are become new" (2 Corinthians 5:17).

The everlasting covenant not only took care of the legal penalty for transgression, it also destroyed the *power* of sin that took root in the human mind when Adam chose to disbelieve God's word. The message of Christ and His righteousness remedies the entire problem.

But we had the sentence of death in ourselves, that we should not trust in ourselves, but in God which raiseth the dead: Who delivered us from so great a death, and doth deliver: in Whom we trust that He will yet deliver us (2 Corinthians 1:9, 10).

The penalty, power and eventually, the very presence of sin are dealt with in the life and death of Christ Jesus promised in the everlasting covenant, revealed from the foundation of the world. When Jesus cleanses this world in the lake of fire and creates a new home for the redeemed, then the very presence of sin will be destroyed forever:—

But the day of the Lord will come as a thief in the night; in the which the heavens shall pass away with a great noise, and the elements shall melt with fervent heat, the earth also and the works that are therein shall be burned up. Seeing then that all these things shall be dissolved, what manner of persons ought ye to be in all holy conversation and godliness, looking for and hasting unto the coming of the day of God, wherein the heavens being on fire shall be dissolved, and the elements shall melt with fervent heat? (2 Peter 3:10-12).

For, behold, the day cometh, that shall burn as an oven; and all the proud, yea, and all that do wickedly, shall be stubble: and the day that cometh shall burn them up, saith the LORD of hosts, that it shall leave them neither root nor branch. ... And ye shall tread down the wicked; for they shall be ashes under the soles of your feet in the day that I shall do this, saith the LORD of hosts (Malachi 4:1, 3).

Since Adam is our first father, we were corporately "in Adam" when he received his probation. The whole human race was, in effect, placed into the Lamb's lifeboat. Probation was extended to us corporately "in Adam." By the power of God working in us we then respond individually to that gift of life by making one of two choices: (1) We can actively throw away that gift by continuing in a life of sin and rebellion. In other words, we can jump out of the lifeboat into the sea of sin and eternal death, or (2) we can receive God's everlasting covenant promise into our hearts by appreciating what redemption cost God.

Contrary to what many people may think, salvation is not "free." No indeed! It cost the precious life of the Son of God to save you from your sin. Once a true heart appreciation of that fact becomes your motivation, overcoming all sin in your life and serving your Lord with all your heart and mind will be your highest joy. Satan can hurl his entire quiver of arrows at you, but you will be able to deflect them, saying, like Joseph, "how can I do this great wickedness and sin against my God?" (Genesis 39:9). You will be able to

... stand therefore, having girded your waist with truth, having put on the breastplate of righteousness, and having shod your feet with the preparation of the Gospel of peace; above all, taking the shield of faith [the faith *of* Jesus] with which you will be able to quench all the fiery darts of the wicked one. And take the helmet of salvation, and the sword of the Spirit, which is the word of God (Ephesians 6:14–17).

Thus yielding to the Holy Spirit's work in us, we will be re-formed through a transformation of our minds. "Let this mind be in you, which was also in Christ Jesus" (Philippians 2:5). Where the mind of Christ dwells, the mind of Satan is driven away.

Be ye transformed by the renewing of your mind, that ye may prove what is the good, and acceptable and perfect will of God (Romans 12:2).

This transforming process will realign our characters with the character of our Saviour, and we will be sanctified and separated from the wickedness of the world. We will be His chosen people, "a royal priesthood, an holy nation, a peculiar people, that [we] should show forth the praises of Him who has called us out of darkness into His marvelous light" (1 Peter 2:9).

Notes

5

Conflict Among Brothers

Genesis chapter four opens with the birth of Adam and Eve's first two sons, Cain and his brother Abel. Some Biblical scholars believe that the text indicates Cain and Abel were twins because there is no mention of a second conception for Abel. "Adam knew Eve his wife; and she conceived, and bore Cain, and she said I have gotten a man from the LORD. And she again bare his brother Abel" (Genesis 4:1, 2). Two births, but only one conception is mentioned. The description of the birth of Cain and Abel is similar to the wording of the twin birth of Esau and Jacob in Genesis 25:21, 24.

Abel was a shepherd while his brother Cain was a farmer, a "tiller of the soil." Both of these occupations are implied in the imprecation Adam received when he sinned. "In the sweat of thy face shalt thou eat bread, till thou return unto the ground" (Genesis 3:19). Adam was the first agriculturalist. Farming is a godly occupation, one that has divine commendation. The blessings God intended the human family to receive through the farming lifestyle would keep their hearts and minds ever focused toward heaven and the Creator, from whence the abundance of the earth's produce comes. Working and cooperating with nature to obtain their food would ensure that the human family remembered their total dependence upon God for all things.

Exiled from their garden home, the first couple no longer had easy access to food by merely plucking fruit from a branch or ripe grain from a seed head. With the fall of Adam, thorns and thistles became abundant and invasive, requiring vigilance in keeping them rooted up.

Thistles spread quickly by seed, the wind blowing them wherever it will. Even though cut down to the ground, bramble vines continue their menace unseen in the soil through their underground rhizome structure, ready to sprout again when conditions are favorable. In both of these plants, we have an object lesson of the insidious pervasiveness of sin. For sin to be eradicated from our lives, it must be dealt with both root and branch. The seed of enmity against God must be destroyed in our hearts.

God told Cain and Abel's father that because of sin, hard work would be a blessing to the human family. "Cursed is the ground for *thy sake*" (Genesis 3:17). Working with their hands would be beneficial in their education about sin and its results. Even though the curse superficially appears to be vengeful, we must never forget that in all He does, God has the well-being of His children as His great objective. Even before they sinned, God gave employment responsibilities in the Garden to Adam and Eve. "And the LORD God took the man, and put him into the garden of Eden to dress it and to keep it" (Genesis 2:15). The Hebrew word translated "dress" means "to render service, to work," and "keep" translates as "watch over or guard; to cherish." Adam and his wife were to perform pleasant work in the garden and cherish all the Lord had given them.

Within God's command to tend the garden, we find a form of worship of the Creator who made all things. The beauty and intricacy in the plants and animals awed Adam as he worked with them day by day. He witnessed God's creative power in every flower and majestic tree, in the most diminutive insect or the largest mammal. The lesson is also for us. While attending to our everyday duties, we can find God's hand guiding and protecting us. Our appreciation and treasuring of His influence in our daily lives become praiseful worship of our Creator. Instead of our work being a drudge, we have peace and happiness when we give "thanks always for all things unto God and the Father in the name of our Lord Jesus Christ" (Ephesians 5:20).

Though marred by sin, the earth and its heavens still declare the glory of God and His creative power so that all who will may know that our Creator is the God of love.

> The heavens declare the glory of God; and the firmament shows His handiwork. Day unto day utters speech, and night unto night reveals knowledge. There is no speech nor language where their voice is not heard. Their line has gone out through all the earth (Psalm 19:1–4, NKJV).

It does not matter what your ancestral heritage is or what language you speak. Just look up over your head on a clear night and you will be awed by the power of the God who flung hundreds of billions of stars and galaxies across the dark canopy above you. Even greater might is displayed in His ability to keep all these in perfect order as they race across the sky at fantastic speeds.

In contrast, Cain did not have this appreciation for the things God gave him. From the accounting in Genesis chapter 4, he seems more focused on the thorns and thistles. Cain was looking at himself instead of beholding his Creator. His self-centeredness caused Cain to lose the blessing that could have been his through praise and admiration for God and what he received from His hand. Pride and resentment hardened his heart against the One who had pronounced the curse on the earth. Because Cain blamed God for his hard life, worship of the Creator became an impersonal formality. He turned his worship into a ritual that showed respect only in outward form. It was devoid of faith and love toward God, and his family.

Familiar with how the sinful human mind operates, we can imagine Cain's line of thought. From the field where he toiled, he might have questioned: "Why does my brother have such an easy workload? All he does is follow a flock of half-witted sheep and goats as they wander along grazing, while I have to push this plow through the earth and then dig my hands into the loosened soil and pull up the stubborn weeds. From dawn to dusk, my work never ceases, but Abel lounges most of the day sitting on a rock or under a shade tree watching his flock!"

Cain might well have entertained thoughts of this sort, for we know from Scripture that there existed bitterness between the brothers. The sacred text indicates a long-standing resentment of some sort. Cain's hostile attitude toward his brother did not spring up in a moment but had been festering for some time.

And then, "in the course of time," there came a day when "Cain brought to the LORD an offering of the fruit of the ground, and Abel for his part brought of the firstlings of his flock, and their fat portions" (Genesis 4:3, 4; NRSV). "In the course of time," or as the King James Version puts it, "in the process of time" means that a specific amount of time had elapsed, and now the narrative has arrived at that point where a foreknown event was to take place. The Hebrew word translated "process" literally means "at the end," a delimiting of something from its related components. The language reveals that this offering was a repeating affair, an occasion they already knew about and which took place at the end of a definite time interval.

"In the course of time" indicates that a specific period had elapsed, and now the time for the event had returned. While this offering could have been a sacrifice brought at the beginning of each weekly Sabbath, more likely it was an annual offering. "In the process of time," it was necessary for God's people to bring an offering to show their faith in His promised Messiah. Since both Cain and Abel brought offerings, the event was most probably held on the anniversary of the Fall, reminding everyone of God's mercy. It was not a "celebration" but a solemn remembrance of what Adam and Eve did to bring sin and misery into the world, and of God's graciousness in pardoning their transgression.

Offerings brought on that day were whole burnt sacrifices made to the LORD, in remembrance of the first bloody offering done by Christ to clothe Adam and Eve before they were expelled from their Garden home. In the lamb was symbolized God's total commitment to save His people from their sin. The offering was also a recognition of the sinner's dependence on God for salvation and their thankful submission to Him.

Later, when God brought His people out of Egypt, He instituted a more extensive and comprehensive sacrificial system through which He taught the message of Christ and His righteousness. Each sacrifice and offering of the ceremonial system typified some aspect of the Saviour's work on behalf of sinners. By participating in God's plan, the repentant sinner showed his faith in God's promise of redemption.

The whole burnt offering originated at the gate of Eden when Christ killed those first two lambs to provide clothing for Adam and Eve. In the whole burnt offering, the entire sacrifice was laid on the altar and burned to ashes (Leviticus 1:2-9). However, until the establishment of the tabernacle and its priesthood, the expanded system of offerings did not exist.

The whole burnt sacrifice was performed by the patriarchs. We read of Noah (Genesis 8:20), Abraham (Genesis 13:18), Isaac (Genesis 26:25), Jacob (Genesis 33:20; 35:7), and Job (Job 1:5; 42:7-9) making whole burnt offerings, which showed their faith in the promised Messiah.

As head of the household, each man served as priest for his family. He offered these whole burnt offerings on behalf of himself and his entire family unit. In this capacity the patriarchs typified the coming High Priest, who would intercede for the human family. The whole burnt offering symbolically showed a complete consecration to God of the person or his family. Job said that he "sanctified" his children through the burnt offerings he made on their behalf. Gideon's extraordinary victories followed his whole burnt offering that demonstrated he was fully surrendered to the LORD (see Judges 6:21-28).

The animals offered in the whole burnt offering were burned on top of a natural stone altar overlaid with firewood. We find only whole burnt offerings in Genesis because all the other offering types needed an official "place" with the various pieces of furniture and curtains etc., for the offering to be carried out. Thus, the amplified sacrificial service was not instituted until the wilderness tabernacle was enacted by God, with its orders of priests and various typical offerings.

Every offering symbolized, in some way, the work of Christ for the sinner. The entire sanctuary service is far more than just a "Jewish" ritual that has passed away. We no longer perform these offerings, for with the sacrifice of Christ all sacrifices and oblations came to an end (Daniel 9:27). Even so, we should study them to appreciate the lessons they can teach us about God's character of love and the horribleness of sin that took the life of the Son of God.

Immediately prior to his expulsion, Adam heard his Maker declare the everlasting covenant promise that He would correct the sin problem through the Messiah, the Lamb of God. When they sinned, the skin coverings placed by Christ on Adam and Eve prefigured the Lamb's robe of righteousness that He will put on every repentant, believing person who appreciates Him as their Saviour. "I will greatly rejoice in the LORD, my soul shall be joyful in my God; for He hath clothed me with the garments of salvation, He hath covered me with the robe of righteousness" (Isaiah 61:10).

A thankful, faithful heart would have discerned in that commemorative offering at the gate of Eden, the tremendous everlasting covenant promise of God "to save His people from their sin" (Matthew 1:21). The whole burnt offering signified faith in God who had redeemed them from immediate death when their father rebelled. The promise included the eventual eradication of the virulent disease of sin and restoration in their Eden home.

But Cain chose to reject the blessing.

"Cain brought the fruit of the ground" as an offering to God, while Abel "brought the first of his flock" as his offering. "And the LORD had respect unto Abel and to his offering: but unto Cain and to his offering He had not respect" (Genesis 4:4, 5). In these verses, the Hebrew word translated "respect" literally means to look at with interest, intensity, and with approval. Abel's offering of a first-born lamb was approved by God, while Cain's fruits and grains found no commendation.

The natural question is: Why?—*why* was one offering accepted and the other, a perfectly good offering, refused? Is God arbitrary, fickle, spiteful?

As a free will or "thank" offering, there was nothing wrong with Cain's gift of grain and fruit. At Sinai, God gave instructions regarding grain as a peace offering, either as the whole grain itself, or as bread baked from the flour. Cain could have made this type of offering any day that he wished. But at this particular time, it was inappropriate because the occasion demanded a burnt offering of a lamb to commemorate the Saviour's work at the Fall of the human race.

Previously we read that there was enmity between the two brothers. Cain brought his offering while harboring hard feelings toward Abel. A resentful attitude is not conducive to worship of the holy God, Creator of heaven and earth. Jesus instructed, "If you are offering your gift at the altar and there remember that your brother has something against you, leave your gift there before the altar and go. First, be reconciled to your brother, and then come and offer your gift" (Matthew 2:23, 24; ESV). No matter what form of offering Cain brought, his hateful attitude toward his brother prevented him from receiving a blessing that day.

More significantly, if Cain intended his offering to be a sin offering that was supposed to point forward to the coming Lamb of God, it was unacceptable because "without shedding of blood, there is no remission of sin" (Hebrews 9:22). Fruit and grain offerings were never acceptable as sin offerings because they were bloodless offerings.

The message is clear: Cain thought the work of his own hands should be sufficient for an offering of consecration to the LORD. Abel brought the same offering that Christ used at the gate of Eden when Adam and Eve sinned. The symbol of Christ's own righteousness is in the shed blood of the innocent lamb. Abel's offering of a lamb from his flock showed faith in God's everlasting covenant. Cain's offering revealed a proud, unbelieving heart; it was an old covenant "works" offering done because it was expected and to gain merit, but devoid of faith.

> And the LORD had respect unto Abel and to his offering: but unto Cain and to his offering He had not respect. And Cain was very wroth, and his countenance fell. (Genesis 4:4b, 5).

The nature of the two offerings reflected the condition of the two men's hearts. Hebrews 11:4 says that Abel's offering was a "more excellent sacrifice" because it was brought in faith. Cain's offering exposed what resided in his heart. For some time before this offering was made, Cain had been developing an evil spirit of discontent. Rebellion against God smoldered in the depths of his heart.

The LORD "had respect" for Abel's offering; God "looked upon it with favor." That "looking" brought fire down from heaven and lit Abel's sacrifice with the divine flame, consuming it as a whole burnt offering. According to the Bible, this was the usual way for the LORD to display His affirmation of an offering. The same thing happened when Moses offered sacrifices at the dedication of the wilderness tabernacle (Leviticus 9:24). When Manoah made his offering on a slab of rock, the Angel of the LORD lit it afire and ascended to heaven in the flames. Likewise, when Solomon dedicated the Temple, at the end of his prayer, fire came down from heaven and consumed the burnt offering and sacrifices on the altar (2 Chronicles 7:1).

The narrative of Elijah's confrontation between the priests and prophets of Baal on Mount Carmel (see 1 Kings 18:17-39), shows the clear distinction between God's rejection of paganism's faithless old covenant approach to worship, and Elijah's faith in the new covenant (also known as the everlasting covenant). God has power; the pagan gods (and man) have none.

> And the LORD said unto Cain, Why art thou wroth? and why is thy countenance fallen? (Genesis 4:6).

Standing near the gate of Eden close by his brother's altar and witnessing what took place, Cain saw his offering in stark contrast to

Abel's. Each man knew the reality of commendation or rejection by God. When nothing happened to Cain's vegetables piled up on his pillar of stones, immediately resentment and anger welled up from his crooked heart and showed on his face.

The Hebrew word translated "countenance fell" literally means "turn toward self." The term is similar to "iniquity," which means "bent toward self." Anger is a self-centered expression revealing that we think we've been mistreated or abused. Anger arises because we want "self" to be vindicated and appeased. The "countenance" (facial expression) displays the character and feelings of the heart. People show their attitudes and emotions through their facial expressions.

A conscience not hardened by rebellion will respond to the power of the Holy Spirit. It is still open to the Holy Spirit's work to convince of blessing or convict of sin. Abel left the altar at peace with God, while Cain became very angry, "and his countenance fell." The expression on his face revealed the true condition of his heart. However, even if Cain had not demonstrated his feelings visibly, God still knows the condition of our hearts. We cannot hide ourselves from His constant, penetrating gaze. God knows all things.

The offerings were made in front of the angels with flaming swords who stood guarding the gate into Eden. They were the visible presence of the LORD on earth.

Whether the LORD communicated through them and they spoke to Cain, or whether the LORD's voice came from the midst of the angel's presence at the gate, or whether it came directly into Cain's mind, we cannot tell from the text.

"And the LORD said unto Cain, Why art thou wroth? and why is thy countenance fallen?" In this question, we hear an echo from the fall of Adam. The omniscient God knew where Adam was hiding when He came searching for him that awful day in the Garden of Eden when sin entered the world. Just so with Cain, God already knew the contemptuous condition of his heart. The question put to Cain offered an opportunity for him to examine his feelings and motives and confess his sin before his benevolent heavenly Father. Gently God explained, "if you do good, will you not be accepted?"

The Hebrew word translated "well" or "good" literally means to have a benevolent attitude toward others, a personal characteristic that signifies the existence of a positive relationship with God. We cannot love our fellowmen without first loving God. The vertical friendship with God exists before the horizontal, human-to-human fellowship can be rightly manifested. With the question presented to him, Cain was brought face to face with the fact that he was out of alignment with his Maker and his brother.

Why are you angry, Cain? What has taken place here that should make you angry? If you had done what you should, wouldn't things have worked out differently?

God was asking Cain to examine the facts of the situation. Who was at fault here? What was the real problem?

At the root of Cain's angry thoughts was jealousy. Abel's offering was accepted, and envy arose in Cain's heart. He desired for himself the approval that God gave to his brother. Why should his "little brother" receive such a blessing while he did not? Wasn't the elder brother the heir to their father's estate? Shouldn't the elder brother be the one to receive the blessings from the LORD? And in this narrative, we find a theme that plays out again and again throughout Genesis—brother against brother, spurred on by jealousy.

Somehow the LORD spoke to Cain, asking him a "good question"— "If thou doest well, shalt thou not be accepted?" And then God gave Cain a warning concerning his attitude. "If thou doest not well, sin lieth at the door." *Watch out, Cain. You're about to commit a grave sin— don't do it! Reconsider your plotting before it is too late.* Our conscience is enlightned by the Holy Spirit, and warns us not to proceed down the path of sin. But like Cain, we can ignore the "still, small voice" that earnestly entreats us to turn from sin.

God already knew that there was murder in Cain's heart even before Cain fully developed the thought in his mind. Anger leads to murder. "Thou shalt not kill; and whosoever shall kill shall be in danger of the judgment. But I say unto you, that whosoever is angry with his brother shall be in danger of the judgment" (Matthew 5:21, 22). Jesus equated anger with murder. In some cases, only the fear of punishment prevents a person's anger from running to the full-grown murderous act. God counseled Cain to submit himself to the LORD's power to deliver him from this anger, and its certain outcome. It was the only way to prevent the inevitable result of Cain's wrath toward his brother.

"And unto thee shall be his [Satan's] desire." Satan wanted to destroy both Cain and Abel. Though part of the prophecy of Genesis 3:15 was a mystery to Satan, he understood that a child of Eve, the One who would destroy Satan, who would "crush" his head, would be a male descendent of Adam and Eve. Satan did not know the time frame for the fulfillment any more than did Eve and Adam. To prevent its fulfillment, it was Satan's "desire," in one way or another, to destroy every male child to prevent his own destruction. Getting Cain to kill his brother would eliminate the first two possibilities of a Messiah who would crush his head.

If Cain would kill Abel, then Satan hoped to have established in Cain a beachhead from which to continue his war against Christ. This is precisely what we read in the rest of the narrative. Cain made the wrong choice, turned his back on the way of escape God generously gave him, and plunged headlong into murder.

There is always a "way of escape" when temptation calls us to commit sin. "God is faithful, who will not suffer you to be tempted above that ye are able; but will with the temptation also make a way to escape, that ye may be able to bear it." (1 Corinthians 10:13).

What follows in the chronicle of the first family is the sad revelation of the end result of cherished sin. Hatred harbored against his brother corrupted Cain's moral compass. His heart was closed to the working of the Holy Spirit trying to convict him of the evilness of his thoughts. If Cain had yielded to God, He would have empowered him to overcome it. The sin lying at his feet, ready to spring to life and devour him, was not resisted. A little over a thousand years later sin and corruption were so pervasive all over the world that God sent a purifying flood to wash the earth clean. The flood reset humanity's probation.

6

Sin lies At Your Door

By refusing the work of the Holy Spirit that draws us to repentance, we stumble into Satan's devious trap. Cain could have chosen to believe God, turned from his wicked thoughts and found the same peace that Abel experienced. Sin might have been lying at his feet and harbored in his heart, but God promised Cain that he could conquer it. "Unto thee shall be its desire, but thou shalt rule over it" (Genesis 4:7).

"Submit yourselves therefore to God. Resist the devil and he will flee from you" (James 4:7). What precious promises of overcoming sin through faith in God's power! God placed two options before Cain. Through faith, he could conquer the evil that compelled him, or he could disbelieve the promise, disdain the power so freely given, and continue in a life of sin. Cain turned his back on God. The "way of escape" was rejected. Repentance is always God's desire for us, but much of the time, we refuse to believe this good news. Cain would have none of it.

"And Cain talked with Abel his brother: and it came to pass, when they were in the field, that Cain rose up against Abel his brother, and slew him" (Genesis 4:8).

Cain's scheme to kill Abel was cunningly deceptive, inspired by the mind of Satan. The Scripture does not indicate any animosity between the brothers during the days following the offering. Conversation between them continued as before, giving no evidence of Cain's murderous thoughts toward his innocent brother. One day when they were both in the field, away from their homes and family,

Cain "talked with his brother" in a non-threatening manner, inducing Abel to dismiss the uneasiness he usually felt when in Cain's presence.

We learn something of Abel's character in this short segment of Scripture. Unlike his brother, Abel had a loving and forgiving heart. He desired to see the good in Cain, to overlook past experiences and harsh words between them, and live in peace with his brother. When Abel was most at ease, not expecting any further problems between them, "Cain rose up and slew his brother" and went his way without the slightest twinge of remorse or guilt. The works of the flesh—strife and envy—bore their baleful fruit of murder, the first premeditated crime the human family ever experienced.

Jesus teaches us, "You have heard that it was said to our ancestors, Do not murder, and whoever murders will be subject to judgment. But I tell you, everyone who is angry with his brother will be subject to judgment." (Matthew 5:21; HCSB). Hatred, envy, strife, and ill will toward anyone poisons our minds and hardens our hearts, allowing Satan to make inroads deep into our character. It was Cain's free choice to turn away from sin, or continue to cherish hatred toward his brother. He chose to continue in his unbelief in God's power over sin, throwing away the gift of God's righteousness.

But God did not leave Cain there. He gave him a chance to repent of the murder and be reconciled with God. "And the LORD said unto Cain, Where is Abel, thy brother?" Just as when Adam fell, God again came searching for the sinner, seeking the lost, desiring to restore him. God came looking for the guilty party, not to condemn, but to give the opportunity for confession and repentance. God presented Cain with a simple question, "Where is your brother?" God knew the deed that had been committed and where Cain hid the body. He had forewarned Cain concerning it. Nothing takes God by surprise.

Asking where Abel was confronted Cain with his sin of murder. If his conscience had responded to God's query, he would have been convicted of his sin, fallen at the feet of his Saviour in repentance, and found forgiveness waiting there for him.

King David was similarly confronted by God when he committed adultery and murder. But unlike Cain, when David was brought to task he immediately confessed, "I have sinned against the LORD," and he repented (see 2 Samuel 12:13ff.). In the psalm of praise written after he sinned, David sang, "create in me a clean heart, O God; and renew a right spirit within me" (Psalm 51:10). David confessed his sin and fell into the open arms of his Saviour, where God desires every sinner to be found.

But Cain sullenly responded, "I don't know: am I my brother's keeper?" (Genesis 4:9). Notice the pride, unbelief, and impenitence of Cain's heart expressed in these words. Arrogantly he denied the crime as if he could conceal it from our omniscient, omnipresent God. Cain tried to cover a deliberate murder with an equally deliberate lie. And that's the way of things once we set foot on the slippery slope of sin. We just keep piling sin upon sin until we are suffocating from the weight of it. Sin squeezes out the life of God from us. "Your iniquities have separated between you and your God, and your sins have hid His face from you, that He will not hear." (Isaiah 59:2). God does not erect a stone barrier between the sinner and Himself. Rather, the pile of sins form the barrier preventing us from hearing His sweet voice calling us back.

The interrogation of Cain was calculated to pierce his hardened mind and reach down into his seared conscience. But he would not yield to the work of the Holy Spirit. His reply differed from Adam's, who initially didn't deny the crime but attempted to blame someone else—his wife and then God.

The intervening years since that first hasty, incautious yielding to Satan in the Garden had hardened the human mind so much that it could commit a deliberate and calculated sin without compunction. No confusion here about what the sin is. Cain knew exactly what he was doing when he took his brother's life. And he didn't care.

A hardened sinner must take a different approach when confronted with his guilt. Cain, therefore, attempted to evade the question, apparently on the vain supposition that no eye, not even that of the omniscient God, was present to witness his dastardly deed. Cain quickly blows off the query, "I don't know," as if to say, don't bother me about such trivial stuff. "Am I my brother's keeper?" *My brother is of no importance to me; what do I care where he's gotten himself?*

The insanity of sin is evident in his flippant attitude toward his crime. In his sin-birthed madness, Cain goes further into sin and disputes the right of the Creator to make any demands concerning the way he is living his life. *Who are You to come along here and interfere in my life? I don't need You, and I don't want You. Go away!*

God's behavior toward Cain proves that He is the "Good Shepherd" who comes seeking the lost, who willingly lays down His life for the sheep. "I am the good shepherd, and know My sheep, and am known of Mine" (John 10:14).

> What man of you, having an hundred sheep, if he lose one of them, doth not leave the ninety and nine in the wilderness, and go after that which is lost, until he find it? And when he hath found it, he layeth it on his shoulders, rejoicing (Luke 15:4, 5).

The merciful Shepherd didn't give up. He was still trying to save His one lost sheep, so God pressed Cain further, saying, "What have you done?" *Confess, Cain! Repentance will save your eternal life. Confess and believe that I forgive you of this terrible sin. You cannot hide it because* "the voice of your brother's blood cries unto Me from the ground." (Genesis 4:10).

Cain stubbornly resisted. His heart was stone, utterly unyielding to the call of his loving Creator, who had no desire to curse him but wanted Cain to turn around and come back into the arms of his Saviour. Instead of confession and repentance, Cain denied any knowledge of what he had done. "And he said, I know not" where my brother is, and why should I care? "Am I my brother's keeper?" (Genesis 4:9). What an arrogant and self-righteous attitude!

Notwithstanding Cain's attitude, God persisted in His desire to save Cain by repeating, "What have you done? The voice of your brother's blood cries to Me from the ground" *where you shed it. By bringing an unworthy offering, you refused to acknowledge your dependence upon Me for all you have. Instead, you brought a bloodless offering of your own design. Moreover, your hard heart suffered no compunction from shedding your innocent brother's blood.*

If we will not believe God's promise to save us from sin, then He is unable to do anything more, and we are left with the wretched results of our choice. We have thrown away salvation with both hands.

> And now are you cursed from the earth, which has opened her mouth to receive your brother's blood from your hand; when you till the ground, it shall not henceforth yield unto you her strength; a fugitive and a vagabond shalt you be in the earth (Genesis 4:11, 12).

No longer would Cain be able to grow his food. The ground would not yield to his bloody hands any produce to sustain his life. He was condemned to wander the world, scrounging whatever he could from the trees and bushes that had fruits on them, or begging from anyone who would be merciful enough to share their food with a murderer.

God placed this curse on Cain to warn others that sin had a terrible cost. Wherever Cain wandered, people would ask him why he had no home; why was he roaming the earth as a "vagabond"? It was the same curse laid on the leper who had to wander, always proclaiming, "Unclean, I am an unclean person!"

Cain stood speechless as he received his threefold judgment. He was condemned personally, "thou art cursed"; the earth no longer would abundantly produce food for him when he worked it; and Cain was sentenced to the unsettled life of a vagabond.

When Adam and Eve sinned, they were not cursed personally—God condemns no one.[1] The entrance of sin into their lives caused shame and guilt and forced them to hide themselves from their Creator. Because sin cannot remain in the presence of the holy God, their punishment was expulsion from their Garden home and thus from direct, face-to-face communion with God.

Divine judgment upon Cain was more severe. Not only was he banished from his home, but he was to be a wanderer all his life, sentenced to live in temporary dwellings, eating whatever food he could find or beg from brothers, sisters, and cousins who populated the earth.

Since Cain thought that the work of his own hands was sufficient for a sin offering, the curse impacted his ability to till the soil with his hands—it "would no longer yield" its produce for him. He would be forever reminded that the works of his own hands could not save him or gain merit with our Holy God.

Confronted as he was, Cain might have been *convinced* of his guilt before God, but he was not *convicted* of his sin. His sorrow was not a "godly sorrow that worked repentance unto salvation, not to be regretted,

---

1. "For God sent not His Son into the world to condemn the world; but that the world through Him might be saved" (John 3:17). "And we have seen and do testify that the Father sent the Son to be the Saviour of the world" (1 John 4:14). "The Son of man is not come to destroy men's lives, but to save them" (Luke 9:56).

but the sorrow of the world [that] works death" (2 Corinthians 7:10). When the unfaithful are rebuked, their pride is injured, their anger is excited, and resentment boils from their heart. "And Cain said unto the LORD, My punishment is greater than I can bear!" (Genesis 4:13).

Cain's statement was not a confession of his sin but a complaint against God for the sentence that was justly pronounced against him for his crime. Just as his parents had done, he was pointing the finger back to God as the source of his misery rather than taking responsibility for the problem that he himself had caused. *You are driving me from my home! You are causing me to suffer! And You are going to bring every person against me!*—was Cain's complaint.

> Surely You have driven me out this day from the face of the ground; I shall be hidden from Your face; I shall be a fugitive and a vagabond on the earth, and it will happen that anyone who finds me will kill me (Genesis 4:14; NKJV).

In his complaint, Cain admitted that God will not countenance sin in His holy presence.

> Your iniquities have separated between you and your God, and your sins have hid His face from you, that He will not hear (Isaiah 59:2).

> When ye spread forth your hands, I will hide My eyes from you: yea, when ye make many prayers, I will not hear: your hands are full of blood (Isaiah 1:15).

Rebelliousness drives the Holy Spirit from us, not because He *will not* save us, but because we *do not want* to be saved. Cain was lost not because God was unjust or arbitrary in condemning Cain's sin but because he refused to believe God's counsel and call to repentance. His curse was not vindictiveness on the part of God but the result of his own willful rejection of God's love and mercy which would have restored him.

Proof of God's love is found in the next verse. "And the LORD set a mark upon Cain, lest any finding him should kill him." Many have speculated concerning the "mark"—a tattoo on his forehead; an external badge of some type that proved repulsive to others; a peculiar kind of clothing; some visible sign of his guilt—but whatever it was, it was a *blessing* from God toward this unrepentant sinner. It was protective, not vengeful.

The "mark" proved the depth of divine forbearance toward sinners. Cain would live the rest of his natural life without fear that anyone would kill him. As long as Cain lived, there was hope for redemption. The door of mercy was still open for him if he would but yield to divine love.

Whatever the curse was that God placed on Cain when He sent him to wander the earth, it was nothing Cain felt ashamed of or kept to himself. Knowledge of Cain's expulsion from the presence of God was well known, handed down through the generations.

The Biblical record informs us that "Cain went out from the presence of the LORD, and dwelt in the land of Nod, on the east of Eden" (Genesis 4:16). If Nod refers to a specific area, it is useless to speculate the location of "the land of Nod." The verse states that it was "east of Eden," and since we cannot locate Eden, it is impossible for us to determine where Nod was.

Furthermore, the Hebrew word translated "Nod" is the same word translated "vagabond" in verse 14. The word means to wander, to be unstable, and denotes a physical going back and forth, such as nodding the head or fleeing from place to place. It is descriptive of the existence God ordained for Cain rather than naming a particular place or area. Such was Cain's sentence. God intended that Cain would not know peace or settlement for the rest of his days.

Cain's rebellion was so deep-seated that he even rebelled against his merciful judgment. Instead of wandering to and fro, he decided to build a city. Prior to this, there had been no cities or even villages. Adam's descendants were country-dwellers living on their farms, as God had intended for His human family from the beginning.

Country life allowed personal contact with God's natural creation. Before sin had so corrupted and damaged God's creation, people could wonder at the marvelous diversity of plant and animal life and observe how all things worked beneficially together. In taking care of animals and growing their own food in a garden, people were constantly aware that God alone provided all the things they needed. Thus, their thoughts were directed heavenward even during everyday employment.

Living in a city among an increasingly wicked population contributed its own disquietude to Cain's unhappy life. To Cain can be attributed the title "founder of civilization" because he was the first to build a city. He became the head of a line of descendants who dwelt in close proximity to each other, developing trades, commercial enterprises, and other professional skills and crafts. Cain thought that the work of his own hands was sufficient for worship, and his descendants expanded that idea into full-blown heathenism. They worshiped the things their hands crafted from wood, stone, and metal, turning them into idols.

"God saw that the wickedness of man was great in the earth, and that every imagination of the thoughts of his heart was only evil continually" (Genesis 6:5). In this verse the Hebrew word translated "continually" is *yom*. It is the basic word for day. In this context, God saw that the descendants of Cain were daily, day by day, and all day, "continually" practicing evil. "The daily" (Hebrew: *ha tamid*) became the descriptive term for exalted paganism, as we find it used in Isaiah 52:5 and by the angel speaking to Daniel in Daniel 8:11-13.

By the fifth generation from Cain, murder and adultery were so common that it engendered bragging rights. Contrary to God's ordained plan for His human family, Cain's great grandson Lamech took two women to be his wives and fathered at least three sons and a daughter through them.

His wickedness did not end with his polygamy. "Lamech said unto his wives: Adah and Zillah, hear my voice; ye wives of Lamech, hearken unto my speech: for I have slain a man for wounding me, a young man for bruising me" (Genesis 4:23; ASV). Referring to and mocking God's promise of protection for Cain, Lamech boasted, "If Cain shall be avenged sevenfold, truly Lamech seventy and sevenfold."

Lamech's third son was a smith and the inventor of brass and iron weapons and other implements of destruction. "Tubal-cain [was] the forger of every cutting instrument of brass and iron" (Genesis 4:22; ASV). Boasting to his wives about murdering a young man who simply insulted him ("wounded" and "bruised"), Lamech was also trumpeting Tubal-cain's skills in creating instruments that could inflict death, tools that made killing easier to accomplish.

"And every imagination of the thoughts of his heart was only evil continually." Puffed up with his self-worth, Lamech mocked God by claiming that there would be no judgment upon him for his sin of murder. If God promised to avenge the death of Cain seven times,

Lamech crowed that he would be avenged ten times over should someone come in retaliation for the death of the young man he killed.

Cain's unrepentant, unbelieving heart bore like fruit down through his descendants until the whole earth was filled with wickedness. God is long-suffering, but there does come an end to His forbearance. He will gladly take away our sins, but He cannot remove what we tenaciously cling to and cherish.

> The LORD, the LORD, a God merciful and gracious, slow to anger, and abounding in steadfast love and faithfulness, keeping steadfast love for thousands, forgiving iniquity and transgression and sin, but who will by no means clear the guilty, visiting the iniquity of the fathers on the children and the children's children, to the third and the fourth generation of them that hate Me (Exodus 34:6, 7; ESV).

This declaration does not mean that God condemned future generations *because* of what their forefathers did. There is no intimation of "original sin" or inherited guilt in these verses. God does not condemn us because of the sins committed by our ancestors, including Adam. We are not condemned because of Adam's or anyone else's sin. Only the iniquity that we personally commit will condemn us if we cling to it instead of believing in the gift of salvation through Christ alone.

What, then, does this verse mean? The inclinations toward sin are learned, reinforced, and even magnified in succeeding generations. The behaviors and attitudes seen in parents and older generations are carried forward through the children's lives. Sins parents and other family members and associates commit without remorse or guilt educate children to think lightly about what sin really involves—that sin is an affront to the holy God, abhorrent in His sight. In this way, the sins of the fathers are "visited" upon the future generations through example.

The lesson from Cain illustrates this truth. Cain's rebellious attitude and unwillingness to repent, even when personally confronted by the LORD, was a living example to his children every day of his life. His children developed characters patterned after their father's arrogant, vindictive, and rebellious attitude toward God until the whole earth was full of wickedness and ripe for destruction.

In the short fourth chapter of Genesis, we see an explicit picture of an affluent, materialistic society that persistently defied God and

His laws. Their only interest was pleasure-seeking and self-indulgence. The iniquity of Cain was passed on to his children unto the third and fourth generation filling the earth with pride, self-centeredness, avarice, corruption, and violence.

When an individual, a family, a people, or a nation continually reject God's love and mercy, He withdraws His protection leaving them to the power of Satan. Wickedness overflowed the earth endangering God's faithful remnant who were descended from Adam through his third son, Seth. It was time for God to perform His "strange act" (see Isaiah 28:21, 22). "And the LORD said, I will destroy man whom I have created from the face of the earth."

After God declared His divine retribution upon the wicked world, the door of mercy remained open for another one hundred and twenty years. When probation closed, the entire globe was covered with a raging flood of water that swept everything to destruction and completely rearranged the surface of the earth.

"But Noah found grace in the eyes of the Lord." He obeyed God's command. When the world had never seen a drop of water fall from the sky, he constructed a massive boat on dry land to prepare for the coming flood that would wash the face of the earth clean.

By faith, Noah was prepared for the day of destruction. From his personal witness of God's power to deliver, recorded as a lesson for all humanity, Noah is an example to God's remnant people who live among similar wickedness at the end of time, for Jesus said, "As it was in the days of Noah, so shall the coming of the Son of man be."

Only Noah and his family survived the Deluge that cleansed the earth from sin and violence. All the works of man's hands that had been raised in self-glory were buried in the deep.

7

Walking With God

For 930 years Adam lived to witness the baneful fruit of his unbelief as sin exponentially increased among his sons and daughters. For nearly a thousand years people lived, married, and had children in abundance. Even without access to the Tree of Life, during this period in earth's early history people did not die young from "natural causes," though with the increase in violence murders did take place.

With each new generation, as sin multiplied, the human stature and noble character deteriorated from the physical as well as spiritual effects of sin. When Adam rebelled God told him: "dust thou art, and to dust thou shalt return" (Genesis 3:19). Eventually, that day came. "And all the days that Adam lived were nine hundred and thirty years: and he died" (Genesis 5:5).

With the death of Adam, his family was undeniably confronted with the raw fact of their naturally perishable existence: sin caused death. It was the unavoidable consequence of Adam's sin of unbelief. As astonishing as Adam's demise was to the human family, another mysterious occurrence happened a short half-century later. The righteous Enoch vanished from the face of the earth; "he was not; for God took him" (Genesis 5:24). Where Enoch went no one at the time could say. He just "was not" to be found anywhere on earth.

In contrast to the purity of Enoch's life, we have Cain and his descendants. Cain defied God's judgment and continued to live a life of contemptible immorality. Through Cain and his sons and daughters, Satan encouraged the idea that God is incapable of carrying out His punishment against sin. "Because sentence against an evil work is not executed speedily, therefore the heart of the sons of men is fully set in them to do evil" (Ecclesiastes 8:11).

Satan reminded sinners that Adam had been warned "in the day that thou eatest [the fruit of the forbidden tree] thou shalt surely die" (Genesis 2:17). But Adam lived 930 more years before he succumbed to the consequences of his sin—the "first death." By instilling doubt about God's ability to immediately carry out the punishment for sin, Satan worked to undermine God's authority and destroy faith in the Creator and His holy law.

After Cain killed his brother Abel, opposing views of God's character coalesced into two distinct tribes of mankind, each tribe further divided into family units and clans as they dispersed across the earth. One group was called the "sons and daughters of men" who followed Cain's example, disregarding God's call to repent and bent on fomenting rebellion of every kind. These chose to develop their evil propensities to the highest degree, indulging every lust without restraint.

Cain's grandson, Lamech, learned from his ancestor's murderous character. By their examples a prideful, boasting attitude quickly gained ground among the world's population. Lamech's double boast of taking two wives and then of murdering a young man who insulted him is a statement of heroism. He had done things no one before him dared to do, setting a new low mark in rebellion.

The ease of committing murder and lack of remorse over the death of a brother caused fear in many. Groups either banded together in walled cities for protection, or moved away from violent neighbors. The growth of pride and ambition in people's hearts, the aspiration for supremacy, as well as fear for one's safety, combined to produce a group of men who were known for their prowess in fighting. They were referred to as "men of renown" (Genesis 6:4).

The thought that people would live and die and no one would remember them caused some men to desire "immortality" through their heroic and daring feats. If they became legendary in this life, they hoped to circumvent the grave's inevitable oblivion. In life they could "make a name for themselves" that would be remembered long after they returned to dust.

Unfortunately, ambitious attitudes did not die in the Flood. Noah's great grandson, Nimrod, is called "a mighty one in the earth" and "the mighty hunter before the LORD" (Genesis 10:8, 9). His ambition was the same as Cain's. He built four cities on the Plain of Shinar and was the founder of a counterfeit religious system that still exists and remains in open opposition to the God of heaven and earth.

A Righteous Remnant

From Seth came all the persons who "walked with God" before the Flood. Just as Cain's descendants learned evil from their parents, Seth's descendants were taught righteousness through the godly examples of their parents and other close family members.

For the most part Seth's branch of the family chose to remain loyal to the Creator and sought spiritual refuge in Him. It was this part of Adam's family who "called upon the name of the LORD" and were referred to as "sons of God" (Genesis 4:26; cf. Luke 3:38). They followed God's will and therefore were at odds with those who refused to live according to God's plan.

However, Satan worked through Cain's wicked descendants to make sin alluring to God's faithful people, enticing them into sin.

A Contrasting Life

Enoch was a righteous man living at a time when total immorality and disregard for God and His Commandments were demonstrated by nearly all who lived in the world. He is also a Biblical "type" of those who will be living at the end of time just before Christ's return. Enoch "was not, for God took him," and that promise of deliverance from the world gone mad in sin encourages the faithful remnant at the end of time. Like righteous Enoch, the end-time remnant will be translated from this world without seeing death.

> In a moment, in the twinkling of an eye, at the last trump: for the trumpet shall sound, and the dead shall be raised incorruptible, and we shall be changed. For this corruptible must put on incorruption, and this mortal must put on immortality. So when this corruptible shall have put on incorruption, and this mortal shall have put on immortality, then shall be brought to pass the saying that is written, Death is swallowed up in victory (1 Corinthians 15:52-54; cf. Isaiah 25:8).

> For this we say to you by the word of the Lord, that we who are alive and remain until the coming of the Lord, will not precede

those who have fallen asleep. For the Lord Himself will descend from heaven with a shout, with the voice of the archangel and with the trumpet of God, and the dead in Christ will rise first. Then we who are alive and remain will be caught up together with them in the clouds to meet the Lord in the air, and so we shall always be with the Lord (1 Thessalonians 4:15-17, NASB).

From Creation to the Flood, Adam and his children produced 18 to 20 generations, and most were still living on the earth when Enoch and Noah preached their message of righteousness by faith.[1] During this time, wickedness increased among Cain's descendants until the world was filled with "strife and discord" of such immense proportions that it brought on the world's destruction. "Every imagination of the thoughts of [man's] heart was only evil continually" (Genesis 6:5).

When people believe that there is no absolute rule of conduct and no authoritative standard by which to live, that there is no punishment for their evil behavior and no reward for faithfulness, then their sinful heart will commit anything it desires without fear of repercussion.

When the Flood came and washed the earth clean, the vast majority of the world's population (a conservative calculation puts it at some three billion people) held just such a delusion about God. They believed they could live as wickedly as they pleased without suffering any consequences. "But it shall not be well with the wicked, neither shall he prolong his days, which are as a shadow; because he feareth not before God" (Ecclesiastes 8:13).

Wickedness will not always be tolerated by our holy God. He does set a limit to evil, and then "sudden destruction" comes. The antediluvians were enjoying their wicked lifestyle without a thought that the rejecters of God's mercy and salvation were facing destruction, just as many are living today.

For when they shall say, Peace and safety, then sudden destruction cometh upon them, as travail upon a woman with child; and they shall not escape (1 Thessalonians 5:3).

For many walk, of whom I have told you often, and now tell you even weeping, that they are the enemies of the cross of Christ: whose end is destruction, whose God is their belly, and whose

1. When the Flood came only about 1650 years had passed since Creation.

glory is in their shame, who mind earthly things (Philippians 3:18, 19).

"Enoch walked with God." That short string of words carries an essential message for us. The world of our day is hardly less wicked than it was in the days of those ancient patriarchs. Daily the news reports murder, theft, rape, drug-related crimes, war in most of the world, and political unrest where war has not yet broken out. Our social fabric is unraveling at an unprecedented rate. Co-habitation without the benefit of a religious or civil ceremony, children born out of wedlock, divorce in more than fifty percent of couples who do choose to marry legally, and abortion[2] have turned this world upside down from God's original intention for a moral and happy society in which the family unit was the stabilizing factor.

> This know also, that in the last days perilous times shall come. For men shall be lovers of their own selves, covetous, boasters, proud, blasphemers, disobedient to parents, unthankful, unholy, without natural affection, trucebreakers, false accusers, incontinent, fierce, despisers of those that are good, traitors, heady, highminded, lovers of pleasures more than lovers of God; having a form of godliness, but denying the power thereof: from such turn away (2 Timothy 3:1–5).

Precious little is written about righteous Enoch, yet we have volumes about Napoleon, Hitler, and the various Roman caesars. Men who conquered and destroyed have their lives studied and analyzed in-depth, yet we have no evidence that any of them ever did a single thing to honor and glorify the Creator of heaven and earth. But of Enoch is recorded the transparent truth: "Enoch walked with God; and he was not; for God took him." The apostle Paul wrote:—

> By faith Enoch was translated that he should not see death; and was not found, because God had translated him: for before his translation he had this testimony, that he pleased God (Hebrews 11:5).

---

2. Statistics from 2020 reveal China has aborted more than 336 million unborn children, India more than 100 million unborn. The United States exceeds 62 million. Since the Supreme Court overturned *Roe v. Wade* in June 2022, abortions have increased, with between 81,000 and 89,000 abortions taking place monthly between July and September 2023.

Since we live in a world of similar political and social conditions as existed just before the Flood (see Matthew 24:37–39), we ought to be curious about what it means to "walk with God." Is this something unique to this one man, Enoch? Or is it something we can all do if we learn to live by faith as Enoch did?

To walk means to move forward, putting one foot in front of the other with forward progress toward a desired goal. For the Christian, it means keeping our eyes focused on Christ, whose perfect character is our goal, and not stopping to indulge ourselves in the side excursions of sin. Walking involves exercising our God-given abilities to learn more about Him and His character. "God has given to every man [woman, and child] the measure of faith"—the tested and proven faith of Jesus. (Romans 12:3).

Faith is not the only gift from God. He has also given us grace. "Unto every one of us is given grace according to the measure of the gift of Christ" (Ephesians 4:7), and what a huge "measure" that is! All these and more than we can think or ask are gifts from our Saviour, and all are intended by God to strengthen our characters in the ways of righteousness.

Grace means loving-kindness of a master toward his servants and especially portrays God's benevolence toward all men. It is preeminently the kindness God has bestowed upon the ill-deserving human race. Since the day of Adam's fall, grace has granted sinners pardon for our offenses. Grace bids us to believe that God loves us, and beckons us to receive eternal salvation through His Son Christ Jesus, the Saviour of the world.

> Now we believe, not because of thy saying: for we have heard Him ourselves, and know that this is indeed the Christ, the Saviour of the world (John 4:42).

> And we have seen and do testify that the Father sent the Son to be the Saviour of the world (1 John 4:14).

As we exercise the gift of faith, it grows in strength through appreciation of all God has done to redeem us from sin. Through faith in His power, we learn to adhere steadfastly to the principles of truth revealed in God's holy Word. Just as those righteous patriarchs in the days of Enoch, we learn to do right because it is right, without looking for reward or benefit from doing right.

Studying the Scripture's record of faithful people like Enoch, Noah, Abraham, Joseph, Moses, Rahab, Hannah, Ruth, David—and yes, God's dear Son, Jesus—we gain valuable knowledge about God's love that empowers us to walk in the footsteps of those who before us have lived to vindicate the character of God.

Rightly understanding the Bible, we find that there is no room for situational ethics in God's plan for His people—it is not "sometimes justifiable" to break God's Commandments, if the situation warrants it. Neither do God's people attempt to "figure out all the angles" and then select the option that will net us the most profit. We do right because it honors our Creator, not because we hope to be rewarded with heaven or spared from the fires of hell.

Enoch maintained continual and simple faith in God's promises. By faith he recognized that he had a constant Companion at his side. Through the work of the Comforter sent by Jesus, we, too, can have a continual awareness of "God with us" ("Emmanuel," Matthew 1:23). "The Comforter, which is the Holy Ghost, whom the Father will send in My name, shall teach you all things, and bring all things to your remembrance, whatsoever I have said unto you" (John 14:26).

This one realization is perhaps the greatest deterrent to sin. Recognizing that God is always with us—near at hand—makes it easier to converse with Him through prayer as we steadfastly uplift our hearts to Him. He is not hiding far away somewhere buried deep in the cosmos, uninterested in our daily struggles. He is our most intimate and trustworthy Friend. Talking with Him should come as naturally as speaking with our closest earthly confidant.

While engaged in our daily labors, we can lift up our voices to heaven. When temptation confounds us, through prayer we have the privilege of seeking divine guidance and strength to resist temptation. In this corrupt world of sin and death, we are not safe unless our petitions continually ascend to the throne of grace, seeking God's power to free us from rebellion and wickedness.

Our Saviour said, "Watch ye therefore, and pray always, that ye may be accounted worthy to escape all these things that shall come to pass, and to stand before the Son of man" (Luke 21:36). Paul the evangelist admonished us to "pray without ceasing" (1 Thessalonians 5:17).

We should never fear that when speaking to God, we can not pray "properly" or say things as they ought to be said. The Holy Spirit is always with us to assist our feeble utterings.

The Spirit too comes to help us in our weakness, for, when we do not know how to pray properly, then the Spirit personally makes our petitions for us in groans [deep unspeakable feelings] that cannot be put into words; and He who can see into all hearts knows what the Spirit means because the prayers that the Spirit makes for God's holy people are always in accordance with the mind of God. (Romans 8:26, NJB).

8

How We Walk With God

Walking by faith is no more difficult for us living just before the second coming of Christ than it was for Enoch who lived a perfect life just prior to the Flood. As we live among the perils of the last days, we have been given the same power Enoch had that enabled him to escape the corruption of his world. "By faith Enoch was translated that he should not see death" (Hebrews 11:5).

By faith in God's power, individuals have always overcome sin. At the second coming of Christ, His faithful people, just like Enoch, will be translated alive from this evil world.

> Then we which are alive and remain shall be caught up together with them in the clouds, to meet the Lord in the air; and so shall we ever be with the Lord (1 Thessalonians 4:17).

As we learn to constantly talk with our Saviour about all aspects of our lives, we come to rely more on His wisdom and ways. Life becomes "not my will, but Thine." When we let the mind of Christ direct our thoughts, and submit to His will, we find it just as easy to do right as it was to do wrong under Satan's control. Making right choices becomes the pattern by which we live, whereas before, we just as easily made wrong choices that were in opposition to God's will.

Through Bible study and prayer, we reflect upon the purity of the character of Christ. Conscientious Bible study acquires knowledge through which we may honor God. Constant focus on the purity of Christ's character transforms our mind. We learn to "let this mind be in [us] which was also in Christ Jesus" (Philippians 2:5).

It is true that the "natural man receiveth not the things of the Spirit of God: for they are foolishness unto him: neither can he know them, because they are spiritually discerned." But the apostle Paul says as followers of Christ "we have the mind of Christ" (1 Corinthians 2:16) and that mind resisted every temptation to sin. The mind of Christ resisted even sinful thoughts that would have blossomed into the act. With the mind of Christ working in us, we can also resist sinful thoughts and actions. The mind of Christ conquers the "natural" enmity of the carnal mind (Romans 8:7) that fights against and resists the purifying work of the Holy Spirit.

Walking with God can only be accomplished by dying to self. Paul said, "I die daily"; and "I am crucified with Christ: nevertheless I live; yet not I but Christ liveth in me: and the life which I now live in the flesh I live by the faith of the Son of God [the gift of the "measure of faith" given to all], who loved me, and gave Himself for me" (1 Corinthians 15:31; Galatians 2:20).

Dying to self means completely surrendering our rebellious will to God's will. It involves a constant struggle with self, denying the lusts of the flesh, the lust of the eyes, and the pride of life, all of which are not of God but of this wicked world (see 1 John 2:16). These were the sins destroying the souls of men in Enoch's day, just as today when most people are "lovers of pleasures more than lovers of God; having a form of godliness, but denying the power thereof." Our admonition is just as it was for Enoch: "from such turn away" (2 Timothy 3:4, 5).

Shockingly, Paul is not in these verses speaking only of those wicked persons who blatantly resist God but also those in the church who refuse to allow their characters to be fully converted. These "have a form of godliness" by claiming to be Christians, by attending church, carrying a Bible in their hands, wearing a cross around their neck, and perhaps even attempting to evangelize others. But their hearts are not wholly with Jesus. Of such people, Christ will say, "I never knew you."

Matthew records this sad commentary:—

Not every one that saith unto Me, Lord, Lord, shall enter into the kingdom of heaven; but he that doeth the will of My Father which is in heaven. Many will say to Me in that day, Lord, Lord, have we not prophesied in Thy name? and in Thy name have cast out devils? and in Thy name done many wonderful works?

And then will I profess unto them, I never knew you: depart from Me, ye that work iniquity (Matthew 7:21–23).

And yet, amid all the violence and lawlessness of the antediluvian world, Enoch "walked with God" and by faith "he pleased God," so that God translated him out of this wicked world without Enoch seeing death. If we, like Enoch, keep ever before our mind's eye the majestic beauty of the Redeemer's love for the sinner, our own characters will also be transformed. By beholding His righteousness, we become changed into His likeness (2 Corinthians 3:18).

All of us, with unveiled faces, seeing the glory of the Lord as though reflected in a mirror, are being transformed into the same image from one degree of glory to another; for this comes from the Lord, the Spirit of God (2 Corinthians 3:18; ESV).

What are the results of "walking with God"? A tremendous change is wrought upon the heart and mind. Our natural inclinations and propensities to evil are conquered through the power of the faith of Jesus, and our characters are molded after Christ's own perfect character.

Under the guidance of the Holy Spirit, as we study our Bible, we increase in spiritual knowledge and discernment. Jesus told us He sent the Holy Spirit to "teach us all things." Daily, our heart appreciation of God's love toward us grows more robust and sure. We become more dependent upon Him for all things. We trust Him explicitly to protect us and provide for all our needs. And through this advancing knowledge of the Son of God, we grow up "unto a perfect man, unto the measure of the stature of the fulness of Christ" (Ephesians 4:13).

The wickedness of the antediluvian world was the result of humanity refusing to walk with God and choosing instead to walk with the deceiver of mankind. For more than sixteen hundred years before the Flood, Cain's descendants listened to Satan's lies about God's character and modeled their lives to conform to Satan's own malignant design. Negatively influencing the sons of Seth, Cain's clan taught many of Seth's sons to compromise and reject God's instructions in righteousness.

Just as in Enoch's time, today's world is filled with "murmurers, complainers, walking after their own lusts" (Jude 16). In marked contrast with the wicked people around him, Enoch's righteous life was one of purity in actions, words, and thoughts. His unswerving moral integrity was the result of his daily walk with God.

If Enoch walked with God in that degenerate age just prior to the destruction of the world by a flood, we should be encouraged and stimulated by his example, realizing that we need not be controlled by evil. Amid all this world's corrupting influences and tendencies, we too may walk with God and be free from sin's power over our lives.

We can have the mind of Christ just as Enoch did. And just like Enoch, we too may see translation at the soon coming of our Lord when He returns to rescue His people from this corrupt world. "And at that time Thy people shall be delivered, every one that shall be found written in the book" of eternal life (Daniel 12:1).

Through surrender to his Lord, Enoch was God's watchman standing firm, like a beacon of light on a hill. He was God's faithful witness to the world that was careening toward total ruin. Through him, God prophesied to the inhabitants of the old world concerning their eminent destruction. All who followed Cain's example in refusing to serve the living God would perish.

But God didn't leave them without hope. God always gives us the way of escape from sin.

> No temptation has overtaken you except such as is common to man; but God is faithful, who will not allow you to be tempted beyond what you are able, but with the temptation will also make the way of escape, that you may be able to bear it (1 Corinthians 10:13).

The Greek word translated "bear" means endure by faith and does not in any way imply succumbing to the temptation. The "way of escape" from sin is open to all who will exercise the gift of faith. By believing that God has power over everything Satan would throw at us to make us dishonor God by trampling on His law, we become overcomers and recipients of the promise to sit with Christ on His throne. We receive as a gift what Lucifer coveted in heaven—the right to sit on God's throne *with* Him. Lucifer thought he could steal the coveted seat, but only righteousness can sit upon the lofty throne of God.

> To him that overcometh will I grant to sit with Me in My throne, even as I also overcame, and am set down with My Father in His throne (Revelation 3:21).

Enoch is our example in living the sanctified life. As we go about our daily duties among those who give no thought to God or heavenly things or eternal life, we can be positive witnesses for God's goodness and mercy and eternal love. When we appreciate what it cost God to save us from sin, we will have a precious message to bear to the lost world. We will find it easy to talk about Jesus and to point sin-weary persons to the One who has all power in heaven and earth, who "is able to keep [us] from falling and to present [us] faultless before the presence of His glory with exceeding joy" (Jude 24).

In the beginning, God made mankind in His image with His perfect law of liberty and peace written upon Adam and Eve's hearts; this they were to pass on to all their posterity. But when Adam fell into sin, face-to-face communion with God was lost.

Precious few since the fall have chosen to follow the Lord with all their heart, soul, mind, and strength (see Mark 12:30). But at the very end of time, God will have a people of whom He will declare before the watching universe, "Here are they that keep the Commandments of God, and the faith of Jesus!" (Revelation 14:12). We have been given "exceeding great and precious promises: that by these [we] might be partakers of the divine nature, having escaped the corruption that is in the world through lust" (2 Peter 1:4). We "keep" the Commandments and the faith of Jesus by treasuring them for all they are worth.

Though most will close their eyes and ears to the good news of overcoming sin, some will respond. The impenitent refuse to hear lest they come to a knowledge of truth that confronts them with the defects of their character. Those cherished defects put them out of alignment with God's holy law. But there will be some who desire truth and eagerly accept it when it is presented to them. Uplifting Christ's beautiful and spotless character as our example will win many back from their degenerate lives.

Jesus left His heavenly home and clothed His sinless nature with our fallen human nature (see Hebrews 2:14-18), that He might give us a trustworthy example of righteous living in a wicked world. While we only have one short sentence in Genesis 5:24 about Enoch and how he lived, we have four Gospels that provide explicit information about how Jesus faced the temptations of this sin-cursed world and overcame them all through faith in His Father's love.

Christ's life is a lamp shining in every direction, even to the ends of the earth. "Jesus spoke to them, saying, 'I am the light of the world. Whoever follows Me will never walk in darkness but will have the light of life'" (John 8:12). That Light refuses to compromise with evil. It cannot allow error to be accepted for truth. It gives no place for vice to be mistaken for righteousness, or for sinning characters to attempt passing for perfection.

Enoch led an active, zealous life as he walked with God. He did not spend time in idle meditation, nor did he strive to gain personal happiness through ordinary amusements. He did not give anyone the opportunity to falsely question his motives or his profession of faith. He was a preacher of righteousness and of God's call to repent.

His life bore the message of forgiveness of sin to the inhabitants of the old world. His life still speaks to us today. His example of holiness is a continual witness in favor of the Gospel truth that we may be washed in the blood of the Lamb and saved from our sin, even while living in this corrupt world in fallen flesh.

Every person who professes to follow Jesus must realize the full responsibility of our high calling. Upon us all rests a personal warfare against besetting sins. Our battles with sin are assured of victory when we let the mind of Christ be our mind. Decisions for right thoughts and actions become part of our daily discipline, transforming our characters through each choice we make. Like Enoch, we are motivated by the desire to vindicate the character of God.[1] The goal is victory through His power. The apostle Paul described our warfare this way:

> Therefore I do not run like one who runs aimlessly or box like one beating the air. Instead, I discipline my body and bring it under strict control, so that after preaching to others, I myself will not be disqualified (1 Corinthians 9:26, 27, HCSB).

We also have an obligation to our Saviour to present His matchless charms to the dying world. We are the foot-soldiers of Christ, marching under His blood-stained banner. Through us, the Sun of Righteousness will shine upon the dark, degraded world, proving the power of God's grace to transform characters into the likeness of His dear Son.

---

1. Overcoming all sin in the lives of God's people through faith in His power, vindicates His name before the watching universe by proving false Satan's lies and accusations about Him.

Enoch was a real man who lived in treacherous times, and as such, he represents to us an example of how we may also live in today's world. He received no human praise or adulation, as Cain and Lamech and the "men of renown" were determined to have. Though not lauded by men, Enoch was exalted by God above any person who then lived. He was translated out of this world and was blessed with the gift of eternal life without first seeing death.

As we near the end of this world's history, we can match Enoch's humility and faith in God and receive the same reward: "he was not, for God took him." God is now preparing His people to welcome His Son's return with open arms.

> Then we which are alive and remain shall be caught up together with [the resurrected righteous] in the clouds, to meet the Lord in the air: and so shall we ever be with the Lord. Wherefore comfort one another with these words (1 Thessalonians 4:17, 18).

Notes

9

Living Righteously for 969 Years

Before the Flood, mankind lived an average of 850 to 900 years, but one man, Methuselah, lived longer than any other human, dying when he was 969 years old. Methuselah was the son of righteous Enoch, the man whose holy life is summed up in one short sentence: "And Enoch walked with God: and he was not; for God took him" (Genesis 5:24). Enoch lived 365 years and, because his character was perfect in the eyes of God, one day the LORD "took him" home with Him. Enoch is God's witness of what it means to live righteously.

Have you been told it is impossible to live righteously in this sin cursed world? or said, "Jesus was the only person to live a sinless life"? Look to Enoch. Or Methuselah, who lived 969 years without any record of sin placed against his name. Methuselah was a man guided by the same faith his father exhibited—faith in the living God who is able to deliver us from all sin.

Prior to the flood, in stark contrast to the evil ways of "the sons and daughters of men," Methuselah's witness (like his father's before him) called the world to repentance and salvation through God's mercy and enabling grace. The Lord does nothing without revealing His plans to His servants. "Surely the Lord GOD will do nothing, but He revealeth His secret unto His servants the prophets" (Amos 3:7). He would not send destruction without a prior warning and a call to repent.

God's everlasting covenant of love and mercy preached to the world through Enoch, Methuselah, and Noah called antediluvian sinners to repentance. Like the final message from God to the sin-filled world just before Jesus returns (Revelation 14:6-12), the message of salvation from sin also warned of coming judgment for those who were hardened in sin and refused His mercy. "God spared not the old world, but saved Noah the eighth person, a preacher of righteousness, bringing in the flood upon the world of the ungodly" (2 Peter 2:5).

Seth's righteous descendants, who were witnesses for God's goodness and power over evil, were "not in darkness, that that day should overtake [them] as a thief. [They were] all the children of light, and the children of the day: [they were] not of the night, nor of darkness." They heeded the warning messages of Methuselah and Noah to "watch and be sober" unto the end (1 Thessalonians 5:4–6). They were the "remnant" who faced the coming destruction with faith in their hearts.

God has always had a remnant people, those who follow Him no matter what the rest of the world does and says. God has never been without a faithful witness of His tender affection toward all His creatures. Enoch and his son Methuselah were both men of moral courage and wisdom, standing as shining beacons in that dark world of sin. Like Noah would later do, they both called individuals to repentance and acceptance of God's forgiveness of their sins.

Methuselah's name has been translated in many fanciful ways attempting to link his name to the timing of the Flood event. What does the name mean? Methuselah is a compound of two distinct Hebrew words with literal definitions: *mat*, which means "man," and *shalah*, "to send," or "to send away," as a person sent on a mission (see Genesis 28:5; 37:13; Isaiah 6:8; Jeremiah 1:7); or "sending away" as of strife and discord. Applying the definitions we discern that Methuselah was a man of action who was "sent away" with a commission from God to bear witness to the message of righteousness by faith so desperately needed in the evil antediluvian world.

Methuselah was the only man in his lineage who knew Adam and also lived until the year of the Flood. Therefore, through his ministry vital truths were preserved and presented to all who would hear. He preached the simple facts about worshipping the one true God, Creator of all that exists; the literal six-day creation; the eternal blessings of the seventh-day Sabbath rest given to mankind; the sanctity of marriage between one man and one woman; and God's unchanging character of love for humanity expressed in the remaining five Commandments.

Right up to the end of probation for the antediluvians, just before the world's catastrophic destruction by flood, the truth of righteousness by faith continued to be preached through a remnant who dedicated themselves to the Creator. As such, Methuselah was a Biblical "type" that will be seen again in God's final remnant people who carry the three angels' messages to the world just before the second coming of Christ.

The Three Angels' Messages

And I saw another angel fly in the midst of heaven, having the everlasting gospel to preach unto them that dwell on the earth, and to every nation, and kindred, and tongue, and people, Saying with a loud voice, Fear God, and give glory to Him; for the hour of His judgment is come: and worship Him that made heaven, and earth, and the sea, and the fountains of waters.

And there followed another angel, saying, Babylon is fallen, is fallen, that great city, because she made all nations drink of the wine of the wrath of her fornication.

And the third angel followed them, saying with a loud voice, If any man worship the beast and his image, and receive his mark in his forehead, or in his hand, the same shall drink of the wine of the wrath of God, which is poured out without mixture into the cup of His indignation; and he shall be tormented with fire and brimstone in the presence of the holy angels, and in the presence of the Lamb: and the smoke of their torment ascendeth up for ever and ever: and they have no rest day nor night, who worship the beast and his image, and whosoever receiveth the mark of his name.

Here is the patience of the saints: here are they that keep the Commandments of God, and the faith of Jesus. (Revelation 14:6–12).

Before the Flood, there were only two spiritual families. One chose to believe the everlasting covenant and kept the faith of Christ given to Adam in Genesis 3:15. These persons demonstrated the fruit of that faith in their daily lives. The second group were those who chose to remain in rebellion against their Creator and Saviour.

The first group will receive a new body and eternal life when Christ comes in His clouds of glory.

> In a moment, in the twinkling of an eye, at the last trump: for the trumpet shall sound, and the dead shall be raised incorruptible, and we shall be changed. For this corruptible must put on incorruption, and this mortal must put on immortality. So when this corruptible shall have put on incorruption, and this mortal shall have put on immortality, then shall be brought to pass the saying that is written, Death is swallowed up in victory (1 Corinthians 15:52-54).

The latter group will receive eternal death:—

> And then shall that Wicked be revealed, whom the Lord shall consume with the spirit of His mouth, and shall destroy with the brightness of His coming: even him, whose coming is after the working of Satan with all power and signs and lying wonders, and with all deceivableness of unrighteousness in them that perish; because they received not the love of the truth, that they might be saved. And for this cause God shall send them strong delusion, that they should believe a lie: that they all might be damned who believed not the truth, but had pleasure in unrighteousness (2 Thessalonians 2:8-12).

The final showdown in this war will be of the same character as that which the antediluvian world faced. At Christ's second coming, only two groups of people will be found on the earth, those who "follow the Lamb wherever He goes" (Revelation 14:4), and those who submit to the Beast power (Revelation 13:7, 8).

The first group believe the messages preached by the three angels. Those three messages are—

(1) A call to repentance and reverent, dedicated worship of the Creator God who judges the world in righteousness. The first angel's message calls for deep commitment and loyalty that includes keeping holy the seventh-day Sabbath given by God at creation—"worship Him that made heaven, and earth, and the sea, and the fountains of waters." The Sabbath is the sign and seal of the faith that finds complete rest in His creative power. "Come unto Me, all ye that labour, and I will

give you rest"[1] from your unholy "works" of attempted righteousness (Matthew 11:28).

> For if Jesus [Joshua] had given them rest, then would he not afterward have spoken of another day. There remaineth therefore a rest[2] to the people of God. For he that is entered into His rest, he also hath ceased from his own works, as God did from His [cf. Genesis 2:1-3]. Let us labour[3] therefore to enter into that rest, lest any man fall after the same example of unbelief (Hebrews 4:8-11; cf. 3:18, 19).

(2) "Babylon is fallen, is fallen, that great city."[4] "Babylon" is the word-symbol for all apostate and pagan religions that preach a false "gospel" about God, maligning His character of self-sacrificing love (*agapé*) by describing Him as angry and vindictive, requiring appeasement of His wrath before the sinner has any hope of acceptance by Him. The method of "salvation" promoted by pagan and apostate religions all claim that works are necessary to appease, or earn merit in payment for transgressions. It is completely fallen because it seeks obedience through ungodly means, following the traditions of men. From its founding by Nimrod, "Babylon" has always been a system that unites religion and state into one dominating, coercive and persecuting power.

(3) The third angel's message warns the world against willingly or unwittingly accepting the lies of the apostate religious system that has united church and state under its coercive power, while counterfeiting the pure Gospel of Jesus Christ. The counterfeit includes a false day of

---

1. The Greek *anapauo* ("rest") means to cause or permit one to cease from any movement or labor in order to recover and collect strength.
2. Here the Greek word translated "rest" is *sabbatismos* and means a literal keeping of the seventh-day Sabbath rest. The word for "rest" in verse 10 is *katapausis*. It is the same Greek word used in Genesis 2:2, 3 in the Septuagint (Greek) version of the Bible's Old Testament. God never changed His fourth Commandment (cf. Exodus 20:8-11; 31:13-18; Ezekiel 20:12, 20).
3. "Labour" means endeavor, give diligence, study (see Ephesians 4:3; 2 Peter 3:14; 2 Timothy 2:15). The equivalent Hebrew word is *shama* translated "obey." It means to hear intelligently, pay careful attention to.
4. The word "fallen" is duplicated to indicate to the reader that it is completely done.

worship as its "mark" of ecclesiastical authority and power to control people's consciences and lives.[5]

Daniel, the Old Testament prophet who lived in ancient Babylon, warned about the catastrophic "time of trouble such as never was since there was a nation" (Daniel 12:1). Jesus described the same time as being fraught with "false christs, and false prophets, [who] show great signs and wonders; insomuch that if it were possible, they shall deceive the very elect" (Matthew 24:24). It is during this tragic and fearsome end-time that God's faithful remnant people will unwaveringly demonstrate to the world that keeping all ten of God's Commandments, including the seventh-day Sabbath, is the greatest joy and pleasure we can experience in this world.

Prior to the falling of the plagues of Revelation chapter 16, the mighty fourth angel will sound the final call to the world, reemphasizing the fallen condition of spiritual Babylon:—

> And after these things I saw another angel come down from heaven, having great power; and the earth was lightened with his glory. And he cried mightily with a strong voice, saying, Babylon the great is fallen, is fallen, and is become the habitation of devils, and the hold of every foul spirit, and a cage of every unclean and hateful bird. For all nations have drunk of the wine of the wrath of her fornication, and the kings of the earth have committed fornication with her, and the merchants of the earth are waxed rich through the abundance of her delicacies. And I heard another voice from heaven, saying, Come out of her, My people, that ye be not partakers of her sins, and that ye receive not of her plagues (Revelation 18:1-4).

Pure faith will produce such deep fidelity and allegiance to God that the true believer, through the power of Jesus' faith working in their lives, will remain steadfast even as societies and governments of the

---

5. "Of course the Catholic Church claims that the change was her act. And the act is a mark of her ecclesiastical power and authority in religious matters." (C.F. Thomas, Chancellor of Cardinal Gibbons, in answer to a letter regarding the change of the Sabbath, November 11, 1895). "The observance of Sunday by the Protestants is homage they pay, in spite of themselves, to the authority of the [Catholic] Church." (Monsignor Louis Segur, *Plain Talk about the Protestantism of Today*, p. 213).

world fall rapidly to total destruction and all seems hopeless. Multitudes will respond to the final call and gather together with the remnant.

After this I beheld, and, lo, a great multitude, which no man could number, of all nations, and kindreds, and people, and tongues, stood before the throne, and before the Lamb, clothed with white robes, and palms in their hands; and cried with a loud voice, saying, Salvation to our God which sitteth upon the throne, and unto the Lamb (Revelation 7:9, 10).

Then, God Himself will declare of His remnant people: "Here are they who keep the Commandments of God and the faith of Jesus." In the darkest hour of earth's history when all seems lost, our Saviour will appear in the midst of heaven with all of His holy angels to rescue us and take us home with Him. "Wherefore comfort one another with these words" (1 Thessalonians 4:18).

Notes

10

Ark of Salvation:
Jesus Christ

And the LORD was sorry that He had made man on the earth, and He was grieved in His heart" (Genesis 6:6, NKJV). When God created this world, everything was perfect. Violence and hatred did not exist in Adam and Eve. Their thoughts and feelings were aligned with the mind of their Maker, who is self-sacrificing love. "He that loveth not knoweth not God; for God is love" (1 John 4:8). But after Adam's fall into sin, their thinking habits and lifestyle changed, and these changes were passed on to their children, whose inclinations increasingly tended toward evil thoughts and wicked actions.

"So the LORD said, 'I will destroy man whom I have created from the face of the earth, both man and beast … for I am sorry that I have made them'" (Genesis 6:7, NKJV). The original language expresses deep anguish, as though God heaved a great shuddering sigh of sorrow over the depraved immorality of His creation. When deep love is injured beyond words, the pain of that rejection is an equally intense, heart-wrenching agony.

That God "repented" or was sorrowful for having created this world might seem to imply that He is capable of changing His mind; that He is fickle and arbitrary in His actions toward mankind, or perhaps He made a mistake. However, in Malachi 3:6, God declared, "I am the LORD, I change not." James 1:17 informs us that in God there "is no variableness, neither shadow of turning." God's Word says His character cannot change; He is always full of mercy and love and very long-suffering. "The LORD God [is] merciful and gracious, longsuffering, and abundant in goodness and truth" (Exodus 34:6).

Nevertheless, if we will not love and honor Him as we ought, He leaves us to the consequences of our choices. He respects our freedom of choice and will do nothing to violate it; God coerces no one. Therefore, because of man's nature and wrong choices, God was forced to use uncharacteristic language to describe what He was about to do in carrying out His "strange act" of destruction (see Isaiah 28:21).

In the days preceding the Flood, God was "not willing that any should perish, but that all should come to repentance" (2 Peter 3:9). As the impious people filled up their cup of iniquity, God sent living witnesses, like Enoch and Methuselah, to warn them that He was about to show Himself a God of justice through a terrible display of His judgment.

> The earth also was corrupt before God, and the earth was filled with violence. And God looked upon the earth, and, behold, it was corrupt; for all flesh had corrupted his way upon the earth. And God said unto Noah, The end of all flesh is come before Me; for the earth is filled with violence through them; and, behold, I will destroy them with the earth. Make thee an ark of gopher wood; rooms shalt thou make in the ark, and shalt pitch it within and without with pitch (Genesis 6:11–14).

Probation for the wicked human race was nearing its end when God called Noah to build a massive wooden structure such as the world had never seen. Explicit instructions were given for the size and type of materials to use in constructing this massive wooden box. Noah did not have any personal input into the design or construction; he simply followed God's plan. "According to all that God commanded him, so did he" (Genesis 6:22). Human wisdom could not have devised a structure of such incredible strength and durability because the human mind could not fathom the terribleness of the impending judgment.

The ark was not a sailing ship. It was a wooden vessel of immense size, 520 feet long, 86 feet wide, and 52 feet high, about half the size of a modern aircraft carrier. When completed, the ark had only one small window at the very top and one large door in the side. It had no steering mechanism, no sails or other power source. No human skills were employed to direct its course or to "sail" the vessel to safety.

Ancient narratives found in the Mesopotamian area tell of a boat built to save the people from a flood, but the boat in the pagan stories was an ordinary sailing vessel that employed boatmen to wrestle with the oars and navigate it through the storm. These stories reveal the sad truth that without a correct knowledge of God, man has always tried to save himself by his own works.

In contrast to all the pagan flood stories, only the power of God could keep Noah's ark and its precious cargo safe amid the tempest raging outside its walls, a storm so fierce that it ripped the surface of the earth apart creating deep canyons for oceans. Then it crashed the parts together in other places to raise high mountains. The violence of water during the Flood, and after as it ran off to allow dry land to appear, left the surface of the earth changed beyond recognition.

As commanded, Noah built the ark and pitched it "within and without with pitch." An interesting word study on "pitch" reveals that the Hebrew word used in Genesis 6:14 is different from the word translated "pitch" in Exodus 2:3 and Isaiah 34:9. In these verses, the word *zepet* is used and refers to the natural substance known as asphalt or tar. In the Noah narrative, the word "pitch" is from the Hebrew word *kapar* meaning "ransom" or "atonement." It is from the same root word translated "mercy seat" in Numbers 7:89.

> And when Moses was gone into the tabernacle of the congregation to speak with Him, then he heard the voice of One speaking unto him from off the mercy seat [*kapar*] that was upon the ark of testimony, from between the two cherubims: and He spake unto him.

Kapar also appears in Job 33:24 translated "ransom." Job said that even as he was going down into the pit—the grave—a ransom (*kapar*) was found to save him. Jesus Christ is the only Ransom that is able to save us from eternal death. Thus, Scripture portrays the ark Noah built as a symbol of Christ and His Righteousness. All who appreciated the gospel message preached by Noah and entered the ark were enveloped in the security of Christ's atoning sacrifice.

At the end of His instructions, God told Noah He was going to "bring a flood of waters upon the earth." Never had any human being seen a "flood of waters." It had never rained on the earth, rivers and streams had always remained within their banks. The Hebrew word *mabbul* is a technical term reserved for a watery catastrophe, but no such thing had ever occurred since the world began.

Nevertheless, Noah did not question nor exhibit any doubt or fear about God's news of the impending devastation of the world by water. Even though he could not fully comprehend the meaning of God's words, "by faith Noah, being warned by God concerning events as yet unseen, in reverent fear [awe of God's power] constructed an ark for the saving of his household. By this he condemned the world and became an heir of the righteousness that comes by faith" (Hebrews 11:7, ESV).

For one hundred and twenty years before the flood came, while he was building the ark, Noah was also employed as a preacher of righteousness. God called him to proclaim salvation to the antediluvian world. Yes, destruction was looming on the horizon, but the love of God would not permit Him to destroy anyone so long as there was hope that even one person might repent, turn from their evil ways, and allow Him to save them. Every hammer blow struck by Noah, his sons, and the many others who assisted in building the ark, was a call to repentance, for the day of judgment was hastening on.

The antediluvians were deceived by the ordinariness of the world around them. Day by day, nothing seemed to change. They still pursued their customary pleasures, lived as usual, and gave no thought to the future. They could not comprehend anything so terrible as a worldwide flood that would sweep away everything they cherished. As Noah stood on the scaffolding surrounding the ark, pleading with those who came to gawk at his handiwork, he received only scorn and ridicule from the assembled mob.

They laughed and mocked to each other that the old man must be insane, blabbering on as he was about a flood of water that was going to wash everything away. A boat built on dry land?—how absurd. Water falling from the sky?—unheard of and impossible to imagine. The very idea of such things was ludicrous to these scoffers. Shaking their heads, they turned their backs on God's last message of mercy to them, saying, "all things continue as they were from the beginning of creation" (2 Peter 3:4). Disbelieving Noah's warning concerning the coming flood, they turned away, proclaiming "peace and safety" to the masses, but then "sudden destruction" came upon them all. There remained nothing more God could do to persuade them, and they were left to reap the consequence of their choice.

The vast majority of the human family had put God far out of their mind. They worshiped creatures of their imagination and objects of their own making. It is a law of the human mind that by beholding, we become changed; what we spend our time on intimately influences who we are and how we think and act. We cannot rise any higher than the thoughts we harbor in our minds. Yet, amid this widespread intellectual and spiritual corruption, Noah was found righteous in the eyes of God. "But Noah found grace in the eyes of the LORD … Noah was a just man and perfect in his generations, and Noah walked with God" (Genesis 6:8, 9). Among that vast population of sinners, God still had His faithful remnant people.

While preaching about the coming destruction, Noah was also telling about the way of escape. Anyone who believed the message, who had faith in God's promise to save, could have gotten on the boat. The only barrier to salvation was their unbelief in God's word. Because of an unwillingness to give up preconceived opinions and the overwhelming desire for self-gratification, the people rejected the solemn message of salvation. Their minds were so blinded by the rejection of light that they readily believed Noah's message was a delusion.

On the day the flood came, of all the billions on the earth, only Noah and his family were willing to let God save them from destruction. Righteous men and women who lived just prior to the flood were mercifully laid in their graves before the flood came. After assisting Noah in building the ark, Methuselah, the oldest person who ever lived, died in the year that the flood came upon the earth.

While scoffers lingered around the completed ark, continuing to harass Noah and his helpers for the foolishness of their faith, a strange thing happened. Creatures from the forest and fields came parading in an orderly fashion to the plain where Noah's "folly" was standing, braced upright by stout timbers. Above them, the sky was darkened by flocks of birds. The mouth of every person was stopped as they witnessed the gathering creatures calmly going through the only entrance to the ark, and finding rest in the pens and corrals prepared for them. The animals sought the safety of the boat the people had ridiculed. "Dumb animals" heard the voice of God and responded.

That single doorway stood open for many months during the ark's construction, ready to receive all who would come though it. Seven days before the flood came, the door of the ark was closed by an unseen hand, and probation ended for the world. For one week, secured in the ark, Noah and his family patiently waited for the event God had foretold. Those outside wondered why nothing happened. Noah had been confident in his dire predictions, even though no one knew what a flood or rain were.

Ominously dark clouds began to pile up over their heads, and the wind rose sharply, snatching at their hair and clothing. Suddenly, bolts of brilliant light flashed across the sky above them, followed by a startling crack of thunder. Great drops of water splashed down on their heads, running in rivulets across their faces. Nothing like this had ever before taken place. In fear and apprehension, the people scattered to their homes seeking safety from the downpour.

As they ran, the ground beneath their feet shook with the blasts of thunder roaring overhead, and then with a violent upheaval, the ground opened up, releasing vast geysers of water shooting upward from the bowels of the earth. Water from above and beneath soon flooded the plain, and the people were forced to seek higher ground above the raging surface of the engulfing sea. No matter how high they climbed, the water rose below them, licking at their feet. Frightened animals competed with the people who were fleeing from the judgment of God, all seeking safety that was no longer available.

Eventually, there was no where else to go. The water had reached the summit of the highest hill, and still it kept rising. For forty days and nights the rain poured down until every square inch of dry ground was covered with hundreds of feet of swirling, frothing, heaving water that drowned every living thing on the surface of the earth.

Incorrigibly disobedient, the people "knew not until the flood came, and took them all away; so shall also the coming of the Son of Man be." The people "knew not" by their own choice. They rejected truth God sent through Noah, intent upon remaining willingly ignorant of the message of salvation.

As the days of Noah were, so shall also the coming of the Son of Man be. For as in the days that were before the flood they were eating and drinking, marrying and giving in marriage, until the day that Noah entered into the ark (Matthew 24:37, 38).

In these words, Jesus was not condemning ordinary consumption of nutritious foods nor marriage as ordained from Creation (Genesis 1:27, 28; 2:23, 24). He is remarking that at the time of the Flood everyone was continuing in the common things of life, paying no attention to the warnings given to them. As it was in the days of Noah, so shall it be at the second coming of Christ.

In every generation, the faithful have found in Jesus Christ a shelter and a sanctuary from the storm of life. Soon a "storm" of human wickedness and violence of frightening dimensions will break upon the earth as the "four angels" release their hold on the "winds of strife" (see Revelation 7:1). "Natural" calamity after calamity—storms, floods, fires and earthquakes—will bring disaster to cities around the world. These will be just as terrifying as the Flood in Noah's day. The unbelieving will have nowhere to go to find safety and relief from the coming worldwide destruction.

> And the heaven departed as a scroll when it is rolled together; and every mountain and island were moved out of their places. And the kings of the earth, and the great men, and the rich men, and the chief captains, and the mighty men, and every bondman, and every free man, hid themselves in the dens and in the rocks of the mountains; and said to the mountains and rocks, Fall on us, and hide us from the face of him that sitteth on the throne, and from the wrath of the Lamb (Revelation 6:14-16).

> And there were voices, and thunders, and lightnings; and there was a great earthquake, such as was not since men were upon the earth, so mighty an earthquake, and so great. … And every island fled away, and the mountains were not found. And there fell upon men a great hail out of heaven, every stone about the weight of a talent: and men blasphemed God because of the plague of the hail; for the plague thereof was exceeding great (Revelation 16:18-21).

Only those residing by faith in the righteousness of Christ will be safe and ready when their Saviour comes to rescue them. "And it shall be said in that day, Lo, this is our God; we have waited for Him, and He will save us: this is the LORD; we have waited for Him, we will be glad and rejoice in His salvation" (Isaiah 25:9).

Noah was saved by faith in God's word. He believed that the destruction would come. He built the ark according to God's instructions without any additions or modifications of his own. He and his family boarded the ark when it was time. In the ark "pitched within and without," they were symbolically wrapped in the righteousness of Christ. By faith in the righteousness of Christ seen in the promises of God, they rode out that storm in perfect safety.

How was salvation accomplished when the flood came and buried all in a watery grave? Was it obtained through sacrifices and offerings? Was it secured by the "works of the law"? No. Then as always, salvation is only through the grace of God and faith in His promises. Since the fall of Adam, God has only had one method of saving people, and that is through His grace and the faith of Jesus. Both the Old and the New Testaments certify this fact. Every saved individual, from Adam to the end of the world, has been saved by grace through faith in the shed blood of Jesus Christ.

> For by grace are ye saved through faith; and that not of yourselves: it is the gift of God: Not of works, lest any man should boast (Ephesians 2:8, 9).

Noah "became heir of the righteousness which is by faith." To become an "heir" means that you are entitled to inherit property, rank, title, or office. It means the thing you inherit has already been established through a promise. The saving righteousness of Jesus Christ was established before the foundation of the world, and Noah became an heir to that salvation "by faith" in God's word. From the foundation of the world, God has only had one plan of salvation. Faith in the blood of Jesus Christ saved Noah, just as it saves you and me.

> Being justified freely by His grace through the redemption that is in Christ Jesus: whom God hath set forth to be a propitiation through faith in His blood, to declare His righteousness for the remission of sins that are past, through the forbearance of God; to declare, I say, at this time His righteousness: that He might be just, and the justifier of him which believeth in Jesus (Romans 3:24-26).

> Therefore being justified by faith, we have peace with God through our Lord Jesus Christ (Romans 5:1).

11

The Unchanged Gospel

Abraham was born 250 years after the Flood in the Babylonian city called "Ur of the Chaldees" (Genesis 11:28, 31). The city was part of an advanced civilization stretching along the Euphrates River in the area now known as Iraq. The major east-west trade route from India to Egypt brought wealth and cultural exchange to the people living on the Plain of Shinar (Genesis 10:8-10).

Innovative construction techniques raised beautiful cities along the twin rivers. As the cities grew, the builders learned to solve the urban sanitation problem. The Mesopotamian Empire was the first civilization to figure out the solution to waste management. Archeologists discovered ruins of homes in Ur and Babylon constructed of brick with indoor plumbing and toilets with septic systems using clay pipe drains that carried sewage to pit latrines or into cesspits.

Chaldean culture was both polytheistic and pantheistic.[1] The primary object of their religious ceremonies was the moon god called

---

1. Polytheism believes in and worships more than one god. Buddhism, Hinduism, and animism are religions that believe many gods (or spirits) exist and are everywhere in the universe. Pantheism is the Greek word meaning everything (*pan*) is God (*theos*). While denying the reality of a personal God, pantheism identifies God with all things that exist, from the stars above to the smallest single-cell organism; "all things" are God. The idea is that the universe manifests God's whole being; God does not exist except through what exists in nature. "God is the explanation of nature,—not a God outside of nature, but *in* nature, manifesting himself through and in all the objects, movements, and varied phenomena of the universe." One variety of pantheism teaches that God is the "soul of the universe"—the life-giving, animating force—"there is present in the tree a power which creates and …

Sin. Known as the "illuminator" or the god of wisdom, he was believed to be the father of the sun god, Shamash. Ishtar (Venus) was the female deity that completed their primary trinity of gods—the three brightest objects in the sky.

Before his rebellion in heaven, Satan's name was Lucifer, or "light-bearer." Satan challenged the integrity of God's creative word with his first lie to the human family: even if you rebel against God, "ye shall not die." The second lie was that by disobeying God, Adam and Eve's minds would be illuminated; they would find "wisdom" that would elevate them to godhood (Genesis 3:4, 5). Thus we see that by worshiping the god called Sin and his two cohorts, the people of Babylon and Ur were, in reality, worshiping Satan and accepting his lies about the nature and character of God.

Temples to the Babylonian false gods were extravagantly decorated with carved statues, mosaics, and embossed metal reliefs. Called ziggurats, the temples were constructed of adobe brick in a semi-pyramidal shape using a series of steps that led the worshiper's eye upward to the sky. The stair towers were an attempt to reach the heavenly realm—a "stairway to heaven"—whereby people could ascend to the gods, and the gods could descend to earth. The columns at the temple's entrance were sheathed with colorful mosaic tiles and polished copper that reflected light, creating a luminous glow, even in moonlight.

The names of Abraham's immediate family indicate that they were idol-worshipers while living in Ur. Abraham's father was called Terah. In the Akkadian language, *yareah* means "moon." Abraham's wife's name, Sarah, is the Hebrew form of the Akkadian *sarratu*, or "queen," the word used when referring to the consort of the moon god—the "queen of heaven." The moon god's daughter's name, *malkatu* or "princess," was the name given to Abraham's sister-in-law, Milcah. Laban was the grandson of Milcah and Nahor, Abraham's brother. His name meant "the white one," an Akkadian poetic expression for the moon.

Both Terah and Laban were known to have kept idols. "And Joshua said unto all the people, Thus saith the LORD God of Israel, Your fathers

---

(footnote continued from previous page) maintains it, a tree-maker in the tree." To the pantheist, the universe is divine and should be held sacred and worshiped. Since the universe is identified with God, the concept denies any personality or transcendence of God. "All is God" and, therefore, everything is sacred.

dwelt on the other side of the flood in old time, even Terah, the father of Abraham, and the father of Nahor: and they served other gods" (Joshua 24:2; cf. Genesis 31:29-32).[2]

Abraham (Abram) was called from the luxurious and fascinating pagan environment of Ur to "walk before" God all the days of his life (Genesis 17:1). When the "God of glory appeared" to Abraham, saying, "get thee out of thy country and from thy kindred" (Acts 7:2, 3), "by faith" Abraham strapped on his walking sandals and, "not knowing whither he went," he obeyed (Hebrews 11:8). He did not question the wisdom of God's call, nor rue the loss of his comfortable existence in Ur. "By faith," Abraham "obeyed." It was a natural response for him to do what the true God of heaven and earth asked of him.

With this in mind, what was it that Abraham "knew not"? He certainly would have known about the existence of Canaan. The major overland trade route from India to Egypt ran through Ur and Babylon, around the "fertile crescent" that followed the River Euphrates northward, and then curved down the Mediterranean coast of Canaan to Egypt. But God did not at first reveal to Abraham where he was going. God simply told him, "follow Me," and Abraham confidently did as God asked.

Even though he was raised in a pagan world, Abraham did not forget the God of his fathers. He was a direct descendant of Noah through Shem. After the deluge, Noah, Shem, and Abraham were contemporaries for 39 years. Abraham was born when Shem was 392 years old, and Shem continued to live for 500 years after the Flood.[3] For more than 110 years, Shem and Abraham would have had ample opportunity to communicate with each other.

It was through Shem that Abraham learned the facts concerning the worldwide flood and its cause. Shem remained God's faithful witness all of his life, preaching the Gospel by sharing his knowledge of Creation; the Garden of Eden; the fall of Adam; the promise of the coming Redeemer; the sacrificial system instituted at the very gate of Eden by the LORD; the first murder committed by Cain and it's terrible results

---

2. "The other side of the flood" refers to the Euphrates River where the city of Ur was located.

3. Shem was 98 years old when the earth was destroyed by the Flood; he died at age 600. Shem outlived Abraham by thirty-five years.

that brought the cleansing flood, resetting humanity's probation.

As a devout follower of God, Shem was distressed to witness how rapidly after the Flood wickedness spread over the world through the influence of his grand-nephew, Nimrod, the founder of the earliest imperial world power. Nimrod was instrumental in renewing pre-flood paganism. He promoted worship of the sun, moon, and the (supposed) powers of nature, and "hero-worship." Instead of worshiping the LORD who created all things, Nimrod defiantly raised his hands against God's holy character, calling himself "a mighty hunter before the LORD" (or "in God's face") turning his back to God in rebellion (Genesis 10:9).

Building the city of Babel (and the other three cities on the plain, see Genesis 10:9, 10) was a direct revolt against God's command to Noah and his sons to "replenish the earth" (repopulate) by scattering the tribes widely over the earth. Building a city reestablished the sin of Cain, who was condemned to wander, but instead, he constructed a city in which evil took root and spread through Cain's children (Genesis 4:13-24). By congregating closely in a city, sin easily multiplied. The cities on the Plain of Shinar bore the same wicked fruit. Their descendants—the Babylonians and Assyrians—became implacable enemies of God.

Shem told people about the horrors of the Flood. In addition to the violence of the water that buried the wicked in a watery grave, catastrophic earthquakes and volcanoes ripped the surface of the earth asunder, pushing up high mountains where none had ever existed. After forty days, when the rise of water came to an end, the receding deluge dug valleys and canyons as it rushed into the deep chasms of the new oceans. Shem warned people about evil and iniquity and the dire results of immorality that wiped humanity from the face of the earth. Keeping the facts of the worldwide flood fresh in the minds of remnant believers—like Abraham—was a warning against sin and its destructive power.

The truth of righteousness by faith was also kept alive through Shem, who proclaimed the work of the coming Saviour, promised in Eden to Adam (Genesis 3:15). All his life, Shem applied his efforts to spreading the life-sustaining truth of Creation and the Fall, and the seventh-day Sabbath rest as the memorial of God's creative and redemptive power. "For in six days the LORD made heaven and earth, the sea, and all that in them is, and rested the seventh day: wherefore the LORD blessed the Sabbath day, and hallowed it" (God made the seventh-day sacred; Exodus 20:11; cf. Genesis 2:1-3).

No pagan god has ever been proven to have creative or redemptive power. They can neither change the weather nor give life. But the LORD declares of Himself: "I am the LORD, and there is none else, there is no God beside Me: I girded thee, though thou hast not known Me: that they may know from the rising of the sun, and from the west, that there is none beside Me. I am the LORD, and there is none else" (Isaiah 45:5, 6).

Shem knew and taught that the LORD God not only created all things "visible and invisible," but He has the power to re-create a repentant and faithful sinner, and give eternal life.

> Therefore if any man be in Christ, he is a new creature: old things are passed away; behold, all things are become new (Colossians 1:16; 2 Corinthians 5:17).

> Of Him are ye in Christ Jesus, who of God is made unto us wisdom, and righteousness, and sanctification, and redemption (1 Corinthians 1:30).

God has never had multiple systems of salvation from sin. The plan of salvation from sin was complete when God gave His promise to Adam; unchanged when Shem preached it in Abraham's day; and still true when the apostle Paul took it to the Gentiles. People may disbelieve and set truth aside, but truth never changes.

> The thing that hath been, it is that which shall be; and that which is done is that which shall be done: and there is no new thing under the sun. Is there any thing whereof it may be said, See, this is new? it hath been already of old time, which was before us (Ecclesiastes 1:9, 10).

Truth never changes because the LORD God who made heaven and earth never changes:—

> For I am the LORD, I change not (Malachi 3:6).

> Every good gift and every perfect gift is from above, and cometh down from the Father of lights, with whom is no variableness, neither shadow of turning (James 1:17).

Jesus Christ the same yesterday, and to day, and for ever. Be not carried about with divers and strange doctrines (Hebrews 13:8, 9).

I am Alpha and Omega, the beginning and the ending, saith the Lord, which is, and which was, and which is to come, the Almighty (Revelation 1:8).

Before the fall of Adam and Eve, the seventh-day Sabbath was a blessed day of rest and a special time for fellowshipping with their Creator. After the Fall, the Sabbath was a sign that God alone can save us from sin; it is the "sign" of the everlasting covenant promise.

Look unto Me, and be ye saved, all the ends of the earth: for I am God, and there is none else (Isaiah 45:22).

I gave them My Sabbaths, to be a sign between Me and them, that they might know that I am the LORD that sanctify them (Ezekiel 20:12).

And hallow My Sabbaths; and they shall be a sign between Me and you, that ye may know that I am the LORD your God (Ezekiel 20:20).

Honoring God by keeping holy His memorial of Creation and redemption sets God's people apart from the world. The seventh-day Sabbath gives us a trysting place for fellowship with our divine Lover.[4] "And [Jesus] said unto them, The Sabbath was made for man, and not man for the Sabbath: therefore the Son of man is Lord also of the Sabbath" (Mark 2:27, 28; cf. Revelation 1:10).

From the first sin committed by Adam, God has only had one means of salvation—Christ and His righteousness; Christ, who is the "Lamb slain from the foundation of the world" (Revelation 13:8; see also Hebrews 4:3; 1 Peter 1:18-20). There is no power in the Law to save us. No matter how much we strive to meet its requirements, of ourselves, we will always fall short. "For all have sinned, and come short of the glory of God" (Romans 3:23). It is impossible for Phariseeism[5]

---

4. A tryst is an agreement, or rendezvous, between lovers to meet at an appointed place and time.

5. Phariseeism was a theological school of thought demanding strict adherence to the "letter of the law" of Moses. In contrast to the Sadducees, the Pharisees accepted all … (footnote continued on next page)

to produce righteousness. So-called "works of righteousness" done by an individual are merely a whitewash seeking to cover the sin underneath.

No matter how diligently one keeps the Law, it can never proclaim a sinner righteous. From the evidence of the sinner's previous life, the Law must continue to judge him guilty—until his sin is removed. And this is the glorious work of Christ for the sinner. "And ye know that He was manifested to take away our sins" (1 John 3:5). Christ "took away" sin, nailing it to He cross. It is the record of sin that is "against us," condemning us, not God's holy Law.

> Buried with him in baptism, wherein also ye are risen with him through the faith of the operation of God, who hath raised him from the dead. And you, being dead in your sins and the uncircumcision of your flesh, hath he quickened together with him, having forgiven you all trespasses; Blotting out the handwriting of ordinances that was against us, which was contrary to us, and took it out of the way, nailing it to his cross (Colossians 2:13, 14).

Before the throne of God, Christ raises His wounded hands, declaring that the believing sinner is innocent through His shed blood. The guilt is placed upon the Saviour, and the repentant sinner stands before God as though he had never sinned. The righteousness of Christ is accredited in the record book of heaven in the debtor's name. The guilty sinner is legally declared free from condemnation.

> And you, that were sometime alienated and enemies in your mind by wicked works, yet now hath He reconciled in the body of His flesh through death, to present you holy and unblameable and unreproveable in His sight (Colossians 1:21, 22).

> God was in Christ, reconciling the world unto Himself, not imputing their trespasses unto them … for He hath made Him

---

of the writings of the ancient prophets, while the Sadducees only felt bound by the first five books, known as the Pentateuch. Most of the lengthy discussions recorded in the four Gospels were between Jesus, the Pharisees and their scribes. The apostle Paul was a Pharisee before believing the good news of Christ's sacrifice for his sin. Paul then realized his legalism was worthless. (Philippians 3:5, 7).

to be sin for us, who knew no sin; that we might be made the righteousness of God in Him (2 Corinthians 5:19, 21).

Jesus "gave Himself for us, that He might redeem us from all iniquity, and purify unto Himself a peculiar people, zealous of good works" (Titus 2:14).

For what the law could not do, in that it was weak through the flesh, God sending His own Son in the likeness of sinful flesh, and for sin, condemned sin in the flesh: that the righteousness of the law might be fulfilled in us, who walk not after the flesh, but after the Spirit (Romans 8:3, 4).

If we walk in the light, as He is in the light, we have fellowship one with another, and the blood of Jesus Christ His Son cleanseth us from all sin (1 John 1:7).

Since the fall of Adam, salvation has always been through the life, death, and resurrection of Jesus. When He entered this world, taking sinful humanity upon Himself, Jesus submitted His will, yielded His heart and its affections to His Father, and thus exhibited and proved faith's power over sin and sin's ultimate outcome.

What the Law could not do because of the weakness of human nature, God did, sending His own Son in the same human nature as any sinner to be a sacrifice for sin, and condemning sin in that human nature (Romans 8:3, NJB).

To "condemn sin in the flesh" Christ had to assume the very same nature in which sin reigned. He must accomplish what He asks us to do in the same "equipment" we have, otherwise His demands are unjust. And so, God "hath made Him to be sin for us, who knew no sin; that we might be made the righteousness of God in Him" (2 Corinthians 5:21).

Jesus was unconditionally surrendered to His Father's will, and through faith in His Father's power over Satan and sin, He "grew, and waxed strong in the Spirit, filled with wisdom: and the grace of God was upon Him" (Luke 2:40; cf. Luke 2:52; cf. John the Baptist in Luke 1:80). Through the gift of the faith of Jesus, we can do the same (Romans 12:1-3).

It was only through faith in His Father that Jesus accomplished righteousness in His human flesh. He modeled His earthly life after the Father's character. Jesus admitted that of Himself, He could do nothing.

> Then answered Jesus and said unto them, Verily, verily, I say unto you, The Son can do nothing of Himself, but what He seeth the Father do: for what things soever He doeth, these also doeth the Son likewise (John 5:19).

> Then said Jesus unto them, When ye have lifted up the Son of man, then shall ye know that I am He, and that I do nothing of Myself; but as My Father hath taught Me, I speak these things (John 8:28).

The Father's gift to every person who has ever lived is Jesus' tested and proven faith. "God has dealt to every man the measure of faith"— not a small portion, but *the full measure* of the faith of Jesus. Those who lived before Christ and had faith in God's promise of redemption were justified by the faith of Jesus as verily as anyone who has lived since the Cross. "Old" testament faith is the same as "new" testament faith, there is no difference.

> Therefore by the deeds of the law there shall no flesh be justified in His sight: for by the law is the knowledge of sin. But now the righteousness of God without the law is manifested, being witnessed by the law and the prophets; even the righteousness of God which is by faith of Jesus Christ unto all and upon all them that believe: for there is no difference (Romans 3:20-22).

> Knowing that a man is not justified by the works of the law, but by the faith of Jesus Christ, even we have believed in Jesus Christ, that we might be justified by the faith of Christ, and not by the works of the law: for by the works of the law shall no flesh be justified (Galatians 2:16).

Writing about the patriarchs' faith, Paul declared: "These all died in faith, not having received the promises, but having seen them afar off, and were persuaded of them, and embraced them, and confessed that they were strangers and pilgrims on the earth" (Hebrews 11:13). Speaking to a group of Pharisees, Jesus said, "Your father Abraham rejoiced to see My day: and he saw it, and was glad" (John 8:56). "Abraham believed God, and it was counted unto him for righteousness" (Romans 4:3; cf. Genesis 15:6; James 2:23). Faith in God's power to deliver from sin has always been the vehicle through which overcoming sin is made possible, and then Christ's righteousness is demonstrated in the life of the believer.

Christ's work, the perfect "righteousness of God" in behalf of the entire human family extends[6] to us. Only this can remove sin and justify the sinner. All who will choose to believe God's promise of redemption from sin will *experience* this reality in their lives—"even the righteousness of God which is by faith of Jesus Christ unto all and upon all them that believe: for there is no difference" (Romans 3:22). We must learn to cease from our own works and rest entirely in the work of Christ in us. Reverence for the seventh-day Sabbath shows our appreciation of God's work in Creation and Redemption. By faith, we rest in God's power to deliver us from Satan's temptations, and we keep sacred the seventh-day Sabbath as a sign of appreciation for God's loving and merciful work of redemption on our behalf.

The fourth Commandment "remains" in place for the "people of God" (Hebrews 4:9)—it has never been rescinded or modified by God. In a world increasingly mired in pantheism and atheism, the Sabbath still announces to all who the Creator is: "For in six days the LORD made heaven and earth, the sea, and all that in them is, and rested the seventh day: wherefore the LORD blessed the Sabbath day, and hallowed it" (Exodus 20:11). The faith of Jesus and Sabbath-keeping go hand-in-hand. At the heart of the Ten Commandments, the Sabbath identifies God's faithful remnant in a world lost in sin and rebellion. "Here are they that keep the Commandments of God, and the faith of Jesus" (Revelation 14:12).

When we recognize all the LORD has done to save us from sin, we then "enter into His rest" by ceasing from our "works of righteousness" in attempting to save ourselves. There "remains a keeping of the seventh-day Sabbath for the people of God" who believe the truth of righteousness by the faith *of* Jesus Christ. "Knowing that a man is not justified by the works

---

6. Extend means to reach to the uttermost.

of the law, but *by the faith of Jesus Christ*[7] (Galatians 2:16, emphasis supplied). The faith *of* Jesus freely given to us works in the surrendered heart to transform the character. We "let this mind"—the "mind" of Christ—work in us, and it *will* change us. Yielding our minds to Christ, we will no longer want to do the wicked things that once controlled our life. When we are yielded to the Holy Spirit we "cannot do the [evil] things" we used to do (Galatians 5:16, 17).

"But unto every one of us is given grace according to the measure of the gift of Christ" for "God hath dealt to every man the measure of faith (Ephesians 4:7; Romans 12:3). The "reasonable" response from us is to "let this mind be in you, which was also in Christ Jesus" (Philippians 2:5). And we do this when we realize, "I am crucified with Christ: nevertheless I live; yet not I, but Christ liveth in me: and the life which I now live in the flesh I live by the faith *of* the Son of God, who loved me, and gave Himself for me" (Galatians 2:20).

The apostle Paul was trained at the school of Rabbi Gamaliel, who was "a doctor of the law" (Acts 5:34; 22:3). His education made Paul a master of the history and theology of the "old testament." When he was converted, Paul spent three years restudying the "old testament" books, contemplating the depth of verses that had been obscured through his preconceived legalistic ideas about salvation (Galatians 1:13-18).

During those three years of study in the peace and solitude of the Arabian desert, Paul compared what he knew about Jesus with his reinvigorated understanding of "the law." Thus Paul gathered the strands of the gospel found throughout the "old testament" that Pharisaical legalism had cast aside in its blind groping for self-righteousness (see Matthew chapter 23).

From this deep well of truth, Paul went forward preaching Christ and His righteousness. In his pastoral letters to fledgling churches, he made frequent references to and quotes from the writings of the ancient prophets, connecting his work directly to the gospel message found in the "old testament."

---

7. There is a significant difference between "the faith *of* Jesus" and "faith *in*" Jesus. The KJV Bible has the accurate translation of the Greek word *pisteos*. Here the word for faith is a noun in the grammatical form called "possessive," meaning it "belongs to" the one being referenced. The faith *belongs to* Jesus; it is His own faith that He gives to us. "Faith *in*" becomes something we do as we desperately grasp for heaven's reward; "faith *in*" is a subtle work.

Particularly in the letters to the congregations at Rome and Galatia, Paul expounded in fresh detail the eternal truth embedded in God's first promise of salvation given to fallen Adam in the Garden. Upon his conversion, Paul reawakened these "timeless truths," gathering "up the fragments that remained, that nothing be lost" (John 6:12).

The message of righteousness through faith alone has never changed. It was first spoken in Genesis 3:15 to sinful Adam by Christ Himself in the promise of the coming Saviour. Righteous Enoch and Noah preached it before the Flood. And "Enoch also, the seventh [generation] from Adam, prophesied of these, saying, Behold, the Lord cometh with ten thousands of His saints," referring to Christ's glorious second coming.

Peter identified Noah as a "preacher of righteousness" (Jude 1:14; 2 Peter 2:5). Noah's son, Shem, learned the good news from his father and the patriarchs Methuselah and righteous Lamech, who personally knew Adam and his son, Seth. Mind to mind and heart to heart, the Gospel's "good news" has been passed down from generation to generation through a faithful remnant people.

God's message of salvation has never been lost or changed. He has always had faithful witnesses. For five hundred years in the face of nearly worldwide opposition to his message, Shem kept alive the truth of the coming Saviour. Because he had learned from Shem, when God appeared to Abraham, he knew precisely who was addressing him, calling him away from a sinful environment to walk in righteousness. Post-flood humanity had no excuse for rebelling against their Creator.

The apostle Paul wrote:—

> Because that which may be known of God is manifest in them; for God hath shewed it unto them. For the invisible things of Him from the creation of the world are clearly seen, being understood by the things that are made, even His eternal power and Godhead; so that they are without excuse: because that, when they knew God, they glorified Him not as God, neither were thankful; but became vain in their imaginations, and their foolish heart was darkened (Romans 1:19-21).

As before the Flood, when only a few were willing to heed God's voice, so at the time of Abraham only a few were worshiping the God who made all things. When God called Abraham to leave Ur, he responded without hesitation, taking his immediate family with him. Abraham's journey from Ur was interrupted by a sojourn in Haran, where his father died. After burying his father, the LORD prompted Abraham again. "Get thee out of thy country, and from thy kindred, and from thy father's house, unto a land that I will show you" (Genesis 12:1).

Haran was not the end of Abraham's journey; he must move on leaving more of his family behind in Haran. He was given a seven-fold promise:—

I will make of thee a great nation, and I will bless thee, and make thy name great; and thou shalt be a blessing: and I will bless them that bless thee, and curse him that curseth thee: and in thee shall all families of the earth be blessed (Genesis 12:2, 3).

1. "I will make you a great nation."

2. "I will bless you."

3. "I will make your name great."

4. "You will be a blessing" to others.

5. "I will bless those who bless you."

6. "I will curse those who curse you."

7. "In thee shall all families of the earth be blessed."

God's message to Abraham was a seven-part promise that pointed to the coming "Saviour of the world," who would "crush Satan's head," and "make reconciliation for iniquity, and bring in everlasting righteousness" (1 John 4:14; Genesis 3:15; Daniel 9:24). Reading these words with Christ as the focus of the promise, it is readily apparent that "in Christ"—*and through no other*—all these points would be fulfilled "in the fullness of time" when "God sent forth His Son" (Galatians 4:4).

The next day John [the baptizer] seeth Jesus coming unto him, and saith, Behold the Lamb of God, which taketh away the sin of the world (John 1:29).

And many more believed because of His own word; and said unto the woman [of Samaria], Now we believe, not because of thy saying: for we have heard Him ourselves, and know that this is indeed the Christ, the Saviour of the world (John 4:41, 42).

The fallen human race's greatest need is a powerful and spotless Saviour who is able to correct the crime committed by Adam and his descendants; who has the righteousness fit to meet the just demands of the broken Law; and who has the necessary righteousness the Law requires to pronounce the sinner "not guilty."

Appreciation of such a life-restoring, pardoning gift will break the heart hardened in sin, changing the sinner's carnal mind that is "naturally" at enmity with God, into a submissive and loving friend (see Romans 8:5-9; 5:8-10). This is the everlasting covenant of Genesis 3:15 spoken to Satan in the hearing of Adam and Eve.

> And I will put enmity between thee [Satan] and the woman, and between thy seed and her Seed; He shall bruise thy head, and thou shalt bruise His heel (Genesis 3:15).

Through this three-part-promise, the Creator set the human family free from the hatred Satan instilled in the human mind, giving us the power to choose between good and evil. We are free to choose willing service to God or bondage to Satan (Romans 6:16). God did not leave His human family in abject slavery and total darkness. Although Adam freely chose to accept the mind of the insurrectionist, the LORD of love and mercy gave Adam and his wife another chance.

In the precise and comprehensive covenant statement in Daniel 9:24, the work of the Saviour is outlined in another seven-fold promise:—

> Seventy weeks are determined upon thy people and upon thy holy city, [1] to finish the transgression, and [2] to make an end of sins, and [3] to make reconciliation for iniquity, and [4] to bring in everlasting righteousness, and [5] to seal up the vision [6] and prophecy, and [7] to anoint the most Holy (Daniel 9:24).

Through Abraham and his descendants, who were first called "the children of Israel" and, after the Babylonian captivity, "Jews" (people from Judea), the message was to be given to the world concerning the coming Redeemer. Abraham's descendants were intended to be a group of people who continued to preach the Gospel of the coming Messiah and thereby prepare the world for the first advent of God's Son.

Thus, Abraham was promised that he would, through his descendants, become a "great nation." It took a long sojourn in Egypt where the family population grew from seventy sons, daughters, and grandchildren of Jacob who went to Egypt to survive a famine, to grow to a clan of nearly a million and a half people by the time of the Exodus, four hundred and thirty years later (see Genesis 15:13, 14).

But contrary to God's desire, this massive group led by Moses refused to learn righteousness by faith. As a result, even after forty more years wandering in the Sinai desert under God's personal guardianship and mentoring, the people were unprepared to be the nation God wanted them to be.

During all those years, the LORD was with them twenty-four hours a day, seven days a week, guiding them, protecting them, feeding them with bread rained down from heaven, watering them from a solid rock, and speaking directly to them from fire on the mountain, but they never learned to appreciate His self-sacrificing love for them. Instead, they grumbled and complained and ran after idols and other gross immorality. Of the original millions who left Egypt only two men entered Canaan: Joshua and Caleb, descendants of the tribes of Ephraim and Judah. It was through the tribe of Judah the Messiah would be born.

The children of Israel's original purpose as a people group was to herald the coming Messiah, who was the promised "blessing" through whom "all the families of the earth [are] blessed" (Genesis 12:3). They were called to live righteously as witnesses of God's power over sin, and to be prepared to receive Him when He entered the human race as the ultimate blessing for the world. What the Son of God came to do, no other human being, or "great nation," was (or is) capable of accomplishing. He would be the "Saviour of the world" (John 4:42).

Through the work of the Messiah, God would make Abraham's "name" great. The Hebrew word translated "name" means to mark or brand and is used to distinguish one person or thing from others. In ancient times, personal names for children were often not bestowed until the child was two or three years of age. The parents waited to name the child until the character became known. The name reflected that character.

A few notable name changes illustrate this. Abraham was originally called Abram, which means "exalted father" (even though he had no children). But God changed his name to Abraham, "father of many nations" (Genesis 17:5). Jacob means "supplanter" or "deceiver." When he finally learned to give his life entirely to God, his name was changed to Israel, "one who has wrestled with God and prevailed" (Genesis 32:28).

Abraham's name would be "great," and he would be remembered as the "father of the faithful" until the second coming of Christ. All who believe God's word, as Abraham did, and give complete allegiance to the God of heaven and earth, are accounted children of faithful Abraham.

"Faith" is not an intellectual or emotional contract or covenant with God. No contractual agreement is based on faith, but on the weak promises of the parties involved. Man's covenants are no greater than the moral frailty and instability of the covenanting parties. In contrast, true faith is a living and transforming fellowship with our Creator that makes His redemptive power effective in our lives.

The Bible teaches us that through the "faith of Christ," we are made heirs of God's eternal kingdom. "And if ye be Christ's, then are ye Abraham's seed, and heirs according to the promise" (Galatians 3:29). "The promise" is God's everlasting covenant made before the foundation of the world (1 Peter 1:18-20; Hebrews 4:3), restated to Noah and then to Abraham. God's promise was given to the whole world, and "especially those who believe" (Titus 2:11; 1 Timothy 4:10). God's mercy and forgiveness was extended to the entire human race from Adam to the end of time, but only those who believe will receive the gift of eternal life and the right to live in the recreated earth—"the Promised Land."

> For the promise, that he should be the heir of the world, was not to Abraham, or to his seed, through the law, but through the righteousness of faith (Romans 4:13).

> And I will establish My covenant between Me and thee and thy seed after thee in their generations for an *everlasting* covenant, to be a God unto thee, and to thy seed after thee. And I will give unto thee, and to thy seed after thee, the land wherein thou art a stranger, all the land of Canaan, for an *everlasting* possession; and I will be their God (Genesis 17:7, 8).

Superficial reading of these verses leads to the limited understanding that the promise refers only to the "land of Canaan." Such is not the case. First, we note that Paul explained that Abraham and his children "should be heirs of the *world*" (Romans 4:13). Secondly, the inheritance is to be "an everlasting possession." In order to "possess" something "forever" the person would need "everlasting" life. Therefore, the promise includes making righteous the heirs who will dwell forever in the New Earth.

> And I saw a new heaven and a new earth: for the first heaven and the first earth were passed away; and there was no more sea (Revelation 21:1).

> And He that sat upon the throne said, Behold, I make all things new. And He said unto me, Write: for these words are true and faithful (Revelation 21:5).

> For, behold, I create new heavens and a new earth: and the former shall not be remembered, nor come into mind. (Isaiah 65:17).

> For as the new heavens and the new earth, which I will make, shall remain before Me, saith the LORD, so shall your seed and your name remain (Isaiah 66:22).

> Nevertheless we, according to His promise, look for new heavens and a new earth, wherein dwelleth righteousness (2 Peter 3:13).

The promise to Abraham did not ultimately concern the land we now refer to as Israel, but pointed to the new earth that will be restored as the dwelling place for all the redeemed of God, regardless of their ethnic heritage.

> That the blessing of Abraham might come on the Gentiles through Jesus Christ; that we might receive the promise of the Spirit through faith (Galatians 3:14).

> There is neither Jew nor Greek, there is neither bond nor free, there is neither male nor female: for ye are all one in Christ Jesus. And if ye be Christ's, then are ye Abraham's seed, and heirs according to the promise (Galatians 3:28, 29).

The promise of inheritance does not concern ethnicity or political boundaries. What matters is faith in the Saviour to save His people from sin and eternal destruction. Only His righteousness demonstrated in the individual can fit the person for heavenly residence and fellowship among unfallen beings. This is the goal of the Gospel's message, that everyone should know CHRIST OUR RIGHTEOUSNESS (see Jeremiah 23:5, 6). "He that overcometh shall inherit all things; and I will be his God, and he shall be My son" (Revelation 21:7).

And since only righteousness will be in the new earth, the covenant given to Abraham and his "heirs" included the *making* righteous of all who will believe God's everlasting covenant. God promised a grant of land in the New Earth to everyone who is willing to have it from His hand and under His condition: faith in Christ as our Saviour.

But, unfortunately, the majority of the world's people spurn and throw away the gift so freely and lovingly given by the Creator. The final judgment will reveal that the lost have deliberately thrown away their birthright possession, preferring instead the temporary things of this wicked world.

> And I saw the dead, small and great, stand before God; and the books were opened: and another book was opened, which is the book of life: and the dead were judged out of those things which were written in the books, according to their works (Revelation 20:12; cf. Daniel 7:9, 10; John 5:29; Exodus 32:33).

Through God's promise to Abraham, "all the families of the earth are blessed" in Christ. Paul echoed this promise when he wrote: "The Spirit itself beareth witness with our spirit, that we are the children of God: and if children, then heirs; heirs of God, and joint-heirs with Christ" (Romans 8:16, 17). Christ alone is the Saviour, and His faith is the only means of redemption and restoration.

> Jesus saith unto him, I am the Way, the Truth, and the Life: no man cometh unto the Father, but by Me (John 14:6).

No "method," no "works" program or sacramental system can save the sinner *from* their sin (see Matthew 1:21). No ethnic or genealogical connection has any power to deliver from the coming destruction of the world in the lake of fire.

And the sea gave up the dead which were in it; and death and hell delivered up the dead which were in them: and they were judged every man according to their works. And death and hell were cast into the lake of fire. This is the second death. And whosoever was not found written in the book of life was cast into the lake of fire (Revelation 20:13-15).

From Genesis to Revelation God has one way through which He saves sinners. Only Christ can save us. In Christ the artificial "middle wall" erected by the remnant Jews returning from Babylon, that separated the "unsavable" Gentiles from themselves, was broken down (Ephesians 2:14). The "chosen people" are those who are grafted into the true Vine (John 15:5, 6).

Not as though the word of God hath taken none effect. For they are not all Israel, which are of Israel: neither, because they are the seed of Abraham, are they all children: but, In Isaac shall thy seed be called. That is, They which are the children of the flesh, these are not the children of God: but the children of the promise are counted for the seed (Romans 9:6-8).

What shall we say then? That the Gentiles, which followed not after righteousness, have attained to righteousness, even the righteousness which is of faith. But Israel, which followed after the law of righteousness, hath not attained to the law of righteousness. Wherefore? Because they sought it not by faith, but as it were by the works of the law. For they stumbled at that Stumblingstone; as it is written, Behold, I lay in Sion a Stumblingstone and Rock of offence: and whosoever believeth on Him shall not be ashamed (Romans 9:30-33).

Then said Jesus unto them again, Verily, verily, I say unto you, I am the door of the sheep. All that ever came before Me are thieves and robbers: but the sheep did not hear them. I am the door: by Me if any man enter in, he shall be saved, and shall go in and out, and find pasture (John 10:7-9).

Notes

12

Out of Weakness, Made Strong

"And he said unto me, My grace is sufficient for thee: for My strength is made perfect in weakness." (2 Corinthians 12:9).

Samson is one of the most tragic figures in the Bible. Consider his story. He was called of God before he was conceived, and raised by dedicated parents who understood the divine purpose of their son's life (Judges 13:1-5). However, when he reached maturity and should have been actively accomplishing his God-given task, he made a U-turn and spent the rest of his life in self-absorption, wasting his potential on the sins of the flesh.

Samson's feats are so fantastic that some modern scholars have attempted to explain him away as a myth. To these Bible critics, Samson's life story appears to have counterparts borrowed from pagan Greek mythological figures. They portray him as a demigod, comparing his life to the astonishing feats of Zeus, Hercules, and Atlas. Bible critics see Samson's exceptional strength and cunning as a reinterpretation of the activities of those ancient Greek gods.

Paralleling Samson's descent from hilltop retreats to interact with Philistines in the valleys below, critics liken the Bible narrative to the stories of the Greek god Zeus who supposedly had many sexual encounters with mortal "daughters of men." Like Samson, Zeus was said to have invincible strength except when succumbing to the siren song of lust. Other re-interpreters see parallels between the Greek Sphinx's three riddles and Samson's use of riddles to confound and tease his opponents. Samson ended his life toiling away at an unending chore, which is likened to the condemned Sisyphus, who had to roll a massive boulder up a hill, only to have it roll down again as soon as he reached the summit. Some critics have also selected texts from the Bible and likened Samson's activities to those of Christ.

Modern assessments of the Bible's narrative seek to undermine the validity of the Word of God, attempting to prove it is a man-made story based on ancient legends. One method of interpretation is a mythical way of dealing with Samson's history, another is a mystical way. Both place the carnal mind of man above the infallible Word of God.

But there is a third way. The apostle Paul writes that the lives of all the Old Testament men and women were recorded as counsel to us that we might learn something vital from their accomplishments and their mistakes. "Now all these things happened unto them for examples: and they are written for our admonition, upon whom the ends of the world are come" (1 Corinthians 10:11).

What saith the Bible about this enigmatic character named Samson? First, according to history, Samson lived more than three hundred years before the Greek civilization came into existence. Samson was a contemporary of the high priest Eli (1 Samuel 1:9) and lived during the early years of the prophet Samuel. Samson was born about 1160 BC, and Eli died in 1141 BC, just as Samson began his work for God (see Judges chapter 14). The Greek civilization began in the eighth century BC. If "plagiarism" took place concerning those ancient tales of Greek gods and the Bible's narrative of Samson, it would have to be the Greeks who got their ideas from the Israelites.

The narrative of the Book of Judges is not strictly chronological, nor is it a complete recitation of ancient Israel's history. It is a compilation of significant events that took place after Joshua's death and before Saul was called to be king. There is some overlap in the lives of the people whose deeds are recorded in the Book of Judges. The compiler who wrote this Book (probably the prophet Samuel) selected from all the events that took place during this period, choosing the ones that suited his narrative purpose. By selecting the stories and organizing them as he did, the author relates the general downward trend in the spiritual condition of Israel. He ends his narrative with the summary epitaph— "everyone did what was right in his own eyes" (Judges 21:25).

During this troubled time in Israel, God called a man from his birth to be separated and set apart for an exceptional work. Samson was to follow a strict Nazarite lifestyle, which included a total dedication to the will and work of the LORD (see Numbers 6:1-8). Usually, when a person took the Nazarite vow, it was for a short period of time and for a specific purpose. But Samson was a life-long Nazarite. The prophet Samuel was the only other person in the Bible who took a lifetime vow. As his contemporary, Samson's life is a blatant contrast to that of Samuel.

The narrative of Samson moves quickly from his birth to manhood. His first recorded act is the trip from his hilltop home to the Philistine village of Timnath in the valley below. In Timnath, he succumbed to the "lust of the eyes." When he returned home, he told his parents, "I have seen a woman in Timnath," and "she pleases me well." Then he demanded, "get her for me to wife" (Judges 14:2-3).

Initially, Samson intended to boldly take the war with the Philistines directly into the heart of the enemy's home territory. But he had not consulted God about how to accomplish this task. He took the matter into his own strong hands, feeling confident in his physical power to accomplish what he intended.

However, less than righteous motives caused him to seek an alliance with the enemies of God through marriage to a Philistine woman. He compromised every principle by which he was raised to be a man of God, and through lust and self-absorption, Samson set his feet on the path of sin. It was a short fall for Samson once he turned his eyes from God to self, and he plunged himself headlong into Satan's snare. Repeatedly Samson sold himself to foreign women, to "the lust of the flesh, and the lust of the eyes, and the pride of life" (1 John 2:16).

Like a roaring lion, Satan constantly seeks a crack in our armor through which he can gain a hold and strengthen his power over us.[1] By casual association with those who despise God and defy His will, through unguarded exposure to and participation in sinful ways, our willpower is weakened until we can no longer resist temptation. When guided by pride and focused on self, it is easy for Satan to lead us off the path of righteousness.

The valley of Timnath was known for its production of vineyards and wine. Traveling with his parents to make the wedding arrangements, Samson veered off to the side of the road into one of these vineyards, and there he met a lion. Confident in his superior strength, Samson ripped the

---

1. "Be sober, be vigilant; because your adversary the devil, as a roaring lion, walketh about, seeking whom he may devour" (1 Peter 5:8).

116

lion apart with his bare hands as though it were no more than a rag doll. When he rejoined his parents, he told them nothing about the incident.

There was a spiritual lesson here for Samson and he failed to recognize it. God gave Samson the strength to dispatch that "roaring lion" with his bare hands, but Samson attributed the power to himself. His pride would be his downfall. He could not conquer temptation through his own strength. Without God's power, Samson was a weakling.

At the appointed time for the wedding, Samson and his parents returned for the marriage ceremony. Curiosity got the better of Samson, and when they approached the place where he had killed the lion, he "turned aside to see the carcass." To his amazement, a swarm of honey bees had built a nest in the rib cage of the dead animal. Dipping out a handful of the golden liquid, he returned to his parents and gave them some to eat. He didn't tell them anything about killing the lion on their previous journey through that place. One of the Nazarite stipulations was thus thoughtlessly compromised: contact with a dead body, whether human or animal.

Like many of us, Samson's desire to be a part of the group caused him to further compromise his spiritual convictions, blinding him to the dangers of his actions. When Samson arrived at the woman's home, because it was the custom, he made a feast inviting friends of the girl's family to attend. He felt it necessary to conform to the habits and sensual indulgences practiced by the Philistines with whom he sought friendship. The party, without a doubt, involved the consumption of alcoholic beverages. During this seven day feast, the perverted characters and customs of these heathen persons worked to break down the spiritual principles that Samson had been raised to uphold.

And now, a second part of his Nazarite vow was compromised: consumption of wine. The Nazarite was forbidden from consuming all products from the vine, including its dried fruit (raisins).

Riddles were a common form of social entertainment at the time. Remembering the dead lion and the hive of bees residing therein, Samson devised a riddle to confound the guests at the party. Samson set up the game, named the prize, then said, "Out of the eater came forth meat [food]; out of the strong came forth sweetness."

Since the riddle was based on an extraordinary and secret personal event, it was not possible for the Philistine men to solve the mystery.

Determined that they would not lose the wager, they began to harass Samson's fiancee to discover the answer.

The townsmen decided that Samson had come to their city to humiliate and pillage them through the use of this unsolvable riddle with its exorbitant wager. Exasperated in their efforts to solve the puzzle, they went to the girl and said, "Entice thy husband, that he may declare unto us the riddle, lest we burn thee and thy father's house with fire." (Judges 14:15). The death threat so frightened the woman that she cried and pleaded with Samson to tell her the answer. Eventually, she wore down Samson's resolve, and he gave her the solution, which she immediately delivered to the Philistine men. Just before the time limit expired for the wager, the men swaggered into the party and said, "What is sweeter than honey, and what is stronger than a lion?"

Samson angrily retorted: "If you had not plowed with my heifer, you would never have figured out my riddle!" Now Samson was fully aware that he had been deceived by the woman he lusted after. In a rage, he left the party and marched twenty miles to the Philistine town of Ashkelon, where he killed thirty men and took their clothes to pay his betting losses. He then abandoned his fiancee and returned home to his parents.

Whatever the original motivation for his alliance with a Philistine woman and her family, his inability to judge character, and his inability to control himself resulted in disaster. In his quest to satisfy the lusts of the flesh, Samson forgot the spiritual principles he had been taught from his birth. The apostle Paul states the issue clearly: "What harmony can there be between Christ and the Devil? How can a believer be a partner with an unbeliever?" (2 Corinthians 6:15, 16).

Through his lack of sound judgment, Samson placed himself where he could not do the work that God called and sanctified him to accomplish. However, through God's gracious mercy, there was still room for him to repent and submit his will to God. Would he do it and thus become a valuable tool in the hand of his Lord?

Though at that time, Samson had been thoroughly convinced of his betrothed's treachery, his lust for her negated his common sense and he soon changed his mind. Samson determined to take his bride and consummate the marriage. Returning with a spirit of generous forgiveness, even bringing a young goat as a gift, he expected to take up the relationship with the woman where he left it. However, upon his return, he found that his unfaithful bride upon whom he had thrown away his love, was wedded to another man. In his absence, Samson's best man had married the woman. Her father felt justified in giving her to someone else because Samson had abandoned her so abruptly. "I assuredly thought that you completely hated her, therefore I gave her to your companion" (Judges 15:2).

Outfoxed at his own game, this time Samson sought revenge against the whole town. It was the time of the wheat harvest. The golden grains stood tall in the spring sunshine, awaiting the sickle. Attracted by the ripened grains, the fields were overrun with mice ... and the foxes that preyed on the mice. Taking assessment of the situation and allowing the Spirit of God to inspire him, Samson devised a novel method for extracting his revenge.

"Samson went and caught three hundred foxes and took firebrands" and tied the foxes in pairs with a torch between their tails. Then, lighting the torches, he turned the frightened foxes loose in the dry grain fields. The resulting inferno was so great it not only burned up the grain fields but also spread into the already harvested shocks. It then spread to the vineyards and the olive groves, destroying them all (Judges 15:4, 5). With one vindictive act, Samson devastated the agricultural economy of the whole region.

And he attracted the attention of more than just the local Timnites. Philistines from the surrounding area who also suffered loss asked, "Who has done this?" The reply was, "Samson, the son-in-law of the Timnite, because he had taken his wife and given her to his companion" (Judges 15:6). Surprisingly, the Philistines didn't retaliate against Samson. Instead of hunting Samson, they turned on the girl and her father as the guilty parties. "The Philistines came up, and burnt her and her father with fire." Thus did the girl suffer the exact fate pronounced upon her by the angry men at the party if she refused to cooperate with them in solving the riddle (Judges 14:15). Deception is never profitable.

Had Samson found his wife waiting expectantly for his return, having a heart open to reconciliation, his whole career would have taken a different path. However, God's sovereign will and purpose would be done despite the failings of His servant. The girl's death freed Samson of his alliance with the Philistine people, and Samson took up the battle in earnest against the enemies of Israel. To avenge the barbarous murder of his bride, Samson attacked the Philistines and "smote them hip and thigh with a great slaughter" (Judges 15:7, 8).

Whatever the original motivation for Samson's alliance with the girl from Timnath, it resulted in disaster and struck a significant blow against the enemies of God. Now it was an outright war between Samson and the Philistines. Leaving the battlefield, Samson went south into the territory of the tribe of Judah. There he took up a defensive position in a crevice in the rock called Etam. The Philistines followed him, positioning themselves in battle array. The Philistines had no argument against the tribe of Judah, but Judah was inadvertently harboring their enemy. Expecting every Israelite tribe to defend and rescue a fellow Israelite from trouble, they positioned themselves for war if it became necessary to capture their foe.

Not knowing what had occurred, the men of Judah were alarmed by this enemy advance against them. Asking the Philistines why they were aligned for an attack, the reply was "to bind Samson are we come up, to do to him as he hath done to us" (Judges 15:10). Like the rest of the tribes of Israel who had compromised their faith in God's power to deliver them from their enemies, through fear of their neighbors Judah had abandoned their allegiance to God and were then serving the Philistines. And the men of Judah were more afraid of the Philistines camped at their door than they were of Samson.

Taking the precaution of three thousand men, they approached Samson in his stronghold at the top of the rock. They rebuked him for causing trouble with the Philistines. "Don't you know that the Philistines are our masters? What is this trouble you've caused for us?"

Samson showed no animosity against his brethren, even though they came to capture him. He was fully aware of his God-given strength and ability to defend himself if necessary. All he asked was that the men of Judah did not attempt to kill him themselves. If they had, he would have been forced to defend himself against them. Even though they were unwilling to put forth the effort to protect Samson, he did not want to hurt any of his brethren.

Allowing himself to be tied with strong new ropes, he was then led down to the valley below. The Philistines thought this would be the end of their nemesis. As he approached them, they shouted obscenities and insults against Samson. This enraged Samson. The Philistines had not yet learned that an angry Samson was impossible to defeat. Snapping the ropes like threads, he grabbed the jawbone of a donkey lying on the ground near him. Using this as a weapon, he single-handedly routed the army of Philistia. "With the jawbone of a donkey I have slain a thousand men" (Judges 15:16). The astonished men of Judah ran for the hills fearing Samson would turn his rage on them.

Spiritually depressed and cowardly, the men of Judah refused to believe in God's power, even after such a demonstration as they witnessed that day in the valley of Lehi. The Lord raised up a powerful deliverer in their midst, but they united with their enemies and deserted Samson. Outnumbering the Philistine army by two to one, the three thousand men of Judah should have rallied behind their champion warrior and carried the battle all the way to freedom from Philistine oppression, as God intended. Instead, what should have been a signal victory for Israel was merely one more adventure in Samson's life.

Israel neglected the work God commanded them to do in driving out the heathen nations. Instead, they adopted their pagan practices, tolerated their cruelty, and through complicity, endorsed their injustices. The failure of Israel to obey God and believe His promises to them is recorded as a warning to us. Once we set our feet on the path of righteousness, we can not deviate without peril to our soul. We are called to be a separate people with the highest moral standard. Refusing to conform to the world's ways, we're to reflect the character of God in our lives.

While Samson was making gallant strides against the enemies of God, he was losing ground in the defense of his own soul. One of the most important lessons for us from the story of Samson is this: It is vitally important that we guard the portals of our minds. What we read, watch, and listen to does have an impact on our spiritual well-being. When we indulge in earthly things, we strengthen our carnal natures and permit Satan to mold our mind to his evil way of thinking.

The beginning of the end for Samson opens with a short factual statement: "Samson went to Gaza and saw there an harlot, and went in unto her" (Judges 16:1). At least with the woman from Timnath, he had professed to love her and wanted to marry her. Here there is no professed love, only a profane desire. This was a blatant act of presumption; he knew it was a sin but did it anyway. He went to Gaza not by the leading of the Spirit of God, but for self-indulgence. If we willfully place ourselves in sin, we cannot hope that God will protect us from the consequences.

The Bible gives no reason for Samson's visit to Gaza, which was in the heart of the Philistine nation, far away from his homeland. Venturing so deeply into the enemy's territory and encountering no harassment, seems absurd when we remember that a few short verses before, the Philistines sent out a thousand-man army to destroy him. Were the Philistines finally learning Samson's weak point? Were they using his weakness for beautiful women to lure him to his destruction?

Once Samson was inside the harlot's house, the men of Gaza locked the city gates, then lay in wait until morning. They planned to capture Samson as he attempted to leave town. However, Samson didn't wait for the sun to rise before departing. At midnight, while the enemies were sleeping soundly, he took his leave of the harlot. Finding the gates locked against him proved no obstacle to his exit from the town. "He took the doors of the gate of the city, and the two posts, and went away with them, bar and all, and put them upon his shoulders" (Judges 16:3).

To add some perspective to Samson's feat, consider these facts. Archeologists discovered that Philistine city gates were constructed in pairs of enormous size, weighing over a ton, constructed of heavy timbers, and then overlaid with bronze. They were hung from upright beams, the lower end of each turned in a stone door socket, while the upper end turned in a metal socket. To secure the gates, bars were laid across the closed doors and anchored in recesses in the walls of the stone towers between which the gates stood.

Samson lifted the gates, their huge safety beam, and the posts on either side "and put them upon his shoulders, and carried them to the top of an hill which is before Hebron" (Judges 16:3). This hill is about ten miles from the city of Gaza—mark it carefully. Samson carried a wooden and bronze gate weighing more than a ton, ten miles and up a hill before laying it down. An amazing accomplishment indeed!

When the Philistines awakened in the morning, they not only found Samson gone, but their fortified gates had been carried away. They knew beyond a shadow of doubt that their tormentor was no ordinary man. However, it was becoming clear to them that it might be possible to destroy this extraordinary man through a quite ordinary sin.

Whether Samson felt remorse for the sexual sins he committed with the Timnite woman, and then the Gaza harlot, is not recorded for us, but those disastrous experiences did not deter him from seeking other sexual encounters. On the contrary, he became emboldened in his lustful sin. Physically strong but morally weak, having stepped over the threshold of the abyss in committing willful sin with the prostitute of Gaza, Samson's complete fall was soon to follow.

Self-assured in his physical strength and confident that he was an unconquerable man, Samson thought himself secure against anything he would face at the hands of Philistines. But to regard the God-given strength as his own, and to abuse it upon his lusts of the flesh, was the crucial step in denouncing the true Source of his power. By his own acts of unfaithfulness and presumption, he would be deprived of his strength and God's protection.

Lust finally conquered Samson when he fell in love with the temptress Delilah who lived in the valley of Sorek. When the Philistines learned that Samson had fallen in love again, and this time with a more accommodating woman, they approached her to "entice him, and see wherein his great strength lieth, and by what means we may prevail against him, that we may bind him to afflict him." Of course, there was also the hefty bribe of "eleven hundred pieces of silver"—a fortune to be had simply for betraying the man who loved her. Again Samson chose to love a woman based on external appeal rather than moral uprightness.

Over a period of weeks, Delilah pressed Samson to give away the secret to his great physical strength. Perhaps he enjoyed playing with her and her co-conspirators by concocting ruses about using various types of ropes to bind him. Whatever Samson's purpose in continuing the game, whether he was amused or just over-confident, one has to marvel at his apparent unawareness during these attempts to capture him. Surely, even if he had been in a drunken stupor, he should have awakened when Delilah securely tied his hands and arms with ropes.

Finally, being weakened through his continued presumption of God's protection, taking credit for his safety among the Philistines, even while living a life of sin, Samson came temptingly close to the true source of his power when he told her to "weave the seven locks of my hair with the web" on a loom. But again, Samson discomfited the woman's plans, and she cried, "How can you say you love me when you have mocked me these three times?"

Delilah continued to "press him daily, and urged him, so that his soul was vexed unto death" by her nagging. The logical solution to Samson's weariness and temptation was for him to return to his home and never come back to this den of shame and iniquity. Why he chose to stay is indeed the beguiling "mystery of iniquity." Once sin ensnares the mind and enfeebles the moral character through indulgence, choosing the right path becomes impossible without God's intervention.

Instead of escaping before it was too late, Samson finally revealed the source of his strength. It was no magical secret, as the Philistines had assumed, but a supernatural enablement from the Spirit of God. But the strength of the Holy Spirit had been driven from Samson by his habitual sinning. It was gone, blinded by lust, and Samson did not realize it.

Revealing himself to be a Nazarite from his mother's womb, he said, "if I be shaven, then my strength will go from me, and I will be weak, and like any other man." Samson revealed his lack of spiritual discernment in this declaration. His physical strength was not in his shaggy uncut hair, but in his continual acknowledgment of God's power working through him. Samson lost the vital connection to God's power by attributing his strength to himself and his hair. He would never have fallen if he had given God all the glory.

Having obtained her objective, Delilah intoxicated him again, and while he slept with his head on her lap, she had one of the Philistine men cut off Samson's "seven locks." Immediately after she accomplished this, she woke him and "began to afflict him" with her taunts while the Philistine men came in, easily bound him with ordinary ropes, and carried him away to prison.

Enslaved by the enemies of God and having lost his God-given strength, Samson was powerless to resist the torture inflicted upon him. Besides beating Samson, the Philistines put out his eyes, the pathway through which he had been tempted to sin against God. They then cast him into a dungeon, forcing him to grind grain like a beast of burden. On their pagan feast days, they brought their prized captive out of his prison and paraded him in front of the crowds gathered at their temple, demonstrating that their gods were stronger than the God of Samson.

Samson was so weak that he could be led like a lamb by a small boy. When the people saw him, they rejoiced and "praised their god: for they said, Our god hath delivered into our hands our enemy, and the destroyer of our country, which slew many" (Judges 16:24).

Before being imprisoned, in all these escapades, Samson was merely listening to the inclinations of his own heart, whether of lust or anger. Though following his own will, he was nonetheless bringing about God's purpose for the deliverance of Israel.

Throughout his sinful life, God did not abandon His wayward servant. He was long-suffering with Samson, never leaving him even when he was committing adultery (both physical and spiritual). You can be certain that the Holy Spirit was there with Samson in that dungeon, wooing him to return to his first love, to the zealousness which characterized his original dedication to God.

The folly of Samson's life of lust and self-absorption became crystal clear to him as he endured the daily grind at the mill wheel. His physical blindness removed the temptations and lusts of the eyes and he was able to see his true condition. An apt description of his spiritual condition is "thou art wretched, and miserable, and poor, and blind, and naked" (Revelation 3:17).

Samson finally surrendered to God in the Philistine dungeon. Regaining not just his physical strength but his spiritual appreciation for God's gift, Samson was willing to surrender his life completely to God. He returned to the battlefield, fully willing to do God's bidding, even if it required his own life.[2]

The work Samson accomplished in the end, exceeded all the work he had done during his entire life. In his death, he killed more of God's enemies at one time than in all his sporadic warfare against the Philistines. With his faith in God renewed, Samson said, "Let me die with the Philistines. And [leaning on the temple pillars that held up the roof] he bowed himself with all his might; and the house fell upon the lords, and upon all the people that were therein. So the dead which he slew at his death were more than they which he slew in his life" (Judges 16:30). His final act of faith got Samson listed in the Bible's "Faith Hall of Fame"

---

2. **NOTE**: Samson *gave* his life to the work of God; his death was not suicide. Samson was a warrior who died on the battlefield.

(Hebrews 11:32, 34). When he fully surrendered to God, then out of his weakness, he was made strong through God's power to deliver.

From the beginning, God foreknew all that Samson would get himself involved in, yet He used His erring servant as a tool to drive a wedge against Philistine oppression. Even before his birth, the angel told Samson's mother, "he shall *begin* to deliver Israel out of the hand of the Philistines" (Judges 13:5). Samson would only be able to begin the work of deliverance. Unfortunately, two things stood in the way of complete deliverance: Samson's own foolishness in following the lusts of the flesh, and Israel's unwillingness to believe that God *could* deliver them if they would place their undivided allegiance in Him.

All Scripture is given for our education in the things of God (2 Timothy 3:16). "Now all these things happened unto them for examples: and they are written for our admonition, upon whom the ends of the world are come" (1 Corinthians 10:11). When we read of the failures of God's people, He intends for us to learn from their mistakes and not repeat them. We're to learn the corollary lessons that reliance upon self leads to bondage and destruction. "Know ye not, that to whom ye yield yourselves servants to obey, his servants ye are to whom ye obey; whether of sin unto death, or of obedience unto righteousness?" (Romans 6:16).

"Be sober, be vigilant; because your adversary the devil, as a roaring lion, walks about, seeking whom he may devour" (1 Peter 5:8). Our only hope is in total dependence upon Christ for deliverance from sin. "Put ye on the Lord Jesus Christ, and make no provision for the flesh, to fulfil the lusts thereof" (Romans 13:14).

Notes

13

Our Kinsman Redeemer

When Adam fell, not only did he bring himself under the Law's condemnation, but he lost the right to eternal life, and lost dominion over this world. Cast out of the Garden of Eden, Adam and Eve were shut away from the Tree of Life and had no access to it (Genesis 3:22-24). It would take the Kinsman Redeemer to rectify the breach of trust committed when Adam sinned, a breach that impacted the entire human race.

God will not restore access to this Tree until the earth is made new after the millennium. The apostle John recorded the description for us. "And I saw a new heaven and a new earth: for the first heaven and the first earth were passed away; and there was no more sea"; and "He shewed me a pure river of water of life, clear as crystal, proceeding out of the throne of God and of the Lamb. In the midst of the street of it, and on either side of the river, was there the tree of life, which bare twelve manner of fruits, and yielded her fruit every month: and the leaves of the tree were for the healing of the nations" (Revelation 21:1; 22:1, 2).

In any kingdom, there can only be one monarch, one absolute authority who rules over all in his realm. At creation Adam was given the office of vicegerent[1] and steward[2] in charge of this corner of God's universe. Adam was trustee of this world, acting on behalf of his Lord.

---

1. A person exercising delegated power on behalf of a sovereign or ruler.
2. Deputy-governor who manages his master's estate; a person employed in a royal household and given administrative power to act in his master's stead.

God is the Monarch of all that exists, but He placed temporal power in Adam's hands to be administered according to his Lord's will.

The Creator told Adam and all of His creatures, "Be fruitful, and multiply, and populate the earth" (Genesis 1:28). Adam was further placed as custodian over "all the fish of the sea, and over the fowl of the air, and over every living thing that moves upon the earth" (Genesis 1:26). As the divinely appointed steward of this world, Adam was to cherish his home and manage all things according to the will of his Creator, protecting the interests of the LORD of the realm.

By tempting Adam to rebel against his Creator and his Lord, Satan planned to establish in this world a base of operations for his cosmic warfare against God. Satan thought, with the fall of one man, he could gain possession of the whole human race and the entire earth would be his kingdom. With Adam's rebellion and fall into sin, all that was intended to be under Adam's dominion was delivered into Satan's hands, and Satan became "prince of this world" (see John 12:31; 14:30; 16:11). The apostle Paul called Satan "god of this world" (2 Corinthians 4:4). Jesus said Satan is the usurper "from the beginning," and a thief and murderer (see John 8:44; 10:10).

During the temptation of Jesus in the wilderness of Judea, the Tempter bragged that the earth was his, but if Jesus would bow down and worship him, he would give it all back. "And the devil said unto [Jesus], All this power will I give you, and the glory of them: for it was delivered unto me [when Adam fell]; and to whomsoever I will, I give it" (Luke 4:6).

In this statement Satan argued that he was the one who "set up kingdoms" under his own power, and there was some truth in his claim. From the time of Nimrod and the establishment of Babylon on the Plain of Shinar (Genesis 10:8-10), Satan has maintained a constant spiritual stronghold in the world through which he has promoted false religions of every stripe, and preserved his presumption to be "god on earth." Through these two falsehoods, Satan has promoted his lie that God is an "angry God" whose wrath must be appeased by human effort.

But, on the eve of His crucifixion, Christ told His disciples, "Now is the judgment of this world: now shall the prince of this world be cast out" (John 12:31). Christ's death on the cross of Calvary proved to the watching universe that Satan's ultimate desire was to kill God (Isaiah

14:12-15). At the cross, all confusion about Satan's claim that God is an exacting and unforgiving tyrant crumbled to the ground when Love laid down His life for His friends—the entire human race (John 15:13; 10:11; cf. Romans 5:6-10).

Room for Only One Master

It is undeniably true that there is only one Monarch in the universe and one LORD of this world. "Wherefore Thou art great, O LORD God: for there is none like Thee, neither is there any God beside Thee, according to all that we have heard with our ears" (2 Samuel 7:22). "That men may know that Thou, whose name alone is JEHOVAH, art the most high over all the earth" (Psalm 83:18). "Remember the former things of old: for I am God, and there is none else; I am God, and there is none like Me" (Isaiah 46:9).

God maintains absolute authority over the heavenly realms and all the kingdoms of this world. When this world was created, God intended to have only one vicegerent in the province of His universe we call Earth. Only through the invasion of sin can Satan claim ownership of the legal title to this world and control its inhabitants. When Adam sinned he and all of his human family lost dominion over this world. Satan now works his own will among the majority of earth's inhabitants, controlling all who are not faithful to God. There is no middle ground. By our free choice, we are either under God's leadership, or the arch-deceiver's control. "Know ye not, that to whom ye yield yourselves servants to obey, his servants ye are to whom ye obey, whether of sin unto death, or of obedience unto righteousness?" (Romans 6:16).

Contrary to Satan's claim (and also many human despots), God is the One who sets up kings and takes them down. All earthly kingdoms have existed to fulfill God's plan of exposing Satan's ultimate desire to destroy everything God has created. "Blessed be the name of God forever and ever: for wisdom and might are His ... He removeth kings and setteth up kings" (Daniel 2:20, 21). Our heavenly Father has permitted Satan's usurpation of this world so that Satan's character as the destroyer will be fully exposed. "He doeth according to His will in the army of heaven, and among the inhabitants of the earth: and none can stay His hand, or say unto Him, What doest Thou?" (Daniel 4:35).

Reconciliation: the Work of Our High Priest

Christ, our great High Priest, is now ministering in the heavenly sanctuary, working to cleanse the hearts of His people from all sin. "In all things it behoved Him to be made like unto His brethren, that He might be a merciful and faithful high priest in things pertaining to God, to make reconciliation for the sins of the people" (Hebrews 2:17).

For "God hath set forth [Christ] to be a propitiation through faith in His blood" (Romans 3:25). "God was in Christ, reconciling the world unto Himself, not imputing [our] trespasses unto [us]" (2 Corinthians 5:19). In fulfilling the eternal covenant promise proclaimed when Adam sinned (Genesis 3:15), the profound reality of Christ's death for our sins, when rightly understood, turns our enmity away from God and toward Satan where it belongs.

God's reconciliation includes reestablishing peace between mankind and the Godhead (Romans 5:1) and reclaiming this world as the home of the redeemed. When Christ has completed His heavenly ministry, His destiny is to be "King of kings and LORD of lords" (Revelation 19:16). "For He must reign, till He hath put all enemies under His feet. The last enemy that shall be destroyed is death" (1 Corinthians 15:25, 26).

When the work of redemption is completed and sin is no more to be found, then "the kingdom and dominion, and the greatness of the kingdom under the whole heaven, shall be given to the people of the saints of the most High, whose kingdom is an everlasting kingdom, and all dominions shall serve Him" (Daniel 7:27). Christ will soon come in heavenly grandeur to claim His prize. Every knee shall bow, and every tongue confess that Jesus Christ is "the blessed and only Potentate, the King of kings, and LORD of lords; who only hath immortality" (1 Timothy 6:15, 16; see also Philippians 2:10, 11).

How Reconciliation Is Accomplished

To accomplish His goals of reconciliation, reclamation, and restoration, Christ had to become our Kinsman Redeemer by assuming an extraordinary position in relation to His creatures. As an object lesson, Christ gave the "typical" [3] laws regarding the kinsman redeemer

---

3. In the Bible, a "type" is an image or symbolic representation of something that will come to pass in the future. An "antitype" is a person or thing that was prophesied, prefigured or represented by a type or symbol in the Old Testament, …

so that all could understand what He was going to accomplish in His life and ministry on behalf of the fallen race of Adam.

Laws regarding the kinsman redeemer were established at Sinai. "If thy brother be waxen poor, and hath sold away some of his possession, and if his kin come to redeem it, then shall he redeem that which his brother sold" (Leviticus 25:25). Adam sold his birthright possession to Satan when he sinned in the Garden of Eden and Christ, as our Elder Brother, is "the nearest of kin" who has the power to redeem what was lost. Long before Sinai, Abraham was a type of kinsman redeemer when he rescued Lot from slavery to Chedorlaomer (see Genesis 14).

In the broadest sense, the term kinsman redeemer refers to a person of the same race, tribe, or family. In the Bible, a kinsman redeemer was to be the nearest blood relation to the person who was in trouble, and it was the obligation of this redeemer to restore his relative's lost property, or forfeited inheritance, or to avenge his murder. Specific stipulations had to be met for an individual to be considered a kinsman redeemer. As we study these from Scripture, we will see they were all realized for the human family in our Elder Brother, Christ Jesus. Let's examine what the Bible says about the work of the kinsman redeemer.

Kinsman must Be the Closest Relative

The kinsman must be a "near" relative, the closest living relative to the person needing redemption. "One of his brothers may redeem him ... or anyone who is near of kin to him in his family may redeem him" (Leviticus 25:48, 49). In the event that the closest relative refused to assist, or was unable to help the person in need, then the next closest individual would be considered. We read of this circumstance with Ruth's husband's nearest of kin. "If you will redeem it, redeem it; but if you will not redeem it, then tell me, that I may know; for there is no one but you to redeem it, and I am the next after you" (Ruth 4:4, cf. vs. 6).

If Christ was to be our Kinsman Redeemer, He had to be the "nearest relative" to those who needed redeeming. In his pre-fall nature, Adam did not need a Saviour to redeem him. Only those who have fallen into sin need saving, and that includes the entire human race

(footnote continued from previous page)
especially a character or event fulfilled in the New Testament. The ancient sanctuary service with its priesthood and animal offerings were a "type" pointing to the antitypical work of Christ who takes away the sin of the world.

(see Romans 3:23; 5:12). When Adam sinned and corrupted human nature, the entire human race was "in his loins." His children could inherit nothing from him except fallen flesh.

The promised Redeemer was to be made of "the Seed of the woman," and "when the fullness of the time had come, God sent forth His Son, born of a woman" (Genesis 3:15; Gal. 4:4). Jesus is the "Son of David" and "was made of the seed of David according to the flesh" (Romans 1:3; cf. Matthew 1:1; 9:27; 20:30). Furthermore,

> … forasmuch then as the children are partakers of flesh and blood, He also Himself likewise took part of the same; that through death He might destroy him that had the power of death, that is, the devil … for verily He took not on Him the nature of angels; but He took on Him the seed of Abraham (Hebrews 2:14-16)

At His incarnation, Christ took upon Himself our fallen nature and assumed the redemptive position of our closest relative. Born of Mary, He became our "Elder Brother." As such, Jesus is closer to every human being than any earthly father, mother, brother, friend, or lover. Christ came to "save that which was lost" (Matthew 18:11; see also the parables of Luke 15). When Christ was born in a human body, He clothed His divine Self with that which needed redeeming: fallen human flesh. At that point in history, the human family had suffered more than four thousand years of physical, mental, and moral degradation caused by sin. Only by assuming our fallen human nature could Jesus Christ qualify Himself to be our Kinsman Redeemer and fulfill the function of "Saviour of the world" (John 4:42; 1 John 4:14).

Redemption from Slavery

The near kinsman could redeem a poor relative from slavery by paying the required debt if he had sufficient resources.

> Now, if a sojourner or stranger close to you becomes rich, and one of your brethren who dwells by him becomes poor, and sells himself to the stranger … after he is sold he may be redeemed again. One of his brothers may redeem him … or anyone who is near of kin to him in his family may redeem him (Leviticus 25:47-49).

For our Redeemer to rescue us from our slavery to Satan and sin, He must have sufficient resources to meet the demands of the ransom.

Mercilessly, the broken Law demands the life of the one who violated its precepts, and nothing less than the eternal life of the sinner will satisfy the just demand of the violated Law. If the sinner paid the price by shedding his own blood, he would lose his life forever (eternally).

To show that death is the end result of sin, God gave the "type" of the sacrificial system as a sandbox lesson. Through the shed blood of a perfect creature (a "type" of Christ), the person who committed the sin was spared from forfeiting his own life. The Old Testament sacrificial system gives us a glimpse of the cost of our redemption from sin.

> For the life of the flesh is in the blood, and I have given it to you upon the altar to make atonement for your souls; for it is the blood that makes atonement for the soul (Leviticus 17:11).

Adam sold himself and his posterity into slavery to Satan. By his one sin, we were all lost (Romans 5:12). In his destitute state, Adam could do nothing to save himself; he was "without strength" to change his circumstances (Romans 5:6). "Know ye not, that to whom ye yield yourselves servants to obey, his servants ye are to whom ye obey; whether of sin unto death, or of obedience unto righteousness?" (Romans 6:16). Adam traded his life and royal inheritance to Satan for a bite of the forbidden fruit. The price for his sinful choice was the life he possessed; eternal destruction was the cost of his rebellion. With no resources, he could not regain his lost estate or salvage his inheritance. How, then, was he to be free from his slavery to Satan? Only through his Kinsman Redeemer could Adam (or any of us) find salvation.

By taking upon Himself our fallen nature and in that defective equipment working out the perfect performance in obedience to all the Law demanded, Jesus proved that it is not necessary for us to remain slaves to Satan and sin. Christ opened the prison doors and set the captives free (Isaiah 61:1, cf. Luke 4:18). Though tempted in every way that it was possible for us to be tempted, Christ did not yield, not even by a thought (Hebrews 4:15; cf. Matthew 5:27, 28).

Adam represented the entire human race when he rebelled against his Maker, casting the whole human race into depravity and sin. "Wherefore, as by one man sin entered into the world, and death by sin; and so death passed upon all men, for that all have sinned" (Romans 5:12). Therefore, it was necessary that the Kinsman Redeemer as our divinely appointed Attorney at Bar,[4] represent all who have fallen "in" their human ancestor, Adam.

Christ was born "in the flesh" to represent corporate humanity, and after thirty-three years battling sin in its own territory, He then took that fallen human nature and paid the ultimate price by surrendering His perfect life on Calvary's cross. When He died, Jesus had sufficient resources to pay the required debt for every man, woman, and child who has or ever will live on this planet. Shedding His precious blood on the cross, Christ emancipated the entire human race from slavery to sin.

Murder Avenged

If a person was murdered through premeditation (not accidentally, but planned in advance),[5] it was the near kinsman's responsibility to avenge his relative's death by watching for and destroying the murderer. "The avenger of blood[6] himself shall put the murderer to death, when he meets him, he shall put him to death" (Numbers 35:19). Far worse than taking the life of an animal, having to slay another human to avenge murder, forced home the terribleness of sin.

Jesus called Satan a "murderer from the beginning" (John 5:44). Satan, in essence, murdered the whole human race with Adam's fall. Satan planned that the human race be lost forever. Having been forewarned of the penalty—"in the day that thou eatest thereof thou shalt surely die" (Genesis 2:17)—when Adam sinned, he forfeited his right to live. Why didn't Adam and Eve die as soon as they ate the fruit? Because, as we learned in chapter one, Christ is the "Lamb slain from the foundation of the world" (Revelation 13:8).

As soon as there was sin, Christ presented Himself as the Kinsman

---

4. "Standing at the bar" is a legal term in common law jurisdictions where persons must be qualified to be allowed to argue in court on behalf of another party.

5. If a person accidently killed another, he could find sanctuary in one of the cities of refuge until the matter could be resolved through an assembly of his countrymen who acted as a jury to hear the facts. If it did turn out to be an accident, the murderer was allowed to return to the city of refuge, and remain there until the high priest died, at which time he was fully vindicated.

6. The "avenger of blood" had to be a family member who was to seek out the murderer in behalf of the victim. Working in behalf of the victim who was unable to avenge himself, he was to bring the murderer to justice.

Redeemer, the Surety[7] for the human race, with as much power as when He shed His blood on Calvary's cross. The Divine Benefactor took the position of Saviour for the fallen race, and mankind was given a second chance, a new probation. Without the work of Christ in behalf of humanity, we would have no existence. The life we live is borrowed from the Son of God, Who "gives to all life, breath, and all things"; "for in Him we live, move and have our being" (Acts 17:25, 28).

The grace-filled blessing of probationary life given to Adam (and to all of his posterity) the moment he sinned, will be replaced by eternal life in Christ when He has completed His work as our High Priest in the heavenly sanctuary. When the last sin has been renounced and removed by Christ's cleansing blood, then He will lay aside His priestly attire, don His kingly robes, and come to claim His own.

Then, at the second coming of our Lord, we will be given the final crowning touch of immortality. The "last Adam," the "life-giving Spirit," will restore His creatures to the full bloom of a never-ending life. "For as in Adam all die, even so in Christ shall all be made alive" (1 Corinthians 15:45; 22).

> Behold, I shew you a mystery; we shall not all sleep, but we shall all be changed, in a moment, in the twinkling of an eye, at the last trump: for the trumpet shall sound, and the dead shall be raised incorruptible, and we shall be changed. For this corruptible must put on incorruption, and this mortal must put on immortality. So when this corruptible shall have put on incorruption, and this mortal shall have put on immortality, then shall be brought to pass the saying that is written, "Death is swallowed up in victory. O death, where is thy sting? O grave, where is thy victory?" The sting of death is sin; and the strength of sin is the law. But thanks be to God, which giveth us the victory through our Lord Jesus Christ. (1 Corinthians 15:51-57).

At the finish of Christ's ministry in the most holy apartment of the heavenly sanctuary, He will come forth as did Aaron on the day of atonement. He shall "lay both His hands on the head of the live goat [which typified Satan], confess over it all the iniquities of the children

---

7. A surety is a security of property, money, or life pledged as a guarantee of the fulfillment of an undertaking or a covenantal agreement.

of Israel, and all their transgressions, concerning all their sins, putting them on the head of the goat [Satan], and shall send it away into the wilderness" (Leviticus 16:21).

At the second coming of Christ, the responsibility for all sin will be placed upon Satan's own head. During the millennium, Satan will wander in the wilderness of this desolate earth destroyed by the last seven plagues (Revelation 16:1-21). Here amidst the destruction he caused, he will be left to ponder his responsibility for the sin problem (Revelation 20:1-3).

During the millennium, the redeemed examine the "books of record" and the "book of life" and learn all that Satan is responsible for (Revelation 20:4; see also Daniel 7:10; Malachi 3:16; Exodus 32:32; Psalm 69:28; Philippians 4:3; Revelation 3:5; 13:8; 17:8). Then, Satan and his evil army of fallen angels, along with all humans who have rejected the gift of salvation, will be destroyed forever (1 Corinthians 6:9, 10). By thus disposing of the "murderer" (Satan), the Redeemer will have avenged the wrong Satan perpetrated upon the human family. God's justice and mercy will be complete through the death of the murderer in the lake of fire (Revelation 20:12-15; Jude 6).

Redemption of Lost Property

Property sold or lost through debt could be redeemed by the near kinsman if he paid what his relative owed against it. "If one of your brethren becomes poor, and has sold his possession, and if his redeeming relative comes to redeem it, then he may redeem what his brother sold" (Leviticus 25:25). Not only did Adam surrender his life, but he lost his inheritance in this world. (Genesis 3:23, 24). By choosing to sin, he sold himself and all of his children into slavery to Satan for the price of a lustful appetite.

God's plan of redemption is based upon one Man who could restore the life and property taken by deception.

After the millennium, when the fires of cleansing have burned out, the earth will be made new. "For behold, I create new heavens and a new earth; and the former shall not be remembered or come to mind" (Isaiah 65:17). "The creation itself also will be delivered from the bondage of corruption" (Romans 8:21).

Then will the prophecy made to Abraham be fulfilled. "I am the Lord, who brought you out of Ur of the Chaldeans, to give you this land to inherit it" (Genesis 15:7). The promise to Abraham included the whole earth, not just the hills and valleys of Palestine. The promise also included the righteousness necessary to possess the territory.

The apostle Paul wrote: "The promise that he would be heir of the world was not to Abraham or to his seed through the law, but through the righteousness of faith" (Romans 4:13). Christ and Abraham are both described as heirs of the world:—

> Yet have I set My King upon My holy hill of Zion. I will declare the decree: the LORD hath said unto Me, Thou art My Son; this day have I begotten Thee. Ask of Me, and I shall give Thee the heathen for Thine inheritance, and the uttermost parts of the earth for Thy possession (Psalm 2:6-8; see also Galatians 3:16; Hebrews 1:2).

The promise concerning "heir of the world" must necessarily mean the New Earth because Abraham remained "a stranger and a pilgrim" all of his life while walking on this sin-filled territory. Abraham looked forward to the "better country" that will come when Jesus reigns as King (Hebrews 11:13, 16).

The primary definition of the Hebrew term translated "heir" in Genesis 15 is "to occupy, by driving out the previous tenants and possessing their place." This was God's plan for His people when they returned from Egypt, but it was never completed because of the nation's continued unbelief (Hebrews 3:17-19). Relying on their own military strength, the Israelites failed to fully drive out the "tenants" that occupied the land. Idolatry remained in the land due to Israel's inability to expel the Canaanite and Philistine tribes along with their false religions.

Eventually, they succumbed to the worship of false gods and rejected the God of heaven and earth (1 Samuel 8:7; Psalm 81:11, 12). Then was the prophecy fulfilled concerning them, if they should fall into apostasy:—

> "And it shall come to pass, that as the LORD rejoiced over you to do you good, and to multiply you; so the LORD will rejoice over you to destroy you, and to bring you to nought; and ye shall be plucked from off the land whither thou goest to possess it. And the LORD shall scatter thee among all people, from the one end of the earth even unto the other; and there thou shalt serve other gods,

which neither thou nor thy fathers have known, even wood and stone. And among these nations shalt thou find no ease, neither shall the sole of thy foot have rest: but the LORD shall give thee there a trembling heart, and failing of eyes, and sorrow of mind" (Deuteronomy 28:63-65).

The ten northern tribes were the first to be overcome by the Assyrians, who repopulated the territory with pagan immigrants from Babylon and the surrounding areas. Never did the Israelites return to their homeland, and for this reason, they are called the "Ten Lost Tribes." Judah failed to learn from their brethren's experience and soon were marched to Babylon, where they endured seventy years of captivity. "And this whole land shall be a desolation, and an astonishment; and these nations shall serve the king of Babylon seventy years" (Jeremiah 25:11). Their crime was too great, there was no one who could turn their captivity. No redeemer came to release them until the sentence God placed upon them had been fully served (Daniel 9:2; 2 Chronicles 36:20, 21).

When the Jews returned from Babylon at the end of their 70 years of captivity, God again placed them on a renewed probation that would last 490 years, at the end of which, because of their continued unbelief, God sent destruction upon the Jews for their rejection of the promised Redeemer (Daniel 9:24-27; Matthew 21:33-41; 23:37, 38; Acts 7:51-53). The city of Jerusalem and the Temple where Jesus walked, taught, healed, and called His people to repentance, were razed to the ground by the Roman army in AD 70, never again to be rebuilt.

After delivering a last scathing rebuke, Jesus turned to the leadership of the Jewish nation and sadly said: "*Your* house is left unto you desolate!" Jesus no longer claimed the Jewish Temple as "*My* Father's house" (Matthew 23:38; cf. John 2:16).

With the death of the Redeemer to whom all the sacrificial offerings pointed, the earthly Temple system was no longer needed. God demonstrated both the rejection of the earthly and the establishment of the heavenly when He tore the curtain between the holy and most holy apartments from top to bottom by His invisible hand. "Jesus, when He had cried again with a loud voice, yielded up the ghost. And, behold, the veil of the temple was rent in twain from the top to the bottom" (Matthew 27:50, 51).

Our Perfect Redeemer

Christ has done a "perfect work" in that He has fully defeated Satan and his evil angels. While in fallen human flesh He lived a faithful life of obedience to all the Commandments of God, and took that life to the cross as our perfect and complete sacrifice for sin. Satan's power over the inhabitants of this slave planet is broken. The cross of Christ destroyed Satan's claim to fallen humanity; it drove out the "tenant rulers" of this world. When the earth is made new, then all of God's redeemed will inherit and possess the land given by promise to Abraham—the whole earth recreated in its original perfection.

At that time, Christ will have fulfilled the final aspect of redemption, restoring Adam's lost Eden. God then will give the inheritance of eternal peace and rest to all His redeemed children. "Then shall the King say unto them on His right hand, Come, ye blessed of My Father, inherit the kingdom prepared for you from the foundation of the world" (Matthew 25:34). With that gift, every last detail of God's plan of redemption will be completed. Christ will have finished every aspect of the work God gave Him to do (see John 4:34; 5:36; 17:4). He will have saved and restored the fallen race and the sin-cursed earth.

The only reminder of sin left in the entire universe will be the scars of the crucifixion in our Saviour's body. "And one shall say unto Him, What are these wounds in Thine hands? Then He shall answer, Those with which I was wounded in the house of My friends" (Zechariah 13:6; cf. John 15:13).

Is the human nature of Christ essential for us to understand correctly? Yes. He could not redeem us if He did not become one with us (see Matthew 1:21, 23). It was fallen humanity that needed redeeming. If Christ had taken the nature of Adam as he was created without a trace of sin or rebellion in his heart, then a great gulf would still exist between fallen mankind and God. The nature Christ assumed at the incarnation is the ladder let down out of heaven, reaching from the throne of grace all the way down to where we are in our lost condition (see Jacob's vision, Genesis 28:10-17). It did not stop one or two rungs short but was firmly planted on the earth. It reaches everyone just where we have fallen and just where we need lifting up.

Christ restored our communion and fellowship with God. We may approach the throne of grace boldly through His holy name (Hebrews

4:16). Jesus is the way, the truth, and the life by which we approach the living Monarch and Sovereign LORD of the universe (see John 14:6). Through His life and ministry on earth, we see God's love for fallen humanity. "He who has seen Me, has seen the Father" (John 14:9). Jesus is the "image of the invisible God" (Colossians 1:15). By studying His life, we gain a living knowledge of God's character of love (Greek, *agape*, self-sacrificing love; 1 John 4:8-10).

A proper understanding of the nature which Christ assumed will bring a deeper appreciation of the cost of salvation. When we see that to be our Kinsman Redeemer, Christ gave up all heaven to take "the form of a bond servant" and die the equivalent of the second death (see Philippians 2:6-8), then we can begin to get a glimpse of the infinite sacrifice made by the Godhead to save us from sin.

How far will *agape* go to redeem fallen man? Look to Calvary for the answer.

14

A Lying Old Prophet

rt thou the man of God that camest from Judah?' And he said, 'I am.' Then he said unto him, 'Come home with me, and eat bread.' And he said, 'I may not return with thee, nor go in with thee: neither will I eat bread nor drink water with thee in this place: for it was said to me by the word of the LORD, Thou shalt eat no bread nor drink water there, nor turn again to go by the way that thou camest.' He said unto him, 'I am a prophet also as thou art; and an angel spake unto me by the word of the LORD, saying, Bring him back with thee into thine house, that he may eat bread and drink water.' But he lied unto him" (1 Kings 13:14-19).

This strange story in 1 Kings chapter 13 opens with the recently anointed king Jeroboam dedicating a new place of worship at Bethel. In this narrative, we find three men who all claimed they were doing the will of God. The first man, Jeroboam, felt that he was doing the will of God in returning the political and religious seats of power back to the worship of Jehovah.

Jeroboam was a man of Judah born in Bethlehem Ephratah, the city of David, and later, the birthplace of the Messiah. He served King Solomon as "a mighty man of valor" and was an "industrious" worker who did his work so well that his talents attracted Solomon's attention. His hard work and honesty were rewarded when Solomon put him in charge of the forced labor group from Ephraim and Manasseh; tribes descended from the two sons of Joseph who now were little more than slaves to Solomon (see 1 Kings 11:28).

As foretold by God's prophet, the king that the people demanded in place of God's leadership would eventually put the people under heavy tax burdens and force the young men into hard labor on his many expansive building projects. Samuel warned the people concerning the evil that would befall them: "And he will take your menservants, and your maidservants, and your goodliest young men, and your donkeys, and put them to his work" (1 Samuel 8:16).

By the time of Jeroboam, great resentment simmered among the people of Israel because of these burdens. Taxes and forced labor were two significant reasons for the revolt against Solomon's son, Rehoboam when he came to the throne.

Even though the LORD God had appeared to him twice and blessed him with godly discernment and phenomenal wealth, Solomon's heart was turned against God by his many foreign wives, who brought about Solomon's moral and spiritual deterioration. He was never supposed to take a foreign woman to be his wife, yet he married the daughter of Pharaoh "and loved many strange women, together with the daughter of Pharaoh" (1 Kings 11:1). "He had seven hundred wives, princesses, and three hundred concubines: and his wives turned away his heart" (vs. 3). Unholy associations destroyed the great king of Israel. Solomon's great pride and wealth blinded him to God's warning.

> Take heed to thyself, lest thou make a covenant with the inhabitants of the land whither thou goest, lest it be for a snare in the midst of thee: but ye shall destroy their altars, break their images, and cut down their groves: for thou shalt worship no other god: for the LORD, whose name is Jealous, is a jealous God: lest thou make a covenant with the inhabitants of the land, and they go a whoring after their gods, and do sacrifice unto their gods, and one call thee, and thou eat of his sacrifice; and thou take of their daughters unto thy sons, and their daughters go a whoring after their gods, and make thy sons go a whoring after their gods. (Exodus 34:12-16).

> For Solomon went after Ashtoreth, the goddess of the Zidonians,[1] and after Milcom, the abomination of the Ammonites. And Solomon did evil in the sight of the LORD, and went not fully after the LORD, as did David his father (1 Kings 11:5, 6; cf. vs. 33).

---

1. Zidonians, also spelled Sidonians, are people living in Sidon, which was a principal city in Phoenicia. Jezebel's father was king of the Zidonians.

Ashtoreth was originally the moon goddess in Babylon. She became the consort of the Canaanite god, Baal. The immoral temple rites used in her worship were supposed to have been exterminated by the Israelites when they conquered Canaan. The male god, Milcom, was also called Molech. The worship of this god consisted of the worst possible abomination: the people roasted alive their infant children in the fire burning in the metal statue of Molech. When the people of Israel sank to this level of wickedness, they exceeded the limit of God's mercy.

> Wherefore the LORD said unto Solomon, Forasmuch as this is done of thee, and thou hast not kept My covenant and My statutes, which I have commanded thee, I will surely rend the kingdom from thee, and will give it to thy servant (1 Kings 11:11).

The oath was not executed during Solomon's lifetime "for David, [his] father's sake." But during the remaining years of his reign, Solomon was plagued by the adversaries that the LORD "stirred up" against him (vv. 14, 23, 26, 27).

When Solomon's son, Rehoboam, mounted the throne of Israel, he was advised by the wise elder statesmen who had served his father, "If thou wilt be a servant unto this people this day, and wilt serve them, and answer them, and speak good words to them, then they will be thy servants for ever" (1 Kings 12:7). But the younger, inexperienced, and power-hungry men of Rehoboam's court advised him to increase the taxes and lay the whip to the resistant workers.

Rehoboam's wicked heart listened to the wrong advice, and the nation was torn asunder by revolution. As God promised, Solomon's kingdom was taken from him and given to his servant, Jeroboam (1 Kings 11:11; 29-31).

Through His prophet, Ahijah, God said to Jeroboam, "if thou wilt hearken unto all that I command thee, and wilt walk in My ways, and do what is right in My sight, to keep My statutes and My commandments, as David My servant did; then I will be with thee, and build thee a sure house, as I built for David, and will give Israel unto thee" (1 Kings 11:38). The promise of God to Jeroboam, if heeded, would have changed the course of Israel's history.

After the death of Solomon and additional oppression by his son, Rehoboam, the northern tribes felt they had a right to rebel.

They intended to return political and religious control to the tribes of Ephraim as it had been from the early settlement of Canaan. Because religion and politics had become corrupted through the incorporation of pagan ideas and practices, Jeroboam felt he was doing the will of God in attempting to correct the matter. But he went about it in his own way. God's promise to Jeroboam (and to all of us) was that obedience brings the blessings.

When he crafted the two golden calves, Jeroboam's desire was to keep the northern tribes free from the pagan influences that brought down Solomon's kingdom. He remembered how God's high priest, Aaron made a golden calf as a visual aide to assist the people in their worship of God. But he forgot God's commandment: "Thou shalt make thee no molten gods" (Exodus 34:17).

Jeroboam didn't stop with just creating idols. Without any authority from the God of heaven, he also commissioned false priests from "the lowest of the people, which were not of the sons of Levi" (1 Kings 12:31). And he initiated a counterfeit day of worship.

Jeroboam was a leader who, if led by God, could have effected a movement of true repentance and reformation in Israel. Reliance upon his own judgment in spiritual matters and without consulting God in fervent prayer caused Jeroboam to fail his trial. Judgment was swift in coming. As he was carrying out the dedication, a stranger approached the altar as Jeroboam and his traitorous priests were making their offering.

A Second Man Doing the Will of God

Then, an unnamed "man of God from Judah" suddenly entered the scene with a message for Jeroboam directly from the LORD. He is the second man who thought he was doing the will of God that day.

Standing with complete confidence in the Master who sent him, the stranger manifested the power of God as he exposed the rebellion taking place in Bethel. Rebuking Jeroboam and the people for their apostasy, he prophesied against the altar and Jeroboam's misdirected reformation, saying, "Altar, altar, this is what the LORD says, 'A son will be born to the house of David, named Josiah, and he will sacrifice on you the priests of the high places who are burning incense on you. Human bones will be burned on you'" (1 Kings 13:2, HCSB).

The stranger added: "This is the sign[2] which the LORD hath spoken; Behold, the altar shall be rent, and the ashes that are upon it shall be poured out."

Jeroboam was stunned by the interruption and raised his hand to direct his guards to arrest the man. But as he did, his hand became withered and useless so that he could not put it down. At the same time, the last words uttered by the prophet came to pass. "The altar was rent, and the ashes poured out from the altar, according to the sign which the man of God had given by the word of the LORD" (1 Kings 13:5).

An immediate reversal of Jeroboam's attitude brought repentance, and he begged the prophet to pray to the LORD for his healing. "And the man of God besought the LORD, and the king's hand was restored to him again and became as it was before" (vs. 6). With his change of heart, the king invited the prophet to come to his home for refreshment and a reward. The prophet's instruction from God was that he must not tarry in his work but return directly home without partaking of any food or drink. "So he went another way," headed back to his home in Judah.

Incredibly, before the sun set that afternoon, he met destruction. This man with a message went from working through complete confidence in the power of God, to becoming a parable and a terrible warning against all who will not stand firm on the Word of God. The Scripture lesson offers a rich mine of material that applies to the day in which we are living. Every person on earth will soon face the same challenge brought to Israel by Jeroboam. Which God is the true God, and how does He command us to worship Him? Will we faithfully cling to His Word, or follow the interpretations and traditions of men?

The challenge brought by Jeroboam was magnified in the days of Elijah when he stood on Mount Carmel and exclaimed: "How long halt ye between two opinions? if the LORD be God, follow Him: but if Baal, then follow him." Because of vast confusion about who the true God was, "the people answered him not a word." God's character and His law had been undermined and compromised for so long that the people could not make an intelligent decision about what they believed.

---

2. The prophecy concerning Josiah was given nearly 350 years before Josiah was born, and was exactly fulfilled. See 2 Kings 23:15-18.

In Elijah's day, tradition and pride had produced a group of people who were content to unresistingly be led down an "easy" path to destruction. We are no different today and are headed for a showdown just as Elijah brought to the people of Israel. Around the globe, people are inundated with misunderstandings about God's character of love. Satan has interwoven subtle deception into the true Gospel so that few can tell the difference between Baal and Jehovah.

A Third Man Claiming to be Sent from God

Our third character is nearly inscrutable from the evidence provided in the Bible narrative. To understand this story, we must gather the crumbs that were dropped for us along the way. The man is called an "old prophet from Bethel." We're told that he had some sons who were part of the dedication ceremony on the mountaintop. The fact that they related the story to their father tells us that the old prophet did not accompany his sons. Apparently, the man was not too frail to attend because he jumped on a donkey and rode after the younger "man of God" as he went on his way home. It was not the distance that prevented him from attending because he lived in the same town where the dedication ceremony was held.

We can wonder why he was not in attendance, if he were a true prophet of God. Even though we're told the old prophet was a liar, perhaps we can construe that, as a prophet of God, his non-attendance at the ceremony was a silent reprimand against the new form of religion. But why was *he* not sent to confront Jeroboam instead of a man from Judah? At the end of the narrative, we find that God used this lying prophet to condemn the younger man who had shown himself weak in faith, even though he stood strong before Jeroboam.

The takeaway for us is, "Beloved, believe not every spirit, but try the spirits whether they are of God: because many false prophets are gone out into the world." (1 John 4:1).

Riding hard on his donkey to catch the fleeing young man, the old prophet quickly came upon him sitting on the side of the road under a shade tree. Lingering instead of hurrying home, as the instructions implied he should do, was the first mistake the young man made. It placed him in a compromised and weakened position. Having carried out God's condemnation of Jeroboam's new method of worship, the young prophet did not flee the scene of idolatry as he should have.

Perhaps the confrontation with Jeroboam was carried out by command, not heart conviction. When the old prophet caught up to him, he had already lost his momentum for determined obedience, and without conviction regarding what he preached, he had no other motive. Therefore, he did not, as he ought to have done, "stay the course" until his assigned task was completed, which included returning home without stopping.

Tempting the young man to question the exactness of the word of the LORD, the old man said, "I am a prophet also as thou art; and an angel spake unto me by the word of the LORD" (1 Kings 13:18). Liar that he was, he couldn't bring himself to claim that God Himself had spoken to him. Instead, he used an indirect method by claiming that an "angel spake unto [him] by the word of the LORD."

There are holy angels and evil angels. We must "try the spirits" against the sure Word of God. The apostle Paul admonishes us: "Though we, or an angel from heaven, preach any other gospel unto you than that which we have preached unto you," we are to reject that "new gospel" (Galatians 1:8). If the "word" from any "spirit" or person does not align with the Word that has proven itself to be the truth of God, we should immediately reject it, no matter how convincing it sounds, and no matter the assumed authority of the speaker.

Just because someone tells us that they have "heard the voice of God" and the message they bring is "new light" we ought to heed, we must have discernment. "Try the spirit" and put what they say against the Word of God. If the "new light" does not match the truth of Scripture, we must reject it. The Holy Spirit does not contradict Himself. He inspired the words of our Bible and will not later present contrary information which would only serve to bring confusion.

The young man from Judah knew precisely what the LORD had instructed him to do. He repeated to the old prophet what he told Jeroboam. "I may not return with thee, nor go in with thee: neither will I eat bread nor drink water with thee in this place: for it was said to me by the word of the LORD, Thou shalt eat no bread nor drink water there, nor turn again to go by the way that thou camest" (1 Kings 13:16-17).

The old prophet's statement that he had "heard" a contradictory instruction from "an angel" (implying that the "angel" was from the

LORD), was accepted by the young man without question. So easily convinced to reverse his conviction of the truth of God's word, the young man got up and, following the old man, went back the way he came, in opposition to the plain word of God.

As they were eating their supper, "the word of the LORD came unto the [old] prophet that brought him [the young man] back." This is now the third time "the word of the LORD" was spoken to these two men. First, the "word of the LORD" was spoken to the young man from Judah instructing him to confront Jeroboam; second, the old prophet said he had received "word" from the LORD that it was permissible for the young man of God to come home with him. The third time, the LORD spoke again to the old man condemning the young man for his disobedience.

> And it came to pass, as they sat at the table, that the word of the LORD came unto the [old] prophet that brought him back: and he cried unto the man of God that came from Judah, saying, Thus saith the LORD, Forasmuch as thou hast disobeyed the mouth of the LORD, and hast not kept the commandment which the LORD thy God commanded thee, but camest back, and hast eaten bread and drunk water in the place, of the which the LORD did say to thee, Eat no bread, and drink no water; thy carcase shall not come unto the sepulchre of thy fathers (1 Kings 13:20-22).

We have nothing recorded as to how the young prophet received his condemnation. Was he stunned beyond words when confronted with his blatant disobedience? Did he understand that by yielding to the desires of the flesh, he was condemned? We can understand that the man was probably tired from his travels and hungry, but that should not have prevented him from obeying God's command.

Was he distraught to learn he'd been tricked? Did he curse the old prophet who lied to him while offering to be his friend? Was his heart stricken with grief for his misrepresentation of God's character?

He willingly believed a stranger's lie rather than cling to the word that had been spoken to him "from the LORD." The Word instructed him not to stay in enemy territory for a moment longer than necessary to carry out God's will. Instead of hastening home, stopping to rest under the shade tree was the opening door for Satan to take action on the young prophet's vacillating character.

Rather than letting his faith in God's word become firmly established through evidence, he chose to discount the evidence presented before him that God was indeed the One who spoke through him to Jeroboam. The counterfeit altar fell apart and spilled its ashes on the ground, just as "the word of the LORD" had said it would (1 Kings 13:2, 5). Despite solid evidence, he defied God's plain commandment to return straight home without stopping for rest or refreshment.

These facts he could not deny. He was undoubtedly guilty of the charges against him and found no room for any objection or plea of innocence.

After pronouncing the young Judean's doom, the old man calmly finished his supper and then sent "the man of God" away on his own donkey. The "man of God" came to Bethel traveling on foot. Why did the old prophet give him his donkey? Was he hoping that haste in returning home might circumvent the curse? Was the old man feeling guilty for bringing this young man to an early death?

"And as he [the young man] went away a lion met him on the road and killed him. And his body was thrown in the road, and the donkey stood beside it; the lion also stood beside the body" (1 Kings 13:24). The lion killed the disobedient man of God, but did not maul or eat any part of the man's body—"the lion had not eaten the body or torn the donkey" (vs. 28).

The obedient lion carried out the pronounced judgment but went no further, not even frightening away the donkey, which also stood nearby awaiting his duty to carry the dead man's body to its burying place. These particulars are given to us to show that the judgment was of divine origin and not an accident. God is in control of His creatures, and they do His bidding when He commissions them.

Soon, other travelers came that way on the road. They must have stopped short as they approached the alarming scene before them: a lion and a donkey standing peacefully together and, between them, sprawled the body of a man. The man being obviously dead and needing no assistance, and having no desire to confront the lion so they could retrieve the body, the group hurried on toward the city of Bethel.

Excitedly, they related the extraordinary sight they had witnessed which became the talk of the town.

"And when the prophet who had brought him back from the way heard of it, he said, 'It is the man of God who disobeyed the word of the LORD; therefore the LORD has given him to the lion, which has torn him and killed him, according to the word that the LORD spoke to him.'" The old man overstated the damage done to the body (he had not actually seen it yet), but knew immediately as he heard the news who the victim was. His sons saddled another donkey for him, and he went down the road until he found the body, with the lion and his donkey standing guard.

> And the prophet took up the body of the man of God and laid it on the donkey and brought it back to the city to mourn and to bury him. And he laid the body in his own grave. And they mourned over him, saying, "Alas, my brother!" (vv. 29, 30).

It seems incongruous to repeatedly refer to the young prophet as "the man of God" when he had been blatantly disobedient, and then mourn him as a brother when the old man's lies were the stumblingstone over which he fell. The lies of the old prophet were not the cause of his disobedience. The cause of the young man's disobedience was unbelief of God's clear word spoken to him.

Further, it seems most cruel to so harshly judge the one and let the other go free. How can we solve the apparent extreme disparity in God's judgment?

The young man's disobedience was inexcusable. He had "the word of the LORD" instructing him to return to Judah without any delay. Yet it is true, he *was* deceived by the old prophet's lie that contradicted the LORD's command.

Here we have the same predicament found with Adam and Eve: explicit instruction with consequences known beforehand, deception of an innocent person, and a subsequent death judgment. The young "man of God" and Eve both listened to the voice of a "stranger" and accepted the lie without question.

Why was the judgment so harsh? Let's consider the purpose for which the man of Judah was sent by God to Bethel. Jeroboam was in the process of initiating Egyptian calf worship, through which the people's hearts would be further turned away from the worship of the one true God, Creator of heaven and earth.

The young prophet's curse of the false day of worship and the pagan idol's altar was to be a standing rebuke against the sin of Israel. It had been accompanied by the sign of God's displeasure when the altar stones crumbled and ashes from the false sacrifice spilled on the ground. Jeroboam was summarily condemned when his hand and arm withered. The prophet's refusal to accept congenial fellowship with the sinners of Bethel was also a rebuke against them. All these miraculous signs from the LORD were intended to bring to the people's attention an awareness of the false path they were treading. The signs were a call to repentance and true spiritual reformation.

Like Adam and Eve, the young man, knowing of a certainty that the word that had come to him "from the LORD" was true, chose to believe a lie instead of remaining firmly planted by faith in that truth. We shake our heads in disbelief over how quickly he turned around and went contrary to the Source of the power he had witnessed earlier in the day when he confronted Jeroboam at the altar. When the evidence was so plain before him, we wonder at his lack of faith.

Accepting fellowship with the old prophet of Bethel, returning with him to the cursed city, and partaking of a meal contrary to the explicit command of God, all worked to destroy the moral purpose of his mission. It might seem that eating and drinking were inconsequential matters and hardly worthy of harsh judgment, but by going contrary to the command of God, especially after he had publicly repeated it, he was doing precisely what Jeroboam and the people of Bethel were doing. They all were ignoring the plain command of God and accepting the ordinances of men instead of following the path of God laid before them. We do the same when without questioning, we abandon God's Word and accept man's religious traditions.

Doubting and changing the word of God is an age-old problem, beginning with Eve in the Garden of Eden. In condemning the manipulation of God's Scriptures done by the Pharisees, Jesus exclaimed: "Ye hypocrites, well did Esaias prophesy of you, saying, This people draweth nigh unto Me with their mouth, and honoureth Me with their lips; but their heart is far from Me. But in vain they do worship Me, teaching for doctrines the commandments of men" (Matthew 15:7-9).

Was "the man of God" guilty of a crime against God worthy of death? Absolutely. As a representative of God, coming "in the name of the LORD," he nonetheless listened to the tempter's voice and followed it. As a result, instead of being a witness for the faith which produces obedience to God's word, he became an example of disobedience and unfaithfulness, the very things God sent him to condemn. As "the man of God," he misrepresented God's character and opened the door to confusion about whether God's word really means what it says.

The lesson?—be careful how you handle God's word when it comes to you. Learn to stand firm on "every word that proceedeth out of the mouth of God" (Matthew 4:4).

Obedience is not optional. In contrast to this unnamed prophet of God, we must stand upon the Word of God alone, never compromising, never yielding the truth as it is in Jesus. Compromise for the sake of so-called "unity" or as an attempt to effect a reformation in God's people, will end in moral disaster. We are called to stand firm upon the truth we have been given in the Word of God. If approached by an "old prophet" who claims to have a message from God that runs contrary to the clear teaching of the Bible, we must remember this lesson.

No matter what stratagem Satan should use; no matter how truthful and appealing the "new" version of the Gospel may outwardly appear; no matter how charismatic the preacher that brings it, we must stand firm. God's word instructs us ever to stand guard against the "wiles of Satan." For lack of vigilance and spiritual discernment, we may fall prey to Satan's deceptions even while calling ourselves Christian.

We are standing on the brink of the Heavenly Canaan and must remain faithful "though the heavens fall." The reward is to "him that overcometh even as [Christ] overcame" every temptation through faith in His Father's power (Revelation 3:21).

15

How Do You Spell BAD?

Notwithstanding, I have a few things against thee, because thou sufferest that woman Jezebel, which calleth herself a prophetess, to teach and to seduce My servants to commit fornication, and to eat things sacrificed unto idols. And I gave her space to repent of her fornication; and she repented not" (Revelation 2:20-21).

How do you spell "bad"? Most people would respond, b-a-d. So, yes, that's how you *spell* it, but how would you *paint a picture* of it or illustrate it? Does the Bible give us any clues?

The Phoenician princess and prophetess of Baal named Jezebel has entered the English language as a descriptive noun portraying wickedness. She was an immoral power-hungry, violent, and whorish woman. The Bible uses her name to symbolize spiritual corruption and apostasy, as in the verse quoted above. Jezebel is the portrait of a totally bad person. The Bible narrative associates her with none of the refined and higher qualities of feminine characteristics. Evil of the worst sort is associated with her name, which embodies seductive power and wholly corrupt sinfulness.

Surprisingly, the definition of her name comes from a Hebrew root word meaning chaste, virtue, or purity, free from a sensual connection. When her father, Ethbaal (1 Kings 16:31), named Jezebel, he must have thought he saw in her these characteristics. Her father was the high priest of Baal and had risen to power as king of Phoenicia through deceit, skulduggery, and murder. The twin Phoenician cities of Tyre and Sidon were so wicked that they are used in the Bible as metaphors for Satan (see Ezekiel 28:11-19).

Jezebel was born of a king and high priest; therefore, she inherited the dual rank of princess of Phoenicia and the high priestess of Baal. She was born in sin, raised in sin, and had both inherited and cultivated tendencies toward evil. She was, by conviction, a devotee of the most base and revolting idolatry the world has ever known.

We can imagine the morally corrupt environment in which Jezebel was raised. Archeology supplies us with great insights into the daily lives of the worshipers of Baal. Known as the sun god, the god of weather, and the male fertility god, Baal's female counterpart was variously known by the names Asherah, Asheroth, Astarte, or Ishtar. Worshiping these two pagan gods required the most licentious activities, including male and female temple prostitutes used by persons who came to the pagan shrine seeking fertility blessings.

Jezebel enters the Bible story through her association with Ahab, the king of Israel. Ahab was the son of Omri, a man who "wrought evil in the eyes of the LORD, and did worse than all that were before him" (1 Kings 16:25). This revealing epitaph is repeated for Ahab (vs. 30). The children of Israel were so deep in their apostasy that they no longer could discern who the real God was.

Apparently possessing great physical beauty and an extraordinary force of character, Jezebel attracted immediate attention when among men. Her charisma captured the lust of Ahab, king of northern Israel.

> And it came to pass, as if it had been a light thing for him to walk in the sins of Jeroboam the son of Nebat, that he took to wife Jezebel the daughter of Ethbaal king of the Zidonians, and went and served Baal, and worshipped him (1 Kings 16:31).

As though his terrible sins against the God of creation were not bad enough already, the Bible tells us that Ahab did something even worse than all those who went before him. He married a Baal worshiper's daughter, bringing revolting sin into his household. The immediate consequence of this ill-fated union was that the religion of Jezebel was declared to be the true religion of Israel.

> And he [Ahab] reared up an altar for Baal in the house of Baal, which he had built in Samaria. And Ahab made a grove; and Ahab

did more to provoke the LORD God of Israel to anger than all the kings of Israel that were before him (1 Kings 16:32, 33).[1]

Ahab proved his lack of discernment and spineless character by marrying such a wicked woman. For the rest of his life, he was dominated and manipulated by his wife, who found no restraint on her murderous designs to eradicate Jehovah from the minds and hearts of all Israelites.

Exceeding even her father's zeal for Baal worship, Jezebel dedicated her entire life to a fanatical promotion of the licentious worship of the sun god. Through seduction and threat of death, she diligently worked to convert all Israel to believe in the presumed powers of the pagan deity, Ashtaroth (Asherah), the Phoenician fertility goddess.

She appointed 450 priests of Baal and 400 priests of Asherah and supported them from her own funds (1 Kings 18:19; 22:6). As a measure of security against an uprising of the Levitical priesthood chosen by the God of heaven, she initiated an extermination program to eliminate all competition against her desire to overthrow the God of Israel (1 Kings 18:13, 19:10; 2 Kings 9:7).

Jezebel put herself forward as the commander in Israel, using her husband's authority in the commission of atrocious crimes. People soon learned to fear the wrath of Jezebel. To her, life was cheap, and one's innocence was no protection against a woman with murder running through her veins.

In her persecution of people who worshiped the God of Abraham, Isaac, and Jacob, she displayed harsh contempt for the rights and consciences of others. She did not shrink from outright murder of all who resisted and opposed her views. Such is the inevitable result of a state controlled by religion. Through this false and unholy union, Israel reached its lowest point in apostasy.

Having conquered Israel for Baal, Jezebel was not satisfied until she also brought down the nation of Judah. By marrying her wicked daughter, Athaliah, to Jehoram, king of Judah (2 Kings 8:16-18; 26), Jezebel spread false worship into the last remaining stronghold of the

---

1. A "grove" in pagan fertility worship was constructed of carved stone pillars or large tree trunks set upright, evoking the idea of an erect phallus. Egyptian obelisks served the same purpose as symbols of power and masculinity.

religion of Jehovah. As a result, Jerusalem and the Temple were polluted with idols to Baal.

Jezebel lives on in infamy. She was crafty, deceitful, and strong-willed. Her zeal for Baal worship resulted in the wholesale murder of innocent men and women. Her use of an abundance of make-up and jewelry in a vain attempt to seduce her enemies, and her domineering attitude in marriage, are all evil traits that have resulted in clichés using her name. The Bible attributes no goodness to her at all.

Every characteristic of this powerful woman was evil and diametrically opposed to God's will. She outlived her husband by eleven years, and her end is one of the most gruesome stories in the Bible. Through Elijah, God sent a prophecy of Ahab and Jezebel's destruction.

> And the word of the LORD came to Elijah the Tishbite, saying, Arise, go down to meet Ahab king of Israel, which is in Samaria: behold, he is in the vineyard of Naboth, whither he is gone down to possess it. And thou shalt speak unto him, saying, Thus saith the LORD, Hast thou killed, and also taken possession? And thou shalt speak unto him, saying, Thus saith the LORD, In the place where dogs licked the blood of Naboth shall dogs lick thy blood, even thine. … And of Jezebel also spake the LORD, saying, The dogs shall eat Jezebel by the wall of Jezreel. Him that dieth of Ahab in the city the dogs shall eat; and him that dieth in the field shall the fowls of the air eat. But there was none like unto Ahab, which did sell himself to work wickedness in the sight of the LORD, whom Jezebel his wife stirred up (1 Kings 21:17-19, 23-25).

Both prophecies were literally fulfilled. God was long-suffering toward these apostates. They had no excuse for continuing to live wickedly, as though they did not know the will of God. After their horrible end was laid before them, God gave them more than 15 years in which to repent, but they refused to hear the call.

They remained defiant in their sin, thinking themselves secure in their dual positions of civil and religious power, unimpeded union of church and state.

Jezebel's life ended when she was thrown from a window by her own servants. As she smashed onto the pavement below, her blood splattered on the wall, horses, and chariot of her conqueror. As he drove away, Jehu ran his chariot over her mangled form. Later wild dogs came and supped on the body of the once proud queen, proving that God's Word is sure (2 Kings 9:30-37).

"Now all these things happened unto them for examples: and they are written for our admonition, upon whom the ends of the world are come." Even in all their wickedness, God never ceased reaching out to Ahab and Jezebel. Through His prophets, Elijah and Micaiah, He provided a continual witness of His power and forgiveness. At any point in their downward spiral, Ahab and Jezebel could have believed in Jehovah as the one true God, turned to Him in repentance, and found rest in His eternal kingdom.

What is the lesson for us from the story of Ahab and Jezebel? We learn that sin has eternal death wrapped up in it. There is no escaping a day of judgment, "for we shall all stand before the judgment seat of Christ" (Romans 14:10).

Like Jezebel, and every person born, we inherit and cultivate tendencies to evil, but unlike her, we don't have to spend our lives clinging to those sins. Through the power of the Holy Spirit, we can learn to say NO! to a life of continual sinning.

"Seeing ye know these things before, beware lest ye also, being led away with the error of the wicked, fall from your own steadfastness" (2 Peter 3:17). A "way of escape" from sin and its ultimate consequence of eternal death has been given to us in Jesus Christ and His righteousness. It is this truth that Ahab and Jezebel rejected at every turn.

Notes

16

Showdown on the Mountain

E lijah, the prophet of God, had been pronouncing judgment upon Ahab and Israel for more than a decade. He first confronted Ahab for his sin of cohorting with evil Baal worshipers. The pagan gods of the Phoenicians and Philistines were thought to control weather, crops and human fertility. The "male" god, Baal, was supposedly in charge of rain which produced the crops. Elijah's first challenge was leveled at this pretense of a god.

> And Elijah the Tishbite, who was of the inhabitants of Gilead, said unto Ahab, As the LORD God of Israel liveth, before whom I stand, there shall not be dew nor rain these years, but according to my word (1 Kings 17:1).

Elijah marched unhindered into Ahab's personal palace and fearlessly confronted him to his face with a direct challenge to the supposed powers of Baal to bring rain. Then the true God of heaven directed His faithful servant to a safe haven where his food and water would not fail, no matter how severe the drought.

God's curse issued through Elijah was a direct affront to Jezebel's authority and her priests of the grove. When people suffering from crop failure due to lack of rain and springs going dry were told to resort to the power of the pagan priests to intervene through Baal, the rain god, they found these sources were impotent. As a result, a chink formed in Jezebel's claim that she and her gods were the ultimate power. For three years, Jezebel hunted for her enemy, and even though God sequestered Elijah right in her hometown, she failed to discover him.

At the end of the predicted years of drought, God ordered a showdown on a mountaintop. The object of the debate was: Who was the true God—the LORD or Baal? On Jezebel's side, 450 priests of Baal and 400 of Asherah climbed the mountain on the designated day. Jezebel did not accompany her husband or her priests to the mountain arena. She remained behind in the safety of her palace.

Standing for God was one man with his assistant.

Ahab arrived and found Elijah standing by the broken-down altar that was once the worship place of the LORD. As Ahab approached in his chariot, he arrogantly exclaimed, "So, here you are, you troublemaker!" Elijah replied, "I have not destroyed Israel, but you and your father's house have, because you have abandoned the LORD's commands and followed the Baals" (1 Kings 18:18, HCSB). With this forthright answer, Elijah laid the ax at the root of the foul tree.

Elijah declared to all the Israelites assembled in the valley below, "I only remain a prophet of the LORD!" Then he pointed to the multitude of pagan prophets and set forth the humble challenge. "If the LORD be God, follow Him: but if Baal, then follow him." Pretty open and easy to understand; he used no confusing theological rhetoric.

But the people were confused anyway. For years they thought they *were* following the God of heaven. They had listened to the priests and the government leaders, never questioning their authority. "Like sheep gone astray," they wandered deeper into apostasy until they arrived at the point where they could not discern the true from the false.

Now Elijah indicated a difference, and they must make a decision.

Every eye was focused on that mountaintop, wondering what would happen. Elijah kept the test simple. Two bullocks were brought to the pagan priests, and he invited them to take their choice. He gave them the entire day to slaughter their offering, lay it on the sacrificial altar, and attempt to get their gods to light the fire.

The priests set to their task. For more than six hours, they danced, shouted, leaped about, jumped on the altar, sang aloud, prophesied, calling on the names of their gods, and when none of these tactics worked, they used knives to cut their flesh, gushing blood everywhere. Elijah watched them closely to prevent one of them from surreptitiously lighting the kindling.

No fire fell from heaven to burn up the offering. And no rain fell to quash the drought.

The priests' antics were so ridiculous that Elijah could not help himself. He taunted them, saying, "Cry aloud, for he is a god. Either he is musing, or he is relieving himself, or he is on a journey, or perhaps he is asleep and must be awakened" (1 Kings 18:27, ESV). His mocking sent the priests of Baal into a greater frenzy so that as the day drew to a close, they were utterly exhausted and fell on the ground around their altar.

It was the time of the evening sacrifice when the sanctuary service for the LORD came to its daily close. At these times, a universal whole burnt offering was made morning and evening, not for anyone's specific sins but for the sin of the world. "Now this is that which thou shalt offer upon the altar; two lambs of the first year day by day continually. The one lamb thou shalt offer in the morning; and the other lamb thou shalt offer at even" (Exodus 29:38, 39). This particular offering of a lamb typified the Lamb of God that would "take away the sin of the world" (John 1:29).

The priests of Baal and Asherah had utterly failed through their extravagant exertions to produce any response from their gods. In great contrast to the carnival of paganism, Elijah confidently gathered the twelve stones of the broken-down altar of the LORD, laying them in order until the altar was reconstructed. He then dug a trench around the altar's base before proceeding with the slaughter of the sacrificial animal.

In times past, the old altar had been a sacred place where offerings were made to the genuine God of heaven and earth. Each stone represented one of the twelve tribes of the children of Israel. Elijah rebuilt this altar "in the name of the LORD," saying, "Israel shall be thy name" (1 Kings 18:31). He purposely recalled to the watching crowd that Jacob's name had been changed to Israel: "thy name shall be called no more Jacob, but Israel: for as a prince hast thou power with God and with men, and hast prevailed" (Genesis 32:28).

Jacob, the Supplanter, wrestled with the LORD and, through faith, gained victory over his fears and self-sufficiency. The name change reflected his conversion experience and was to be a reminder for all time to his children, generation to generation, that the "just shall live by faith alone" (Romans 1:17; cf. Habakkuk 2:4).

Jacob's children had forgotten their history and relied on tradition and the "commandments of men" as their source of truth. Consequently, when challenged by Elijah to decide who the real God was, "the people answered him not a word." As darkness rapidly brought the day to an end, they stood at the foot of Mount Carmel, confused, fearful, and curious about what would happen next.

Then Elijah did an extraordinary thing. After piling the kindling wood on the stones, butchering the LORD's bullock, and laying the pieces on the wood, he next instructed his helper to fetch four barrels of water and pour the water down over the animal parts, the wood, and the altar, until it ran onto the dry ground. Elijah had his helper repeat this two more times, a total of twelve barrels of water, one for each tribe of Israel. Everything was thoroughly saturated with water, and the surrounding trench overflowed.

Elijah was confident his prayer would be answered and proved his faith through careful preparation. His demonstration would erase all doubt in those watching that his God was able to do more than was asked of the pagan priests. Elijah's God could make fire that would burn through water.

A simple prayer was all Elijah needed. Eyes lifted toward heaven, he said, "LORD God of Abraham, Isaac, and of Israel, let it be known this day that Thou art God in Israel, and that I am Thy servant, and that I have done these things at Thy word" (1 Kings 18:36).

Elijah purposely used Jacob's new name, Israel. In his prayer, he wanted everyone to know that faith was the issue. The people of Israel had lost their faith in the LORD and were chasing after false gods devoid of power. Only the God of heaven and earth could save them, and they needed to become reacquainted with Him. Elijah desired Israel to repent and be fully restored as God's people. "Hear me, O LORD, hear me, that this people may know that Thou art the LORD God, and that Thou hast turned their heart back again" (1 Kings 18:37).

As soon as Elijah finished his short prayer, the fire of the LORD rained down "and consumed the burnt sacrifice, and the wood, and the stones, and the dust, and licked up the water that was in the trench" (1 Kings 18:38). Nothing was left except a smoking scar on the ground. The fire "licked up" the water, and even the dust around the altar was gone in that brilliant flash of God's incredible power.

"And when all the people saw it, they fell on their faces: and they said, The LORD, He is the God; the LORD, He is the God" (verse 39). No more indecision. The showdown came to a dramatic ending.

The Bible does not say how the priests and prophets of Baal responded to the LORD's phenomenal display of His power, but it does indicate that they didn't have much time to think about it. Retribution for their sin was swiftly administered.

Elijah commanded the people to grab the "prophets of Baal; let not one of them escape." One by one, those lying priests who had taught and seduced God's people to commit spiritual fornication were slain by Elijah. Eight hundred and fifty evil priests lost their lives that evening. Their blood flowed into the Brook Kishon, which ran down the Jezreel Valley to where Jezebel was sitting in her palace awaiting news of her priests' victory. What she received was a firsthand report from her husband, who told her all that Elijah had done (1 Kings 19:1).

Before Ahab returned home Elijah told him the drought was at an end. "And Elijah said unto Ahab, Get thee up, eat and drink; for there is a sound of abundance of rain"(1 Kings 18:41). The coming of rain at the word of God's prophet confirmed the power of the LORD, Creator and Sustainer of all things. In this Ahab was invited to renounce his paganism and return to true worship of God.

The challenge to discern between the false religions and worship of the Creator is before the world today just as it was in Elijah's day.

And I saw another angel fly in the midst of heaven, having the everlasting gospel to preach unto them that dwell on the earth, and to every nation, and kindred, and tongue, and people, saying with a loud voice, Fear God, and give glory to Him; for the hour of His judgment is come: and worship Him that made heaven, and earth, and the sea, and the fountains of waters (Revelation 14:6, 7).

There is a God in heaven, and He *will* be vindicated, even in the face of what appears to be insurmountable opposition, craven rebellion, and blasphemy of His holy character.

Notes

17

Another Lying Prophet?

Despite widespread political and religious corruption throughout the land, a God-fearing Israelite, Naboth, lived near Ahab's palace. He possessed an inheritance of land composed of very fertile soil, which had not greatly suffered from the three years of drought. It grew an abundance of grape vines and other desirable crops. One day Ahab took notice of Naboth's property and invited him to the palace to negotiate a purchase.

Naboth explained why he was not authorized to sell it, a fact Ahab should have known, being a fellow Israelite. "And Naboth said to Ahab, The LORD forbid it me, that I should give the inheritance of my fathers unto thee" (1 Kings 21:3). Naboth's refusal was not personal. He had inherited the property and was not at liberty to dispose of it. Naboth's refusal relied on the commandment of his God, who is the true owner of all that exists. "The land is not to be permanently sold because it is Mine, and you are only foreigners and temporary residents on My land" (Leviticus 25:23 HCSB).[1]

Like a spoiled child denied a new toy, Ahab took to his bed in a pout. When Ahab refused to come to dinner, Jezebel went to his room, and finding him distraught, she said, "Why are you so upset that you refuse to eat?" (1 Kings 21:5 HCSB).

As the king makes his excuse, a picture comes to mind. With his lower lip stuck out, sniveling, he replied, "Because I spoke to Naboth the Jezreelite and I told him: give me your vineyard for silver, or if you

---

1. This is the reason behind God's command for humanity to be proper stewards of the earth and all that dwells upon it, animals and plants. The world does not belong to us; it belongs to the LORD. We are merely His resident caretakers.

wish, I will give you a vineyard in its place. But he said, 'I won't give you my vineyard!'" Ahab thought he'd been equitable in his generous offer, and Naboth's refusal hurt his childish feelings.

Standing beside his bed, Jezebel looked at the pitiful excuse for a king, thinking how she might turn the situation to her purpose of destroying all who clung to the worship of Jehovah. You can almost hear the scorn in her reply: "Don't you govern the kingdom? Some king of Israel you make! Get up, eat and take heart; *I myself* shall get you the vineyard of Naboth the Jezreelite." And she concocted an evil plot through which her lying accomplices falsely accused a guiltless man. Naboth was dragged outside the city and stoned to death on dual charges of "blaspheming God and the king." Union of church and state is always a persecuting power.

When word was returned that her plot had been carried out, Jezebel went to her husband and told him, "Arise, and take the vineyard of Naboth, for he is dead." Without a single inquiry about how or why Naboth died, Ahab "rose up to take possession of it." His sulk vanished as fast as it appeared. Covetous gloating flooded his heart as he hastened to claim the prize.

But not for long. God is the Avenger of His faithful people, the true corrector of heretics, and will not suffer the abuse of His people without taking action in their defense. "And the word of the LORD came to Elijah. 'Go to Samaria, and meet Ahab where he is standing in Naboth's vineyard. He's gone to take possession of that which is not his" (1 Kings 21:17, 18).

Jezebel had induced her husband to commit crimes of injustice, idolatry, and persecution, to which was now added murder. Insolent disregard for God's Commandments places a person's feet on the slippery slope to perdition. Unrepentant sin closes the heart to the work of the Holy Spirit, eventually leaving the person wholly ensnared by Satan. Ahab had reached that point when God sent His spokesperson to confront him.

> And thou shalt speak unto him, saying, Thus saith the LORD, Hast thou killed, and also taken possession? And thou shalt speak unto him, saying, Thus saith the LORD, In the place where dogs licked the blood of Naboth shall dogs lick thy blood, even thine (1 Kings 21:19).

The same curse was leveled against his murderous wife. "And of Jezebel also spake the LORD, saying, The dogs shall eat Jezebel by the wall of Jezreel" (vs. 23). Ahab and Jezebel's cup of iniquity was full and overflowing.

"And Ahab said to Elijah, Hast thou found me, O mine enemy? And he answered, I have found thee: because thou hast sold thyself to work evil in the sight of the LORD" (vs. 20). At the beginning of the narrative section concerning Ahab and Jezebel, Elijah had waltzed into Ahab's palace and confronted him regarding his idolatry. After three years of drought, Elijah called for the showdown on Mount Carmel.

Near the end of the drought, while searching for water, Ahab met Elijah. He accused Elijah of being the "troubler of Israel," to which the prophet answered: "I have not troubled Israel; but thou, and thy father's house, in that ye have forsaken the Commandments of the LORD, and thou hast followed Baalim" (1 Kings 18:17, 18).

The confrontation on Mount Carmel between the priests and prophets of Baal and the LORD God of heaven and earth was intended to bring Ahab to repentance. The prophet Malachi said that Elijah's work was to "turn the heart of the fathers to the children, and the heart of the children to their fathers" (Malachi 4:5, 6).

If Ahab had heeded the call to repent, reformation in Israel could have taken place. Israel needed a strong leader who would reject Baal worship, destroy the idols and abominable places where sacrilegious orgies took place, and guide the people to turn their hearts back to Jehovah. But Ahab did not listen.

God does not give up until the individual (or nation) has committed the "unpardonable sin" of total rejection of the Holy Spirit's work. Unbelief is unforgivable because the sinner refuses to listen and believe the good news of salvation from their sin. Choosing to continually reject salvation creates a barrier to the work of God and leaves the Holy Spirit without access to our heart.

Ahab was the "troubler in Israel," he and his pagan wife. With the murder of Naboth, they exceeded the limit of wickedness and God's forbearance expired. Judgment was pronounced upon them.

Behold, I will bring evil upon thee, and will take away thy posterity. And will make thine house like the house of Jeroboam the son of Nebat, and like the house of Baasha the son of Ahijah, for the provocation wherewith thou hast provoked Me to anger, and made Israel to sin (1 Kings 21:21, 22).

So horrible was the judgment that when Ahab heard it, he was frightened. "He rent his clothes, and put sackcloth upon his flesh, and fasted, and lay in sackcloth, and went softly" (vs. 27).

The king of Israel might have cringed before these terrible words of denunciation, but there is no evidence of any character change in the man. He repented for fear of the punishment, but there was no godly conversion experience, no demonstration of true faith in God. He made no move to restore what he stole from Naboth's family. He did not destroy the idolatry in Israel nor attempt to control his villainous wife. No change was made in his life of wickedness. He only showed fear of coming judgment.

However, our God is ever a merciful Saviour. Ahab's repentance was based in fear of punishment rather than love for God. Nevertheless, the God Ahab hated granted him a stay of execution. God then remarked to his faithful servant, Elijah, "Seest thou how Ahab humbleth himself before Me? because he humbleth himself before Me, I will not bring the evil in his days: but in his son's days will I bring the evil upon his house" (1 Kings 21:29).

God did not reverse the judgment; He just delayed it through three years of peace in Israel. And during that delay, God gave Ahab one last chance to turn from his wicked unbelief. "The Lord is not slack concerning His promise, as some men count slackness; but is longsuffering to us-ward, not willing that any should perish, but that all should come to repentance." (2 Peter 3:9).

During the third year, Ahab and Jezebel conduced the marriage of their daughter to the son of the king of Judah, truly an unholy alliance that brought Jezebel's wickedness right into the heart of Judah. As a result, Jehoshaphat, king of Judah, paid a state visit to Ahab, who thought to take advantage of the friendly gesture by attempting to lure Jehoshaphat to join him in a war against Ben Haddad of Syria.

Ahab claimed that Syria was occupying a city that belonged to him. "Know ye that Ramoth in Gilead is ours, and we be still, and take it not out of the hand of the king of Syria?" (1 Kings 22:3). He then turned to his friend, Jehoshaphat and said, "Wilt thou go with me to battle to Ramothgilead?" (vs. 4).

Jehoshaphat replied that he was willing to lend his army in the effort to restore what was rightfully Ahab's, with one precondition. Before he was willing to give his hand in this adventure, he wanted the LORD's guidance on the matter. "Enquire, I pray thee, at the word of the LORD to day" (vs. 5). "Then the king of Israel gathered the [pagan] prophets together, about four hundred men" (vs. 6), which was not what Jehoshaphat had asked Ahab to do.

These prophets were employed by the king, advisors for his court, and of the same sort of character as Jeroboam had installed—"the lowest of the people"—when he split the ten northern tribes away from Judah. They sallied forth and assembled themselves before the two thrones. Ahab asked them, "Shall I go against Ramothgilead to battle, or shall I forbear?" (vs. 6). Without consulting one another or making any delay for prayer to enquire of the LORD, they answered unanimously: "Go up; for the Lord shall deliver it into the hand of the king."

We must pause here to consider the word Ahab's prophets used when speaking of the "Lord." The Hebrew word used by the prophets was *adonay*, which is the common word used when addressing a master. Sarah referred to her husband as *adonay* in Genesis 18:12. "Therefore Sarah laughed within herself, saying, After I am waxed old shall I have pleasure, my lord being old also?" The same word was used when referring to Pharaoh. "And it came to pass after these things, that the butler of the king of Egypt and his baker had offended their lord the king of Egypt" (Genesis 40:1).

"Go up; for the Lord [master] shall deliver it into the hand of the king." Praying to their fickle god, they could not say for certain how the battle would go. Maybe what Ahab's prophets said would come to pass, and maybe it wouldn't. They had a fifty-fifty chance of being right. There were only two possible outcomes: Ahab would win the battle, or he would lose it. Since they were paid from the king's coffers, it was advisable to give the king an answer he already wanted to hear.

However, Jehoshaphat intended that they should enquire of the LORD—Jehovah, the Mighty King of the universe—the only One who knows all things. The LORD's prophet would tell them the truth. Judah's king had no interest in the counsel of men. And so, when Ahab's prophets made their pronouncement, he persisted in determining God's will in the matter. "Is there not here a prophet of the LORD besides, that we might enquire of Him?" (1 Kings 22:7).

Ahab had a prophet of the LORD kept under guard by the governor of the city (1 Kings 22:26). But he hated him and did not trust him. "And the king of Israel said unto Jehoshaphat, There is yet one man, Micaiah the son of Imlah, by whom we may enquire of the LORD: but I hate him; for he doth not prophesy good concerning me, but evil" (1 Kings 22:8). Jehoshaphat was horrified to hear Ahab speak evil of the LORD's servant. He said, "Let not the king say so!" Then the king of Israel called a guard and said, "Hurry and bring Micaiah, the son of Imlah, before us."

While they waited for Micaiah to arrive, Ahab's chief prophet, Zedekiah, hastily hammered out a pair of iron horns similar to those on the golden calf idols at Bethel and Dan. Showing them to Ahab, he prophesied, "Thus saith the LORD, With these shalt thou push the Syrians, until thou have consumed them" (vs. 11). The rest of the prophets continued with their antics, chanting, "Go up to Ramothgilead, and prosper: for the LORD shall deliver it into the king's hand" (vs. 12).

But notice that after hearing Jehoshaphat demand to know Jehovah's will in the matter, the false prophets changed the word they used for God. After hearing Jehoshaphat's request for counsel from the true LORD, they decided to change their approach.

As the king's messenger ushered Micaiah to where the kings were waiting, he advised him that it might be a good idea for the beleaguered prophet to go along with what the king's prophets were saying. Perhaps, if he would speak kindly to the king, Micaiah could, in that way, get released from jail. But a true prophet (or any child of God) is faithful to his LORD and can do nothing contrary to God's character, no matter the cost to himself. Micaiah answered the guard, "As the LORD liveth, what the LORD saith unto me, that will I speak" (vs. 14).

Having declared that he could offer nothing except absolute honesty, Micaiah stood before the two kings. "And the king said unto him, Micaiah, shall we go against Ramothgilead to battle, or shall we forbear? And he answered him, Go, and prosper: for the LORD shall deliver it into the hand of the king."

Does it seem strange that the LORD's prophet appears to echo what the false prophets proclaimed? Remember, they had a fifty-fifty chance of being right no matter which outcome they offered the king. The fact that the LORD's prophet said Ahab's adventure would be successful was not an agreement with the false prophets. His "agreement" concerned the result but had nothing in common with the source of the victory. Because both prophets predicted success does not mean that Micaiah lied. Neither does it mean the false prophets were speaking for the LORD in giving their answer to Ahab's question.

When Zedekiah instructed Ahab to rely on the empty power of the "horns" of an idol, he was not speaking for the LORD God of heaven. He was using God's name in vain. Micaiah said, "*the* LORD shall deliver it into the hand of the king." If Ahab had moved forward in faith that the LORD was marching before him to give the victory, the Syrian army would have turned heels and fled into the mountains.

The incredible part of the narrative is Ahab's response to Micaiah's declaration of victory. His anger is almost visible in his response. Leaning forward Ahab shouts, "How many times shall I make you swear that you speak to me nothing but the truth in the name of the LORD?" (vs. 16).

Ahab did not complain or threaten when his four hundred prophets gave an optimistic prediction. On the contrary, from the beginning, he seemed convinced that with Jehoshaphat's assistance, retaking the town was an assured outcome. He claimed idleness on their part was the only reason Israel had not already recovered possession. The king of Israel previously lamented to his servants, "You know Ramoth-gilead belongs to us, yet we are doing nothing to take it out of the hand of the king of Aram" (1 Kings 22:3). And now he had a second army at his disposal to wage war against Syria. How could he possibly fail in his endeavor?

How could he fail?—the only way anyone ever fails to gain victory over the enemy: unbelief of God's word. When the LORD promised victory, Ahab saw a curse. Micaiah told Ahab, "go and prosper: for the LORD shall deliver it into the hand of the king" (vs. 15). But the king immediately rejected the good news and screamed at Micaiah, "You always lie to me and tell me bad things are going to happen to me!"

And with that response, Ahab reached the limit of God's gracious forbearance and mercy. His probation came to a screeching halt. Ahab did not use the additional three years of peace-filled probation to learn how to give complete allegiance to the true God of heaven and earth.

He did not seek a deeper repentance, nor did he desire and pursue a vibrant fellowship with his loving Creator, who mercifully stayed his execution and extended Ahab's life three more years.

If he had experienced a heart appreciation for God's gift, in addition to political peace, Ahab could have known tranquility in his innermost being, not just for three years but for the rest of his life. However, Ahab repeatedly blocked the mighty rivers of mercy that poured from the throne of grace above. He would not yield to God's call. Though regretting the consequences of his fiasco over Naboth's vineyard, Ahab continued his hedonistic lifestyle with the wicked Jezebel.

Furthermore, during those last probationary years, he continued to hate and persecute God's holy prophets, who would have assisted the king in his conversion if he had let them do the work God sent them to accomplish. Instead, Ahab resisted God's love which was so freely given to him (see 1 Kings 21:29), threw away his salvation, and instead chose certain destruction.

God's pronouncement of justice was swiftly given. Standing before the two kings, one of whom was determined to kill him, Micaiah solemnly pronounced, "I saw all Israel scattered upon the hills, as sheep that have not a shepherd: and the LORD said, These have no master: let them return every man to his house in peace." Ahab was going to die, leaving Israel without a king.

Ahab's sins so blinded him to truth that he could not accept the impending doom rising before him. Instead he attacked Micaiah calling him a liar, false prophet, and bearer of evil. "See, I told you so! Micaiah is a liar. He can only say evil things about me." Micaiah told no lies or half truths that day. Every word was a revelation from the throne of grace. If Ahab had believed the first truth Micaiah had delivered, "Go up, you will win the battle," then the second truth, "You are going to die," would not have been told that day.

For more than 20 years, God had been working through His prophets to call Ahab to repentance. Each intervention resulted in either a total rejection of God's mercy or a minor and fleeting modification in Ahab's attitude. Now, confronted one last time by God's prophet, Ahab flatly refused God's mercy.

It is true that by beholding, we become changed (2 Corinthians 3:18). By beholding evil continually, we become so morally desensitized and confused that we can call evil good and good evil. Harboring cherished sins clouds our moral vision and causes us to lose spiritual discernment. As a result, the Holy Spirit is blocked from accomplishing His work in convicting us of sin and unrighteousness and bringing us to repentance (see John 16:7-11).

With Ahab's final rejection of God's mercy, Micaiah then related a vision he received from God.

> Hear thou therefore the word of the LORD: I saw the LORD sitting on His throne, and all the host of heaven standing by Him on His right hand and on His left. And the LORD said, Who shall persuade Ahab, that he may go up and fall at Ramothgilead? And one said on this manner, and another said on that manner.
>
> And there came forth a spirit, and stood before the LORD, and said, I will persuade him. And the LORD said unto him, Wherewith? And he said, I will go forth, and I will be a lying spirit in the mouth of all his prophets. And He said, Thou shalt persuade him, and prevail also: go forth, and do so.
>
> Now therefore, behold, the LORD hath put a lying spirit in the mouth of all these thy prophets, and the LORD hath spoken evil concerning thee (1 Kings 22:19-23).

The question is: Who lied?—the four hundred false prophets who told Ahab what he wanted to hear: that he would win the battle; or Micaiah who told Ahab he would "prosper; for the LORD shall deliver it into your hand"?

Who was the one at that heavenly counsel meeting who stepped forward, volunteering to deceive Ahab? Was it Micaiah? Would a man who understood and exhibited the character of God in his daily life, volunteer to misrepresent God's righteous character by telling a lie about their king?

The Bible answers our dilemma. Jesus told us that Satan is the liar and murderer and has been "from the beginning" (John 8:44). Satan appeared before the counsel of God and falsely accused righteous Job (Job 1:9-11; 2:4, 5). King Saul consulted a lying spirit[2] when he visited

---

2. Samuel was dead. He slept in his grave and had no knowledge of anything taking place in this world. The idea that the dead can communicate with this world is

(footnote continued on next page)

the witch of Endor, seeking advice from a dead man (see 1 Samuel 28:5-20). The apostle Paul confronted a liar who was trying to turn the people listening to Paul away from his good news message about Jesus Christ, the Saviour of all mankind. Paul called him, "You son of the Devil, full of all deceit and all fraud, enemy of all righteousness! Won't you ever stop perverting the straight paths of the Lord?" (Acts 13:10, HCSB).

Satan inspired the four hundred false prophets to lie to Ahab. And they *did* lie because they had no knowledge of what God was willing to do for Ahab that day. What they spoke was not inspired by the LORD God of heaven and earth. They told the king what they believed the king wanted to hear: Go forward to battle and you will win through the power of Baal.

On the other hand, Micaiah did possess inside knowledge from the throne room of grace, and he said: "the LORD shall deliver it into the hand of the king." If Ahab had listened and been willing to submit to the power of God to transform his wicked life, then he would have gone to battle against Syria in the strength of faith, and he would not only have won the battle but found eternal life instead of destruction.

It is unbelievable how stubborn is the evil heart filled with pride and rebellion. Even after being told he was going to die in the battle, Ahab thought by deception and craft he could circumvent God's judgment. He disguised himself as an ordinary charioteer, but the enemy's arrow, guided by the sure word of God, found the chink in his armor. He died a condemned and lost man, having thrown away every opportunity God gave him to repent and submit to His cleansing power.

(footnote continued from previous page)

based on the lie Satan told our first parents. When Eve said she would die if she ate the fruit he was tempting her with, Satan (using the snake as his ventriloquist's dummy), flatly contradicted God's word when he said, "You shall not surely die! You will become like God if you eat this fruit" (Genesis 3:3-5; cf. 2:17). The "person" rising up before Saul in that dark cave acting and sounding like Samuel, was an evil demon spirit intent on one thing: destroying demented Saul forever. The evil spirit lied when he told Saul the LORD had become his enemy. God is never our enemy, but always seeks to save. The demon told the truth when he said God had taken his kingdom and given it to David. And he did not lie when he revealed his evil plot to kill Saul at the hand of the Philistines. Satan uses a combination of twisted truth and outright falsehood to confuse us and cause us to disbelieve God's Word.

How gracious is our ever-loving Father who deals in boundless mercy even with thankless and thoughtless rebels. Remember, "The Lord is not slack concerning His promise, as some men count slackness; but is longsuffering to us-ward, not willing that any should perish, but that all should come to repentance."

Notes

18

A Metal Man and Four Beasts

Some of Scripture's most fascinating chapters are found in the Book of Daniel. They contain five separate yet harmonious and parallel prophecies concerning the history of the world. The first was given in 603 BC to the pagan king of ancient Babylon. He conquered the remnant of the children of Israel living in Jerusalem and Judah and transported them to his capital city. Among the first taken captive were cousins of the king of Judah, Daniel, Hananiah, Mishael, and Azariah. Of these four, Daniel eventually attained the highest political position in the realm, next to the king (Daniel 6:1, 2).

Nebuchadnezzar was blessed by the God of heaven long before he recognized that God was the Creator and Saviour of the world. God raised up the pagan king to do a work for Him, and the king of Babylon responded even though, at the time, he knew not that there was One mightier than he who motivated him and gave him the power to accomplish the task. God called this unbeliever "My servant." [1]

> Behold, I will send and take all the families of the north, saith the LORD, and Nebuchadnezzar the king of Babylon, *My servant*, and will bring them against this land, and against the inhabitants thereof, and against all these nations round about, and will utterly destroy them, and make them an astonishment, and an hissing, and perpetual desolations (Jeremiah 25:9). [2]

---

1. See Daniel chapter 4 for Nebuchadnezzar's conversion story.
2. "North" in the Bible indicates the direction from which an invading army would approach the land of Canaan. No one ventured to traverse the vast desert between Canaan and the rivers of Babylon, which were to the east. For example,… (con't. next page)

The first prophecy concerning world events was given to Nebuchadnezzar. It was a brief overview, a sort of graphic shorthand, that illustrated what would take place from the days of Babylon until the second coming of Christ when He will smash all earthly powers and establish His own eternal kingdom. In Nebuchadnezzar's "metal man" dream, the statue was composed of four different metals used to designate the series of empires that would rise and fall after his time (Daniel 2:31-33).

In his dream, the king saw a large figure of a man composed of four different metals and clay. The metals changed in a descending fashion (and value) from the figure's head to its feet. The head was of pure gold, the chest and arms were silver, the belly (abdomen) was brass, and the legs were iron. In the feet of it, the iron was mixed with clay down to its ten toes. When Nebuchadnezzar's "wise men" could not guide the king in solving the mystery of the forgotten dream, God gave Daniel "understanding" of the metal man image (see Daniel chapter 2).

Some modern Bible interpreters present an unsubstantiated assumption that the prophecies begin with Assyria's kingdom and include Egypt. But the Bible itself states that the prophecy begins with Babylon and flows through history uninterrupted. "Thou, O king, art a king of kings; for the God of heaven hath given thee a kingdom, power, and strength, and glory … thou art this head of gold" (Daniel 2:37, 38).

From Daniel's simple explanation, there is not a shred of doubt that Babylon was the "golden head," not ancient Assyria. Thus Babylon is the starting point for the historical parade of nations depicted in the prophecies recorded in Daniel chapters 2, 7, and 8. The Books of Daniel and Revelation parallel each other, confirming the events of world history from Daniel's day to the end of the world.

Nebuchadnezzar's pride was great, and he gave himself credit for all God had given him. In a subsequent dream, God revealed the danger of Nebuchadnezzar's arrogance and the future collapse of his mighty

---

2. (con't) … Isaiah 41:25; Jeremiah 1:14, 15; 6:22, 23; and 46:6, all tell of an invasion from the "north." When the Babylonian captivity ended, God said He would "bring them [the remnant of His people] from the north country" (Jeremiah 31:8). Even though geographically, Babylon was east of the land of Judah, God would "bring" His people home "from the north country" because the travel route between Babylon and Judah made a northward arch around the Arabian Desert.

kingdom. The second dream was of a magnificent tree that spread over the earth. Under its protection, all things lived and flourished. But after a time, the tree was cut down, leaving only a stump and its roots.

Even after Daniel interpreted the second dream for Nebuchadnezzar, he persisted in his vanity, failing to acknowledge that he was truly God's servant in all he did and attained in conquering the nations around him. He was obliged to God for everything.

One day, while standing on the balcony of his palace overlooking the city, Nebuchadnezzar exclaimed: "Is not this great Babylon that *I have built* for the house of the kingdom by the might of *my power*, and for the honour of *my majesty*?" (Daniel 4:30, emphasis supplied). And with that boast, Daniel's interpretation of the tree being cut down came to fulfillment.

> While the word was in the king's mouth, there fell a voice from heaven, saying, O king Nebuchadnezzar, to thee it is spoken; the kingdom is departed from thee. And they shall drive thee from men, and thy dwelling shall be with the beasts of the field: they shall make thee to eat grass as oxen, and seven times shall pass over thee, until thou know that the most High ruleth in the kingdom of men, and giveth it to whomsoever He will. The same hour was the thing fulfilled upon Nebuchadnezzar: and he was driven from men, and did eat grass as oxen, and his body was wet with the dew of heaven, till his hairs were grown like eagles' feathers, and his nails like birds' claws." (Daniel 4:31-33).

After suffering from insanity for seven years ("seven times" in the prophecy, Daniel 4:32; a "time" is one prophetic year), Nebuchadnezzar finally recognized God for all He is and does for humanity. The acknowledgement brought Nebuchadnezzar to a spiritual crisis, and he repented and chose to worship the true God of heaven and earth. "Now I, Nebuchadnezzar, praise and extol and honor the King of heaven, all whose works are truth, and His ways judgment: and those that walk in pride He is able to abase" (Daniel 4:37).

God desired that Nebuchadnezzar would be saved eternally, but the king's pride stood in the way. Humbled and humiliated by seven years of self-inflicted insanity, Nebuchadnezzar finally "came to his senses" and submitted to the God who loved him.

After Nebuchadnezzar passed from the scene, another prophecy was given in 555 BC directly to Daniel. It is recorded in chapter 7 as a succession of vicious and powerful beasts representing the same four kingdoms in Nebuchadnezzar's metal man image. The second prophecy also outlined the ancient world's superpowers from Babylon down to the end of the world, portraying them as a lion, a bear, a leopard, and a terrible nondescript beast with iron teeth and ten horns. From among the ten horns, there emerged a "little horn" that remained until the second coming of Christ.

Because the first three nations were already in existence and familiar to him, Daniel readily grasped the significance of the lion, bear, and leopard kingdoms. Media and Persia were nations to the northeast of Babylon, and Daniel, as Nebuchadnezzar's ambassador, had visited those kingdoms on state business. Daniel was more than 85 years old when Cyrus conquered Babylon in 538 BC, and he lived at least until the third year of the reign of Cyrus (Daniel 10:1). He survived the transfer of power from Babylon to Medo-Persia, serving as a high administrative official in both governments (Daniel 2:48, 49; 6:1-3). "He prospered in the reign of Darius, and the reign of Cyrus the Persian" (Daniel 6:28). At that time, Greece was a nation of city-states, not yet a world-dominating power, but through trade and its philosophy and educational methods, it communicated with surrounding kingdoms and made itself known on the world scene.

The first three beasts representing kingdoms made sense to him, but Daniel could not comprehend the fourth power, an enormous iron beast with ten horns on its head. The fourth beast looked like nothing Daniel had ever seen before, and it greatly astonished him. Even more confusing, the beast sprouted a "little horn" among the ten and, in the process, uprooted three of the original horns. Daniel confessed, "I Daniel was grieved in my spirit in the midst of my body, and the visions of my head troubled me" (Daniel 7:15). An angel came and told Daniel the interpretation: "These great beasts, which are four, are four kings, which shall arise out of the earth" (vs. 17). The last power, the "little horn," extends until the end of earthly time and will be destroyed when Jesus returns.

> The judgment shall sit, and they shall take away his dominion, to consume and to destroy it unto the end. And the kingdom and dominion, and the greatness of the kingdom under the whole heaven, shall be given to the people of the saints of the

most High, whose kingdom is an everlasting kingdom, and all dominions shall serve and obey Him (Daniel 7:26, 27).

The prophecies in Daniel chapters 7 and 8 are parallels of what John saw in Revelation chapters 13, and 16 through 19 concerning the activities of the "little horn" as a persecuting power.

Daniel's high moral standards and ethics impressed the kings of Babylon, Media, and Persia. Daniel's constant and consistent spiritual witness over his more than 70 years of service to kings Nebuchadnezzar, Cyrus, and Darius resulted in the incorporation of Daniel's wise principles into their own diplomatic standards (see Daniel 1:19-21; 2:48; 5:11; 6:1, 2, 25-28).

The writings left behind by the noble statesman Daniel, revealing the power of the Creator God, were of great value to those who followed him as religious and political counselors to the monarchy. Through Daniel's influence, the Persian religion was the most ethical pagan religion ever developed.

While serving in Babylon, religious accommodation[3] was given by Nebuchadnezzar to Shadrach, Meshech, and Abednego when their God demonstrated His superior power to protect them from the fierce fire Nebuchadnezzar cast them into for disobeying the king's demand regarding worship (Daniel 3:24, 25, 28).

Then Nebuchadnezzar spake, and said, Blessed be the God of Shadrach, Meshach, and Abednego, who hath sent His Angel, and delivered His servants that trusted in Him, and have changed the king's word, and yielded their bodies, that they might not serve nor worship any god, except their own God. Therefore I make a decree, That every people, nation, and language, which speak any thing amiss against the God of Shadrach, Meshach, and Abednego, shall be cut in pieces, and their houses shall be made a dunghill: because there is no other God that can deliver after this sort. (Daniel 3:28, 29).

Daniel's religious commitment was challenged after Nebuchadnezzar's kingdom fell to the Medes and Persians. Because he was still

---

3. "Religious accommodation" is an adjustment to the work or social environment that allows an individual to practice their religion unencumbered. Religious freedom is embedded in the First Amendment of the US Constitution.

a captive and foreigner, when Daniel was elevated above the Persian diplomats ("presidents and princes") jealousy drove them to devise a plot to bring Daniel into disfavor with the king. These wicked men knew Daniel's devotion to and faith in the God of heaven.

> Then the presidents and princes sought to find occasion against Daniel concerning the kingdom; but they could find none occasion nor fault; forasmuch as he was faithful, neither was there any error or fault found in him. Then said these men, We shall not find any occasion against this Daniel, except we find it against him concerning the law of his God. (Daniel 6:4, 5).

The men then approached King Darius, urging him to pass a law forbidding anyone from worshipping or praying to any person or god except the king, for thirty days. The proposal appealed to the king's arrogance and pride. Without taking time to consider the implications of such a law, Darius readily consented to the idea.

However, Daniel never varied in the worship of his God, praying every morning, noon, and night. He was fully aware of the plot against him, but did not change one iota of his worship practice. Neither did he seek to hide his faith or protect himself from the murderous intent of his enemies.

> Now when Daniel knew that the writing was signed, he went into his house; and his windows being open in his chamber toward Jerusalem, he kneeled upon his knees three times a day, and prayed, and gave thanks before his God, as he did afore time (Daniel 6:10).

As the jealous men had anticipated, they spied and "found Daniel praying and making supplication before his God" (Daniel 6:11). They hastened to the king and tattled, "that Daniel, which is of the children of the captivity of Judah, regardeth not thee, O king, nor the decree that thou hast signed, but maketh his petition three times a day" to his own God (Daniel 6:13).

King Darius was trapped. A decree issued by the king of the Medes and Persians was "everlasting" and could not be amended or cancelled. Even the king could not break his law, and so he was forced against his will to have Daniel arrested and thrown in the pit that held voracious lions waiting to devour whatever was thrown down to them.

Then the Persian king did an astonishing thing. He refused his dinner feast and fasted and prayed all night to Daniel's God that He would spare His faithful servant (Daniel 6:18-20). "Then the king went to his palace, and passed the night fasting: neither were instruments of music brought before him: and his sleep went from him" (Daniel 6:18).

Early the next morning the king hastened to the pit of lions. Was the God of Daniel willing to hear the prayers of a pagan king? Had He been able to deliver his faithful servant from certain death?

> And when he came to the den, he cried with a lamentable voice unto Daniel: and the king spake and said to Daniel, O Daniel, servant of the living God, is thy God, whom thou servest continually, able to deliver thee from the lions? (vs. 20)

Darius' distress exposed his compassion for his faithful servant. He knew he'd been duped into the attempted murder of Daniel. As he peered into the darkness of the pit he was uncertain whether his intercessory prayer had been acknowledged by "the living God." This short phrase tells us a great deal about Darius' mind at that crisis moment. He recognized that Daniel's God was real, living, and able to respond to human needs, unlike his gods made from metal, stone, and wood. He used the same phrase when he composed the legislation commanding worship of Daniel's God.

> Then king Darius wrote unto all the people, nations, and languages that dwell in all the earth; Peace be unto you. I make a decree, that in every dominion of my kingdom men tremble and fear before the God of Daniel, for He is a living God, and steadfast forever, and His kingdom that which shall not be destroyed, and His dominion shall be even unto the end. (Daniel 6:25, 26).

The Persian government supported Daniel's religion by making another decree similar in intent to the one issued by Nebuchadnezzar after God saved the three Hebrew worthies from the fiery furnace. However, legislated religion does not give freedom of conscience. Union of church and state has always been a great evil resulting in persecution of non-conformists.

Strictly speaking, religious liberty comes from God through His gift of free choice, not from any government, church decree, or man-made law. To attain its goal of universal compliance, any attempt by civil or religious law to mandate or control worship, or control the consciences of the populace, must necessarily use coercion and/or persecution of those who choose to believe differently.

What was the source of Daniel's contentment? He had shown no fear or doubt as he was lowered into the pit the night before. How had he been able to demonstrate perfect peace?—because Daniel knew his God was the God of justice and love, who would not allow His faithful servants to be tested beyond what they are able to endure. He always provides a way of escape (see 1 Corinthians 10:13). The firm foundation of Daniel's faith was God's love that had proven its power to keep him safe from harm. Daniel praised God always for the myriad blessings that had been poured out on him all of his long life.

Daniel raised his voice from the murky pit, informing Darius: "My God hath sent His angel, and hath shut the lions' mouths, that they have not hurt me: forasmuch as before Him innocency was found in me; and also before thee, O king, have I done no hurt" (Daniel 6:22). Daniel first gave all glory to God for preserving him from certain death. Then he declared the obvious: "I am innocent of the charges laid against me."

Daniel's innocence was established before God and the pagan king. He concluded his greeting by adding, "and also before thee, O king, have I done no hurt." He was not an enemy of the state or an insurrectionist. His conformity and commitment was to a higher law outside the control of earthly governments. He honored the law of heaven in ignoring the king's law that interfered with his right to freedom of worship and his service to God.

19

"Exceedingly Prideful"

In chapter 8, Daniel's second vision opens the aperture wider to bring into greater focus three of the four kingdoms. Babylon was approaching its sudden destruction when the vision of this chapter was given to the aging prophet. Chapter 7 opened with: "in the first year of Belshazzar king of Babylon," and chapter 8 opens with a similar remark: "in the third year of the reign of king Belshazzar." History shows that Belshazzar's reign was short. Early in his third year, the young Babylonian king was killed during the night invasion of Cyrus, king of Persia (see Daniel chapter 5). Babylon, as a nation, was ready to depart the scene when Daniel received the vision recorded in chapter 8.

The prophecy now zeros in on the next two kingdoms. While the symbols change, the kingdoms remain the same as in the visions of chapters 2 and 7. The Medo-Persian kingdom is now depicted as a "two-horned ram" that "pushed westward, and northward, and southward," perfectly describing the path of Medo-Persia's conquests as its army marched from the east toward the Mediterranean Sea, following the ancient road along the "fertile crescent." One horn was "higher" than the other indicating the disparity of power in the "united kingdom." Cyrus' Persian army was the military force going forth to conquer and control, while Darius the Mede ruled the homefront.

Passing quickly to the next scene, the vision showed the second beast coming to its end when it ran head-on into the third world power, Greece. The "shaggy goat" with a single "prominent horn between its eyes" smashed the Medo-Persian kingdom, and Alexander the Great became master of an empire that stretched from Greece to India, and southward to Egypt, more vast than any kingdom or empire that had ever existed up to that time (Daniel 8:5-7). Alexander's conquest brought the Greek language, education, and philosophy into universal usage.

Alexander's kingdom was soon destroyed through his own lack of self-control. In his arrogance, he declared himself the son of the Greek god Jupiter. After conquering all that stood before him, he died of a drunken fever two years after he gained universal reign. As foretold, four of his generals divided his kingdom among themselves. The one "notable horn" of the shaggy goat was broken, and four more "notable" (but less glorious) powers rose in its place.

But on the western horizon (from one of the "four winds of heaven," or four directions of the compass, vv. 8, 9), a previously unknown power was developing on the Italian peninsula. This kingdom was unlike any before it in that it was not a monarchy but a senatorial republic. With its highly trained military strategies, the new form of government conquered all of the then-known world, from the Atlantic Ocean to the Indus River, north to the Rhine and Danube rivers in Europe, and south across the Mediterranean Sea to the north coast of Africa. No place where her armies marched could stand against the Roman Empire's iron rule. Cities that resisted were blotted out of existence. Nowhere was this more graphically seen than in the conquest of Judea and the destruction of Jerusalem in AD 70.

Rome's civilization and commerce advanced along its superior system of stone-paved roads and large sea-going vessels. Everywhere the Roman army went, through conquest or culture, it spread its form of peace administered through Roman political justice. Rome developed and established laws that had universal effect throughout the environs controlled by the emperor. Law and justice were closely administered through governors and magistrates who swore allegiance to the Roman emperor, the supreme religio-political guardian of the empire.

After the death of Jesus, Rome's civilization facilitated the promulgation of the Gospel's message. Jesus commissioned His disciples, "Go ye into all the world, and preach the gospel to every creature" (Mark 16:15). Safe roads made over-land travel easier, shipping on the Mediterranean Sea was unhindered by pirates and warring nations. Civil peace in the various regions of the empire all simplified the missionary work of Jesus' apostles (apostle means one who is "sent").

The formal structure of pagan Rome's government and religion laid the foundation for the "little horn" to "magnify itself." Leopold von Ranke, in his extensive work, *History of the Popes, Their Church and State*, volume I, First Chapter, "Epochs of the Papacy," writes that the Roman Empire gave its outward form to Latin Christianity as it rose phoenix-like from the ashes of pagan Rome (Daniel 8:10, 11). The form and constitution of the Roman church hierarchy were built on that of the Roman Empire's religio-political structure. [1]

"…With that transition, Imperial Rome faded away, and the papacy came to the forefront, occupying the position of leadership in Rome vacated by the political power. The historical point at which the papal power began to be realized was when the Ostrogoth's control of [the city of] Rome was lifted in AD 538. Prior to that time, the bishop of Rome had been under the control of barbarian tribes for more than sixty years. Now, free of that encumbrance, his authority, both civil and religious, began to increase until the medieval papacy reached its zenith in the eleventh through the thirteenth centuries." [2]

The prophecies concerning the "little horn" forebode evil for God's people. It would be an arrogant authority, proclaiming itself equal to the God of heaven. It would be a persecuting and destructive power:—

And [the "little horn"] waxed great, even to the host of heaven; and it cast down some of the host and of the stars to the ground, and stamped upon them. Yea, he [the "little horn"] magnified himself even to the prince of the host, and from him the daily was *taken away* [Hebrew *rûm*: "lifted up"; to be high, or to exalt], and the place of his sanctuary was *cast down* [Hebrew: "throw" or "set in place"]. And an host [3] was given him against the daily by reason

---

1. In Roman Catholicism, the mythical phoenix symbolizes the resurrection and eternal life. The legend tells of a magnificent multicolored bird that was thought to periodically sacrifice itself in flames and then reemerge from the ashes. It renewed itself through fire every 500 years. Nearly every pagan culture uses a similar bird symbol to represent eternal life.
2. William H. Shea, *Daniel, A Reader's Guide*, 2005, p. 123.
3. The first nation to support the rising "little horn" was France (known as Gaul in ancient times). King Clovis converted from his purely pagan religion to the compromised form of Christianity in AD 508, pledging his army to defend papal Rome. Clovis was the "prince of the host" and the "host" was his army.

of transgression, and it cast down the truth to the ground; and it practised, and prospered (Daniel 8:10-12).[4]

In these verses the word "daily" is the Hebrew word *tamid* meaning "continual." It is a Hebrew adjective and when used with the definite article it functions as a noun. In Isaiah 52:5, the same word is used to describe the constant blaspheming of God's name by the pagan nations surrounding Israel. "They that rule over them make them to howl, saith the LORD; and My name continually [*tamid*] every day is blasphemed."

In Daniel 8:11-13, the Hebrew noun is prefaced by the definite article, *ha* (the)—"*the* continual" or "*the* daily." Here it refers to a particular entity that took a form of Christianity but would "daily, and every day" blaspheme God's holy name through its mingling of Christian terms with mystical pagan rituals, exalting this union of church and state above pure, simple, unadulterated worship of the God of heaven and earth. "The daily" is used here to identify the infiltration and exaltation of paganism that crept into the early Christian church in the first centuries of the Roman church's existence.

The beloved apostle John was also shown the transition from pure faith in Christ to, first, a compromised faith, then gradually devolving into an apostate religion. The vision of the seven churches in Revelation chapter 2 shows the fall from the pure church of Ephesus that resisted the incursion of heresy (AD 31 to about AD 100); through the church of Smyrna, that experienced a time of terrible persecution by the Roman emperors who demanded unconditional worship from all citizens (about AD 100 to AD 313). Further compromise came under Constantine the Great when paganism was wedded to the Christian church during the Pergamos church period (AD 313 to 538).

The fourth church period, Thyatira (538 to 1798), is described as "Jezebel," the wicked queen who sought through persecution and

---

4. Confusion concerning the interpretation of these verses arises from the time when the Hebrew religious texts were translated into the Greek Septuagint. Commenting on verse 11, one authority of that time stated, "The Septuagint as it at present stands is utterly unintelligible." Scribal misreading during translation and the scribe's addition of marginal commentary, attempting to provide clarity, led to later mistranslations when the Septuagint went from the Greek language into the Latin Vulgate.

threat of death to destroy all worship of the one true God. This church period parallels the time of Daniel's "little horn."

The word "sanctuary" does not appear in the original Hebrew text. It is interesting to note in the King James Version, the word is *italicized*, indicating it was supplied by the translators to complete their interpretation of the text. There is no support from the context to conclude that *"the daily"* refers to anything in the Jewish temple services or sacrificial system.

> The principle of trusts and monopolies, of unions and leagues, which had always characterized pagan society, twined its tendrils about the new organization of Christians, and choked its life. Paganism—the "daily" of Dan. 8:12—was taken away, it is true, and Rome became nominally a Christian empire. Her emperor [Constantine the Great] professed the name of Christ, and carried before his army the banner of the cross. Decrees were issued causing all men to worship according to the dictates of Rome. Then it was that man—the emperor—and the empire attempted to exalt themselves above the God of heaven." [5]

The first civil law mandating a universal day of worship was issued by Constantine the Great on March 7, AD 321, in which he declared that *dies Solis Invicti* (the invincible sun) would be the "sun-day" of rest throughout the Roman Empire. Constantine referred to the Sun-deity as the "Unconquered Sun, my companion." On July 3, 321, Constantine issued his second Sunday law. The second law gave people freedom from most types of legal business and physical work on the first day of the week, the "sun-day."

> And his [the "little horn"] power shall be mighty, but not by his own power: and he shall destroy wonderfully, and shall prosper, and practise, and shall destroy the mighty and the holy people. And through his policy also he shall cause craft [6] to prosper in his hand; and he shall magnify himself in his heart, and by peace shall destroy many: he shall also stand up against the Prince of princes; but he shall be broken without hand (Daniel 8:24, 25).

---

5. S.N. Haskell, *The Story of Daniel, the Prophet*, 1908, p. 128.
6. "Craft" is beguiling fraud, deception, mysticism.

"And he [the "little horn"] shall speak great words against the most High, and shall wear out the saints of the most High, and think to change times and laws: and they shall be given into his hand until a time and times and the dividing of time" (Daniel 7:25). In Bible prophecy several terms are used to indicate periods of time. Here in Daniel 7:25 and in 4:25, the term is "time" and indicates one prophetic year of 360 literal days.[7] The plural "times" means two prophetic years or 720 literal years. A "divided time" is half a prophetic year, or 180 literal years. Therefore, "a time and times and the dividing of time" is literally 1260 years. In Revelation 13, this same power, described as a composite beast that was part leopard, lion, and bear with seven horns and ten crowns, would remain in power for "forty and two months." Forty-two months consisting of 30 days each is equal to 1260 literal years. No matter which term is used, they are all of equivalent value.

History firmly establishes God's word concerning the succession of four world empires: Babylon, Medo-Persia, Greece, and Rome. Each, in turn, fell from glory to an invading and more powerful empire. Here there is no mystery. As the prophetic clock ticked down and the fourth terrible, nondescript beast sprouted its "little horn" onto the world's stage of action, those persons attentive to the Scriptures became aware of the prophetic significance of the Roman Empire.

In AD 50, the apostle Paul identified the beginning of the "little horn's" work in his second letter to the congregation at Thessalonica. He wrote: "For the mystery of iniquity doth already work: only he who now letteth will let, until he be taken out of the way. And then shall that Wicked be revealed, whom the Lord shall consume with the spirit of His mouth, and shall destroy with the brightness of His coming." (2 Thessalonians 2:7, 8, KJV).[8]

---

7. God defined the day-for-a-year Bible principle in Numbers 14:32-35, where the punishment for apostasy was a "day for a year" … "after the number of the days in which ye searched the land, even forty days, each day for a year, shall ye bear your iniquities, even forty years." God again used the principle of a day for a year in prophecy in Ezekiel 4:5, 6. "I have appointed thee each day for a year."

8. A more precise translation that avoids the old Elizabethan word "let" which means "to hinder," is: "The mystery of wickedness is already at work, but let him who is restraining it once be removed, and the wicked one will appear openly" (2 Thessalonians 2:7, 8 NJB).

By AD 96 when the apostle John was a prisoner of Rome on the island of Patmos, all the prophecies concerning these four empires had been fulfilled completely, except the final one. Pagan Rome was beginning to crumble and would be overrun by ten barbarian tribes invading from northern Europe and southwestern Asia. They were represented by the ten toes of Nebuchadnezzar's metal man image, by the ten horns of the great and dreadful fourth beast of Daniel 7:7, 8, and the ten crowns in John's vision of the amalgamated beast in Revelation 13:1. The fulfillment of the rise of the "little horn" was in its early stages at the time of the apostles, who recognized and warned against the subtle infiltration of Gnostic and pagan ideas into the pure Gospel given by Jesus.

Serious conflicts existed between Christianity and gnosticism concerning vital doctrines, primarily the deity and humanity of Christ, and the creation of all that exists as acts of the holy God wrought through His divine Son. Gnosticism also taught the Eastern mystical idea that "knowledge" of one's "inner self" would bring eternal life. Paganism denied sin and actively promoted gross immorality, hedonism, and the exaltation of man's ideas above any divinely inspired authority. Man was a law unto himself, without moral or ethical restraints.

The apostle Paul denounced paganism in his letter to the Romans (1:18-32). He confronted gnosticism in many of his pastoral letters, including 1 Corinthians chapter 15, in which he dealt with the misunderstanding of the death and resurrection of Christ. In Colossians 1:13-22; and 2:8, 9, Paul admonished the early church to believe that Christ is not a created being but the divine Creator of all things. The apostle John addressed the Gnostic idea that it was not possible for Christ to come into the world in fallen human flesh. He called such an idea "antichrist" because it undermined the work Christ came into the world to accomplish—saving us *from* our sin, not *in* our sin (see Matthew 1:21, 23; cf. 1 John 2:18-22; 4:1-3; 2 John vv. 7, 10, 11).

The "little horn" was beginning to emerge even in the early years of Christianity. What was "restraining" or "hindering" the rise of the "little horn" was the absolute control of pagan Rome over government and religion. It was this despotic repression of freedom of religion that brought persecution to Christians during the first three centuries of the new era. The "little horn" arose as the political Roman Empire was crumbling, and it assumed the scepter of autocratic power over religion and government through the gifts and privileges of Constantine the Great (AD 312 to 337) and Justinian I (Eastern Roman emperor from 527 to 565).

In AD 313, Constantine built the St. John Lateran Cathedral in the city of Rome and gifted it to Bishop Miltiades, thus sanctioning the Roman system as the official religion of the empire. In the same year, Constantine issued the Edict of Milan, giving Roman Christianity full legal status within the empire. From that time, the cathedral—not the Vatican—has been the "home church" of all the popes. When speaking *ex cathedra*, the pope is seated upon the throne located in the apse behind the altar of the St. John Lateran Church.[9]

In March AD 533, Emperor Justinian dispatched a letter to the Bishop of Rome in which he officially stated to John II that all affairs touching the church should be referred to the "Pope at Rome" (John II and his successors). In this letter, Justinian said that the bishop of Rome was "head of all bishops and the true and effective corrector of heretics."

The religious laws contained in this Codex were intended to regulate religious practice throughout the empire by banning any worship not controlled by Rome. Not only did the law threaten excommunication from the church, but non-conformists would lose their citizenship and be declared outlaws in all realms of the empire, afforded no legal protection anywhere they went.

With this decree from the emperor, the formation of the "little horn" was finished. The state (government) gave its seat and authority to the bishop of Rome. All that remained for the complete fulfillment of the prophecy of Daniel 7 and 8 concerning the "little horn" was the extermination of the remaining "horns" that resisted its authority. The prophecy showed three of the ten horns disappearing as the "little horn" rose to prominence.[10]

One of the "ten horns" on the head of the "great and terrible beast" (Daniel 7:7, 8) had already been eliminated. The Heruli were defeated

---

9. In Roman church architecture, the apse is a vaulted semicircular or polygonal closure of the choir, usually located behind the altar. First used in pre-Christian Roman architecture, in a temple the apse often functioned as an enlarged niche to hold the statue of a deity.

10. The ten tribes were: Ostrogoths, Visigoths, Heruli, Suevi, Burgundians, Allemani, Vandals, Lombards, Franks, and Anglo-Saxons.

in AD 493. From AD 533 to 538, the Roman army waged war against the remaining enemies of the Roman bishop. The Vandals were destroyed in AD 534, and the Ostrogoths in AD 538.

The pagan power obstructing the full development of the papacy was completely removed. Nothing remained to "restrain" the "little horn" from carrying out its ambitions of world dominance through union of religion and government under the leadership of the pope at Rome. The prophetic clock was started in AD 538 and began to tick down 1260 years to the time when a deadly wound would be inflicted upon the beast, crippling it but not destroying it.

The American Constitution, particularly the First Amendment, and the French Revolution, severed the church from the state in those two nations. No longer did the church control the consciences of the citizens. The people were free to believe what they would about God and religion, without fear of persecution.

But the Roman system was not then completely destroyed. Its destruction will not take place until the second coming of Christ (see Daniel 2:44; 7:25-27; Revelation 19:19-21). Like the phoenix, it will rise again to inflict its will upon a world that will "wonder" at the restoration of its power to persecute "heretics" (see Daniel 7:19-26; cf. Revelation 13:1-9).

Daniel was stunned by the implications of his vision. The prophecy would be many centuries in coming to a conclusion; the wickedness of the "little horn"; its destructive work in paganizing God's church; and centuries of persecution of God's people, so overwhelmed him that he "fainted and was sick for many days" (Daniel 8:24, 25, 27).

Notes

20

End of a Prophecy, and a Nation

When Daniel had sufficiently recovered, the angel Gabriel came and comforted him, saying, "I am now come forth to give thee skill and understanding" concerning the vision recorded in chapter 8 (Daniel 9:21, 22). Gabriel told Daniel he was "greatly beloved" by the God of heaven and earth, who wanted His faithful servant to "understand the matter and consider the vision."

Gabriel explained that after a period of 490 years ("seventy weeks" in prophetic time are 490 literal years), the most stupendous event ever experienced by the world would take place. Seven things are listed as part of its fulfillment. Daniel 9:24 lists these identifying points.

"Seventy weeks are determined upon thy people and upon thy holy city, to—

(1) finish the transgression, and to
(2) make an end of sins, and to
(3) make reconciliation for iniquity, and to
(4) bring in everlasting righteousness, and to
(5) seal up the vision and
(6) the prophecy, and to
(7) anoint the most Holy"

To "seal" means to bring something to a conclusion. The "vision" and the "prophecy" are two separate identifiers. A "vision" is a divine gift through a dream in which the individual foresees something that will come to pass. For example, King Nebuchadnezzar saw a vision in chapters 2 and 4. The vision of the metal man concerned the coming of the Messiah during the time of the fourth, "iron" kingdom.

Prophecy is given by God through a chosen human being, and provides spiritual guidance for living in compliance with the will of God. A prophet also receives warnings about impending divine judgment upon rebellion and apostasy. Daniel's prophecy concerning the Messiah is recorded in chapter 7 and expanded in 9:24-27. They are both calls to repentance and warnings against apostasy.

Only one Being could accomplish the seven great achievements outlined in Daniel 9:24. They all concerned the promised Messiah who would come "at the time appointed" by this prophecy. "When the fullness of the time"—a particular "time"—"was come, God sent forth His Son" as the Saviour of the world (Galatians 4:4; John 4:41, 42). Jesus was born "on time" in fulfillment of the prophecy of Daniel 9:24-27.

We find several astute Persian magi (prudent philosophers) among the ancient scholars who had access to Daniel's writings.[1] Important documents were housed in a Babylonian fortress and protected there for many centuries. Magi living at the time of Herod the Great, king of Judah, heard reports of the extraordinary virgin birth of the Babe named Jesus,[2] and correctly interpreted various prophecies in the Jewish scrolls left in Babylon concerning the coming Messiah. These scrolls are mentioned in Ezra 6:1, 2.

An example of what they would have examined are the prophecies found in Numbers 24:17—the "Star out of Jacob" (descendant of Jacob) had risen; and Isaiah 7:14—a Son born of a virgin who would be named Immanuel, "God with us" (cf. Luke 1:34; Matthew 1:23); and Micah 5:2—the Messiah would be born in Bethlehem Ephrathah, "to be ruler in Israel, whose goings forth have been from of old, from everlasting." Micah's prophecy would have been particularly intriguing because it predicted Someone who must be divine to have lived "from of old, from everlasting."

As chronologers, the magi's interest also would especially have been aroused by the time prophecy of Daniel 9:24-27—the Messiah

1. Magi were Zoroastrian priests who studied the movements of the heavenly bodies and kept the chronology (historical) records of the kingdom. The title "magi" was first used by Darius the Great in his multilingual inscription carved into the rock mountain in Persia known as Behistun.
2. Luke 2:8-20. The shepherds to whom the angels announced the birth of Jesus would not have remained silent concerning that stupendous event.

King would come near the end of Israel's 490 years of probation that began in 457 BC as a result of the decree of Artaxerxes (Ahasuerus), king of Persia. Well aware of the starting point, the "wise men" knew it was time for the fulfillment of that specific prophecy given to Daniel.

After Cyrus conquered Babylon, three decrees were issued, each releasing the Jews from their captivity and obligations to Babylon. First, the Persian king, Cyrus, recognized that "the LORD God of heaven hath given me all the kingdoms of the earth; and He hath charged me to build Him an house at Jerusalem, which is in Judah" (Ezra 1:2). A second decree was issued by King Darius, who ordered the cessation of all interference from local tribes surrounding Jerusalem that were hindering the rebuilding of the temple (Ezra 6:7, 8).

The reluctance of the Jews to leave the comfort of their established existence in Babylon and return to the desolated land of Judah necessitated a third decree and the threat of death if they remained in Babylon (then controlled by the Persians; see the Book of Esther).

The decree issued by Artaxerxes in a letter, recorded verbatim in Ezra 7:11-26, released the Jews from their suzerain contract[3] placed on them by Nebuchadnezzar. The third decree restored the Jews as a political nation with full sovereign rights to govern themselves. After "rightly dividing the Word of God," the Persian wise men traveled "from the east" to Jerusalem near the time of Jesus' birth and inquired of the Jewish "wise men"[4] where He had been born (Matthew 2:1-5).

Jesus connected Daniel's prophecy to Himself when He asked His disciples, "Who do men say that I, the Son of man, am?" (Matthew 16:13), linking the words of Daniel 7:13, 14 to His ministry. "One like the Son of man came with clouds of heaven … and there was given Him dominion, and glory, and a kingdom." The Gospel of Matthew contains thirty-one statements made by Jesus in which He used the phrase "kingdom of heaven" to refer to some aspect of His work.

---

3. The suzerain contract was first developed by the ancient Hittites. It was used to control conquered nations and consisted of a list of stipulations through which the conquered king became a vassal, or feudal tenant. Under treaty he was forced to give full allegiance to the suzerain in order for him to continue in nominal control of his own realm.
4. Jewish scribes and priestly scholars.

Shortly after asking His disciples who people thought He was, Jesus took Peter, James, and John up on a mountain where they saw His glory vividly revealed. "His face did shine as the sun, and His raiment was white like the light … and "while he [Peter] yet spake, behold, a bright cloud overshadowed them: and behold a voice out of the cloud, which said, This is My beloved Son, in whom I am well pleased; hear ye Him" (Matthew 17:2, 5). Their experience on the mountain recalled to their minds Daniel's vision.

> Then I lifted up mine eyes, and looked, and behold a certain Man clothed in linen, whose loins were girded with fine gold of Uphaz: His body also was like the beryl, and His face as the appearance of lightning, and His eyes as lamps of fire, and His arms and His feet like in colour to polished brass, and the voice of His words like the voice of a multitude (Daniel 10:5, 6).

Nebuchadnezzar identified the fourth Man in the fiery furnace walking with the three Hebrews as "the Son of God" (Daniel 2:25).

The prophecy of Daniel 9 began with seven things the Subject of the prophecy would accomplish. To review, they were: (1) finish the transgression, (2) make an end of sins, (3) make reconciliation for iniquity, (4) bring in everlasting righteousness, (5) seal up the vision, (6) seal up the prophecy, and (7) anoint the most Holy (Daniel 9:24).[5]

Only the Son of God, who became the Son of man, could bring an end to the sin problem caused by Adam's fall.[6] Only the Son of God, who became the Son of man, could make reconciliation between the Godhead and rebellious mankind. He alone could bring in everlasting righteousness and, in doing so, fulfill every vision and every prophecy and every sacrificial type given since Adam rebelled that pointed to His work for fallen humanity. At His baptism in the Jordan River in AD 27, He would be "anointed" by the presence of the Holy Spirit and the voice of the Father, commissioning Him to complete His work.

---

5. The verb "seal" used with the conjunction "and" applies equally to both of the nouns in this phrase, thus indicating two separate things. The coming Messiah would fulfill both the vision and the prophecy.

6. "Then as one man's trespass [Adam's sin] led to condemnation for all men, so one Man's act of righteousness [Christ's life and death] leads to acquittal and life for all men." (Romans 5:18, Revised Standard Version). See also 2 Corinthians 5:18, 19; Luke 3:21, 22; John 17:4.

The prophecy of Daniel 9:24-27 begins with an absolutely verifiable historical event. God's messenger angel, Gabriel, stated: "Know therefore and understand, that from the going forth of the commandment to restore and to build Jerusalem" (Daniel 9:25), the final probation for the Jewish nation would play itself out.

Upon their return from Babylonian captivity, the Jews were to prepare themselves, and be a witness to the world concerning the impending arrival of the world's Redeemer. The actual year the "commandment to restore" went into effect has been well established by four historical facts:[7] a published cuneiform tablet from Ur of the Chaldees; a papyrus discovered at Elephantine; the Egyptian calendar; and the Jewish civil calendar, all of which affirm the date of 457 BC, and the historicity of the Bible's narrative in the Books of Ezra and Daniel.

Standing firmly on established and verifiable facts, we can now examine the remainder of the prophecy recorded in Daniel 9:24-27 in

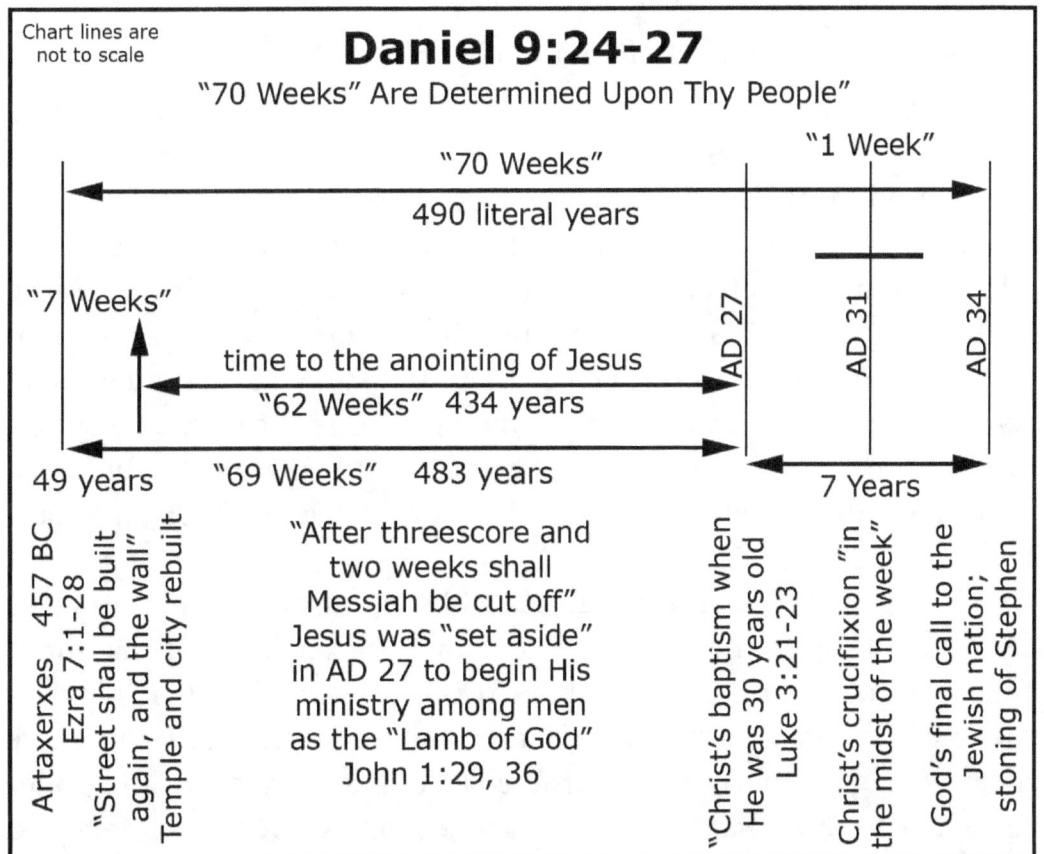

---

7. See Siegfried H. Horn and Lynn H. Wood, *The Chronology of Ezra 7* (1953).

light of this history. In the quotes below, inserted explanations found in brackets will aid the reader in understanding the meaning of the prophetic terms.

> "Know therefore and understand, that from the going forth of the commandment to restore and to build Jerusalem" [Artaxerxes' decree issued in 457 BC; see Ezra 7:11–26] …
>
> "unto Messiah the Prince shall be seven weeks" [seven prophetic "weeks" of seven days each equal 49 literal years; rebuilding the Temple and city took 49 years] …
>
> "and three score and two weeks" [62 prophetic "weeks" of literal years, for a total of 483 literal years from Artaxerxes' decree to the beginning of Christ's earthly ministry in AD 27] …
>
> "and after three score and two weeks" [62 "weeks" added to the initial "seven weeks" yields 69 prophetic "weeks" leaving one "week" for the work of the Messiah] [8]
>
> "… shall Messiah be cut off, but not for Himself" (Daniel 9:25, 26).

History provides us with accurate information concerning the arrival of the Messiah in human flesh, which He assumed in His incarnation through Mary's womb (Luke 1:30-35).

Augustus Caesar, formerly called Octavius, was Julius Caesar's adopted son. He defeated Marc Antony and Cleopatra in the Battle of Actium in 31 BC. He was, as the Bible refers to him, "a raiser of taxes" to support the empire (Luke 2:1). Augustus also instituted social reform by banning promiscuity in an effort to reduce the conception of illegitimate children who were aborted or killed at birth. His social reform was the reason for taking the census that sent Joseph and Mary to Bethlehem in 3 BC (Luke 2:3-7).

The date of Jesus' birth is also established by other events, such as the death of Herod the Great in 1 BC, which is fixed by a peculiar lunar eclipse in that year. Jesus was about two years old when the "kings of the east" (the magi) arrived at Herod's palace inquiring about where the new king was born. Herod ordered all children aged two and under to be killed. Being warned by an angel, Joseph escaped with Mary and

---

8. See Nehemiah chapter 4 and Haggai chapter 1.

Jesus to Egypt. Herod died shortly after issuing his murderous decree against the innocent babes (Matthew 2:1-18).

For many valid reasons, we can affirm that Jesus was not born on December 25. For example, shepherds would not have been "abiding in the fields, keeping watch by night" in the middle of winter. More importantly, Jesus was crucified on Passover, which verifies His death occurred in the spring of the year. According to the Biblical record, His ministry lasted three and a half years. Therefore, if it ended in the spring, counting backward three and a half years takes us not to December but to late September or early October, the season when the Jewish ceremonial year ended with the Day of Atonement. Christ's ministry was to bring an end to the earthly system of types, all of which pointed toward Him.

Christ began His earthly ministry at the beginning of the seventieth week (at the end of 483 literal years covered by the prophecy). Jesus lived with His family in Nazareth until He reached the age of 30 years. "And Jesus Himself began to be about thirty years of age" (Luke 3:23). He then presented Himself to John the Baptist to "fulfill all righteousness" (Matthew 3:13-15). From this evidence, the conclusion is that the final "week" of Daniel's 490 years began in the autumn of AD 27.

At His baptism, the Messiah was "cut off" or "set aside" to begin His ministry in "confirm[ing] the covenant with many." The covenant Jesus preached was the "everlasting covenant" given by Him initially to Adam (Genesis 3:15), restated to Noah (Genesis 9:8-17), and confirmed with Abraham (Genesis 12:1-3; 15:17, 18). His covenant is the promise of redemption *from* sin (Matthew 1:21).

The everlasting covenant, first revealed to mankind in Genesis 3:15, promised the human race that a Son would be born who had the power to destroy the hatred ("enmity") Satan implanted in the human heart by Adam's fall into sin. "And I will put enmity ["intense hatred"] between thee [Satan] and the woman [not Eve literally, but humanity in general], and between thy seed and her seed [those who follow Satan are his "seed"; God's people throughout time are His "seed"]; it ["He," the promised Messiah, Christ] shall bruise [or "crush"] thy head, and thou shalt bruise ["snap"] His heel."

The promise was spoken to the snake in the tree, but was directed at Satan who had used the snake to deceive Eve. God promised that He would send a Saviour who would crush Satan's head, even while Satan struck a blow to the Saviour's human flesh (His "heel").

In His life and death, by being God's atoning sacrifice, Jesus "confirmed" or ratified[9] the promise of the everlasting covenant already given from the foundation of the world. He was the last Passover Lamb the world would ever need. The "Seed" of the woman, Christ, would destroy the "seed" of the devil, root, and branch.

> For, behold, the day cometh, that shall burn as an oven; and all the proud, yea, and all that do wickedly, shall be stubble: and the day that cometh shall burn them up, saith the LORD of hosts, that it shall leave them neither root nor branch (Malachi 4:1).

In Jesus' sermons and parables, He strove to bring the Jews to repentance and acceptance of Him as their promised Messiah. At the end of His ministry, with great pathos in His voice, Jesus cried, "O Jerusalem, Jerusalem, thou that killest the prophets, and stonest them which are sent unto thee, how often would I have gathered thy children together, even as a hen gathereth her chickens under her wings, and ye would not!" (Matthew 23:37).

During those three and a half years, Jesus was constantly confronted with negativism, hatred, and resistance from the religious authority of the Pharisees, priests, and scribes. Their dissension confused the majority of the people and caused disbelief in His message. If the people showed interest, they were met with sneers: "Then answered them the Pharisees, Are ye also deceived? Have any of the rulers or of the Pharisees believed on Him? But this people who knoweth not the law are cursed" (John 7:47-49).

The Pharisees expressed open opposition to the faith of the "uneducated," indicating they thought such were entirely unfit to discern truth from error. Resistance by the leaders of the church instilled doubt in minds of the "common people," and fear of denouncement and stoning, caused the people to turn away from Jesus. "From that time many of His disciples went back, and walked no more with Him" (John 6:66).

The Gospel of John paints a more complete picture of Jesus' rejection by the leadership of the Jewish people.

---

9. Validated or certified.

Jesus answered them, I told you, and ye believed not: the works that I do in My Father's name, they bear witness of Me. But ye believe not, because ye are not of My sheep, as I said unto you. My sheep hear My voice, and I know them, and they follow Me. ... Then the Jews took up stones again to stone Him. Jesus answered them, Many good works have I shewed you from My Father; for which of those works do ye stone Me? The Jews answered Him, saying, For a good work we stone Thee not; but for blasphemy; and because that Thou, being a man, makest Thyself God (John 10:25-27; 31-33).

After the phenomenal display of divine power in the resurrection of Lazarus, some people did believe Jesus.

But some of them went their ways to the Pharisees, and told them what things Jesus had done. Then gathered the chief priests [the Sadducees] and the Pharisees a council, and said, What do we? for this Man doeth many miracles. If we let Him alone, all men will believe on Him: and the Romans shall come and take away both our place and nation (John 11:46-48).

Their fear of destruction by Rome came to pass in AD 70, not because they "let Him alone" but because they rejected their only Saviour and crucified Him. Their 490 year probation was ended; God no longer protected the Jewish nation as His "special people."

The death and resurrection of Lazarus occurred just a week before the Passover; it was "nigh at hand" when Lazarus walked out of his tomb (John 11:55). The stupendous event roused the priests and Pharisees to action. In their anger and fear of Jesus' power they issued an edict.

Now both the chief priests and the Pharisees had given a commandment, that, if any man knew where He were [Jesus], he should shew it, that they might take Him (John 11:57).

Harboring their enemy would render severe consequences upon the offender. Moreover, any known associate of Jesus would also be guilty of treason. And therefore, Jesus "walked no more openly among the Jews" (John 11:54).

But Jesus made one last visit to His friends, Mary, Martha, and Lazarus, at their home in Bethany (John 12:1). There He received an anointing by Mary, who poured out the emblem of her extravagant love for her Saviour. She spent her entire life savings on the precious bottle. "Then took Mary a pound of ointment of spikenard, very costly, and anointed the feet of Jesus, and wiped His feet with her hair: and the house was filled with the odour of the ointment" (John 12:3).

Of all Jesus' followers, Mary alone grasped what Jesus meant when He said, I "must go unto Jerusalem, and suffer many things of the elders and chief priests and scribes, and be killed, and be raised again the third day" (Matthew 16:21). Jesus acknowledged her profound, unquestioning faith when He told the quibbling disciples, "Let her alone: against the day of My burying hath she kept this" (John 12:7).[10]

> And it came to pass, when Jesus had finished all these sayings, He said unto His disciples, ye know that after two days is the feast of the Passover, and the Son of man is betrayed to be crucified (Matthew 26:1, 2).

Another report from Luke further establishes the time.

> Now the feast of unleavened bread drew nigh, which is called the Passover. And the chief priests and scribes sought how they might kill Him; for they feared the people (Luke 22:1, 2).

The hatred of the Jewish leadership for Jesus was briefly tempered by their fear of an insurrection of the common people that would bring the Roman army against them.

Nonetheless, hatred—and the necessity of fulfilling God's prophetic timing—brought the Pharisees and Sadducees to their fateful decision.

> Then the high priest [Caiaphas] rent his clothes, saying, He hath spoken blasphemy; what further need have we of witnesses? behold, now ye have heard His blasphemy. What think ye? They answered and said, He is guilty of death (Matthew 26:65, 66).

And "in the midst of the [seventieth] week," Jesus was delivered to the Roman judge to be condemned and crucified.

> And He [Christ] shall confirm the covenant with many for one week: and in the midst of the week He shall cause the sacrifice and the oblation to cease (Daniel 9:27a).

---

10. Matthew 26:6-13; Mark 14:3-9; and Luke 7:36-50; Jesus said that "everywhere" the Gospel was preached, Mary's story would be told as a memorial of her love and appreciation of her Saviour (Matthew 26:13).

Christ's ministry began with His baptism in the fall of AD 27. Therefore, "in the midst of the week" takes us to the spring of AD 31, three and one-half years after John the Baptist identified Jesus as "the Lamb of God which takes away the sin of the world" (John 1:29, 36).

Jesus Christ was crucified as God's Passover Lamb, bringing the sacrificial system to an end. At the moment Christ died on the cross, the curtain separating the two apartments in the Temple was torn from top to bottom by a mighty unseen hand (Matthew 27:50, 51), demonstrating openly that the prophecy was fulfilled: "And He shall cause the sacrifice and oblation to cease" (Daniel 9:27). Through God's own Lamb, the way to the throne of God was wide open, without any barrier or encumbrance.

> The Holy Ghost this signifying, that the way into the holiest of all was not yet made manifest, while as the first tabernacle [the temple in Jerusalem] was yet standing. ... But Christ being come an high priest of good things to come, by a greater and more perfect tabernacle, not made with hands, that is to say, not of this building [the temple in Jerusalem]; neither by the blood of goats and calves, but by His own blood He entered in once into the holy place, having obtained eternal redemption for us. (Hebrews 9:8, 11, 12).

With the death of Christ, the Temple and its rituals were no longer needed because the One to whom they all pointed had come and died. All the symbolic sacrifices typified a coming Saviour who would shed His precious blood for the sin of the world. In Christ was fulfilled all the types of the Old Testament ceremonial services, sacrifices, and feast days. He is the "new and living way" through which we approach the throne of grace (Hebrews 10:19–23; cf. 4:14–16). No earthly temple or animal sacrifice could accomplish what Jesus did in His life and death.

> But Christ being come an high priest of good things to come, by a greater and more perfect tabernacle, not made with hands, that is to say, not of this building; neither by the blood of goats and calves, but by His own blood He entered in once into the holy place, having obtained eternal redemption for us. For if the blood of bulls and of goats, and the ashes of an heifer sprinkling the unclean, sanctifieth to the purifying of the flesh: how much

more shall the blood of Christ, who through the eternal Spirit offered Himself without spot to God, purge your conscience from dead works to serve the living God? (Hebrews 9:11-14).

However, the popular enthusiasm generated by a misunderstanding of the work of the Messiah caused the majority of the Jewish population in Judea to reject Him. Contrary to their expectations, Christ did not come in earthly power and glory to overthrow the Roman oppressors, as they hoped the Messiah would do. Neither did He come to assume an earthly monarch's throne or a high priest's robe and miter. His purpose was to fulfill the seven points of Daniel 9:24, bringing redemption to all who would believe in Him as their Saviour from sin.

The early rain was poured out at Pentecost upon the repentant and converted disciples. Thus empowered through the Holy Spirit, they traversed the Roman Empire preaching Christ and Him crucified for the sin of the world. Thousands were converted in a day as their eyes were opened, and they recognized their complicity in rejecting Jesus and consenting to the crucifixion of their Messiah (Acts 2:36-41). But not all were willing to give up their pride or position.

The prophetic clock was winding down, and the Jewish nation's final probation was drawing to a close. Clinging to their preconceived opinions about the Messiah, and their pride of position and power, the rulers of the Jewish people "stopped their ears" from hearing the truth that they were "stiffnecked and uncircumcised in heart and ears" and had "always resisted" the Holy Spirit's attempts to bring them the truth and, through it, repentance for their sins (Acts 7:57, 51).

Three and one-half years after the crucifixion of His Son, God sent one last messenger to the religious authorities of the Jewish nation with a final call to repentance. The contentious Jews accused Stephen of the same crime by which Jesus had been falsely convicted.

We have heard him speak blasphemous words against Moses and against God. And they stirred up the people, and the elders, and the scribes, and came upon him [Stephen], and brought him to the council [the Sanhedrin] (Acts 6:11, 12).

Before that distinguished assembly, Stephen gave God's final appeal to the Jewish nation as a corporate people to repent and accept Christ as their Saviour (Acts 7:1–53). His message was vehemently condemned (vv. 54–60).

With the rejection of this final call, the Jewish nation's probation ended in AD 34 as the "seventy weeks" prophecy came to a close, precisely 490 years after Artaxerxes's degree was issued in 457 BC. Jesus "confirmed the covenant" with the Jewish nation through His three and a half year ministry. He further extended His mercy to the rebellious Jews through His apostles as they preached Jesus in Jerusalem and throughout Judea for the remaining three and a half years of the "seventieth week."

The parable of the householder was thus fulfilled (Matthew 21:33-46). Jesus told this parable to a group of caviling "chief priests and elders of the people." The story described a situation in which a wealthy landowner left his property in the hands of "husbandmen," who were supposed to tend the land and make it profitable for the owner. When the landowner sent his stewards to collect his profit, the husbandmen beat them and stoned and killed them, one after another. Finally, the landowner decided to send his beloved son, saying, "They will have reverence for my son." But when he came, they said, "let us kill him, and let us seize on his inheritance. And they caught him, and cast him out of the vineyard, and slew him."

The parable leaves no doubt as to the meaning Jesus intended. He is the "Son" in the parable who was killed. The "householder/landowner" is God the Father, and the "servants" were God's prophets sent to bring repentance to apostate Israel. When Jesus asked them what the "Householder" would do to the "wicked men" who failed to take care of His vineyard (the lost world), return unto Him a profit (by preaching to those who needed salvation), and ended up killing His Son, they correctly responded, "He will miserably destroy those wicked men, and will let out His vineyard unto other husbandmen, which shall render Him the fruits in their seasons" (Matthew 21:41). Saying this, the "chief priests and Pharisees" condemned themselves. Then they "perceived that He spake of them." [11]

Saul, the self-righteous Pharisee, stood by when Stephen was stoned to death for his witness against the unbelieving Jewish authorities. After his conversion (see Acts 8:1; 9:1-20), Saul became Paul, the most enthusiastic preacher and defender of the faith in the early church,

---

11. Jesus used a passage from Isaiah 5:1-7 as the foundation for this parable. Those listening to Him would have been familiar with this text from Isaiah.

traveling everywhere proclaiming to the Jews the Gospel of the crucified and risen Saviour. But in town after town, Paul's message was rejected by the Jews even as it was enthusiastically received by the Gentiles (see, for example, Acts 13:14-51).

Arriving in Antioch with his traveling companion, Barnabas, Paul "went into the synagogue on the Sabbath." When he was given permission to speak, he "beckoned with his hand, saying, 'Men of Israel, and you that fear God [the Gentiles present in the congregation], give me your attention'" (Acts 13:16). He then preached a sermon to them that was similar to what Stephen had presented before the Sanhedrin, calling them to repentance, and pleading with them to accept the risen Saviour as their Lord.

The Gentiles in the congregation were receptive, but when the Jews saw the multitudes who were coming out to listen to Paul's message, "they were filled with envy, and spake against these things which were spoken of by Paul, contradicting and blaspheming" what Paul was preaching (Acts 13:45).

> Then Paul and Barnabas waxed bold, and said, It was necessary that the word of God should first have been spoken to you: but *seeing you put it from you, and judge yourselves unworthy of everlasting life*, lo, we turn to the Gentiles (Acts 13:46, emphasis supplied).

God's forbearance is long, but not forever. The Jews again, "judged themselves as unworthy" by their continued resistance of truth. God turned "to the Gentiles"—the more worthy "husbandmen" of the parable's interpretation (Matthew 21:41). Quoting from Isaiah, Paul exclaimed:—

> For so hath the Lord commanded us, saying, I have set Thee [Christ] to be a light for the Gentiles, that Thou shouldest be for salvation unto the ends of the earth. And when the Gentiles heard this, they were glad, and glorified the word of the Lord: and as many as were ordained to eternal life believed (Acts 13:47, 48).

In a final expression of the rejection of the Jews as a nation, Paul and Barnabas "shook the dust off their feet against them" and passed on in their evangelism tour. Later, Paul would write in his letter to the believers in Rome that the Jews, though genetically children of Abraham, were not guaranteed salvation through that lineage.

> What then are we to say? Gentiles, who did not strive for righteousness, have attained it, that is, righteousness through faith; but Israel, who did strive for the righteousness that is based on the law, did not succeed in fulfilling that law. Why not? Because they did not strive for it on the basis of faith, but as if it were based on works. They have stumbled over the Stumbling Stone. (Romans 9:30-32, NRSV).

To refresh and define, here are the verses with explanation:—

> And after threescore and two weeks shall Messiah be cut off, but not for Himself: and the people of the prince [Titus, the Roman general, and son of Emperor Vespasian] that shall come shall destroy the city and the sanctuary; and the end thereof shall be with a flood, and unto the end of the war desolations are determined. And He [Jesus] shall confirm the covenant with many for one week: and in the midst of the week [three and a half literal years] He [Jesus] shall cause the sacrifice and the oblation to cease, and for the overspreading of abominations he [the Roman army] shall make it desolate, even until the consummation, and that determined shall be poured upon the desolate (Daniel 9:26, 27).

In His final sermon preached in the Temple to the Pharisees, Jesus used the same word to describe the condition of the Jews. "Behold, your house is left unto you desolate" (Matthew 23:38). Their faithless, legalistic system of religion was ripe for destruction. To His disciples, Jesus referred to Daniel 9:27 when He said, "When ye therefore see the abomination of desolation, spoken of by Daniel the prophet, stand in the holy place, (whoso readeth, let him understand)" (Matthew 24:15). His warning was pointing forward to AD 70.

Continued resistance and censure of the Gospel and its missionaries resulted in the destruction of the Jewish nation in AD 70. Just as the priests feared, the "prince" of imperial Rome was no longer restrained by God's hand, and the Roman army led by Titus, the future emperor, "came and destroyed the city and the sanctuary" (Daniel 9:26), leaving not "one stone upon another," exactly as Jesus told His disciples (Matthew 24:2).

By contextually regrouping the two pairs of thought in Daniel 9:26 and 27, the prophecy is easy to understand. "And after threescore and two weeks shall Messiah be cut off, but not for Himself; and He shall confirm the covenant with many for one week: and in the midst of the week He shall cause the sacrifice and the oblation to cease."

Thus the two thoughts concerning the work of the Messiah are complete. Jesus began His ministry—was "cut off" or "set aside" at His baptism in AD 27. He "confirm[ed] the covenant with many"—ratified the everlasting covenant through His death as God's sacrificial Lamb—and in "the midst of the [seventieth] week," He was crucified, bringing the temple ceremonial "sacrifice and oblation" to an end.

Likewise, grouping the two thoughts about the work of Rome, we read: "And the people of the prince that shall come [pagan Rome] shall destroy the city and the sanctuary [accomplished in AD 70 by Titus]; and the end thereof shall be with a flood, and unto the end of the war desolations are determined. For the overspreading of abominations he shall make it desolate, even until the consummation, and that determined shall be poured upon the desolate." The Jewish nation is a "desolate" people because they threw away their only hope of salvation.

Flavius Josephus was a Jewish slave to the Roman general named Vespasian, who waged war against the Jews, and became Emperor in AD 69, leaving his son, Titus, to complete the work of conquest in Jerusalem. In this capacity, Josephus was a first-hand witness to Rome's destruction of Jerusalem and the Temple.

In his seven-volume history of Rome's war against the Jews, titled *The Jewish War; or, The History of the Destruction of Jerusalem*, he recorded the horrendous events and conditions of the Jewish people during the final siege of the city. Most certainly, by "the overspreading of abominations," the Roman army made it "desolate until the consummation," as graphically presented in the quote below.

> Thus did the miseries of Jerusalem grow worse and worse every day; and the seditious were still more irritated by the calamities they were under, even while the famine preyed upon themselves; after it had preyed upon the people. And indeed the multitude of carcasses that lay in heaps one upon another was an horrible sight; and produced a pestilential stench; which

was an hindrance to those that would make sallies out of the city, and fight the enemy. But as those were to go in battle array, who had been already used to ten thousand murders, and must tread upon those dead bodies as they marched along, so were not they terrified, nor did they pity men as they marched over them. Nor did they deem this affront offered to the deceased to be any ill omen to themselves. But as they had their right hands already polluted with the murders of their own country men, and in that condition ran out to fight with foreigners, they seem to me to have cast a reproach upon God Himself; as if He were too slow in punishing them. For the war was not now gone on with, as if they had any hope of victory: for they gloried after a brutish manner in that despair of deliverance they were already in. (Book VI, chapter 1, par. 1).

In Deuteronomy chapter 28, God forewarned His people what would befall them if they rebelled against Him. It was literally "poured upon the desolate" in AD 70 by Rome.

Because thou servedst not the LORD thy God with joyfulness, and with gladness of heart, for the abundance of all things; therefore shalt thou serve thine enemies which the LORD shall send against thee, in hunger, and in thirst, and in nakedness, and in want of all things: and he shall put a yoke of iron upon thy neck, until he have destroyed thee. The LORD shall bring a nation against thee from far, from the end of the earth, as swift as the eagle flieth; a nation whose tongue thou shalt not understand; a nation of fierce countenance, which shall not regard the person of the old, nor shew favour to the young: and he shall eat the fruit of thy cattle, and the fruit of thy land, until thou be destroyed: which also shall not leave thee either corn, wine, or oil, or the increase of thy kine, or flocks of thy sheep, until he have destroyed thee. And he shall besiege thee in all thy gates, until thy high and fenced walls come down, wherein thou trustedst, throughout all thy land: and he shall besiege thee in all thy gates throughout all thy land, which the LORD thy God hath given thee (Deuteronomy 28:47-52).

In verses 48 to 50 we find unmistakable descriptors of the Roman Empire. The oppressive nation would "put a yoke of iron" on their necks. Iron is the metal depicting Rome in Daniel chapters 2 and 7 (iron legs and teeth of iron). The new nation would "come from afar." At no time in history prior to the rise of Rome had any people from the Italian peninsula (principally, the Etruscans) had military dealings with the nation of Israel. Rome conquered swiftly, "as the eagle flieth." The eagle was used as a symbol of military victory and appeared on banners, insignia, and buildings in ancient Rome. The language of the Roman conquerors was Latin, a "tongue thou shalt not understand." Roman law promoted *Pax Romana* (Roman peace), but presented a "fierce face" to rebels and insurrectionists.

The prophecy in Deuteronomy continues:—

> The tender and delicate woman among you, which would not adventure to set the sole of her foot upon the ground for delicateness and tenderness, her eye shall be evil toward the husband of her bosom, and toward her son, and toward her daughter, and toward her young one that cometh out from between her feet, and toward her children which she shall bear: for she shall eat them for want of all things secretly in the siege and straitness, wherewith thine enemy shall distress thee in thy gates (Deuteronomy 28:56, 57).

As recorded by Josephus, God's punishment was fully carried out.

> She then attempted a most unnatural thing: and snatching up her son, which was a child sucking at her breast, she said, "O thou miserable infant! for whom shall I preserve thee, in this war, this famine, and this sedition? As to the war with the Romans, if they preserve our lives, we must be slaves. This famine also will destroy us, even before that slavery comes upon us. Yet are these seditious rogues more terrible than both the other. Come on. Be thou my food: and be thou a fury to these seditious varlets, and a by-word to the world. Which is all that is now wanting to compleat the calamities of us Jews." As soon as she had said this, she slew her son; and then roasted him; and did eat the one half of him; and kept the other half by her concealed. (Book VI, chapter 3, par. 4).

The Jewish nation expired its final probation by rejecting and stumbling over the Chief Cornerstone, and salvation went "unto the Gentiles" (Acts 13:46; 18:6; Romans 11:11). The Old Testament never taught the form of religion that developed after the return from Babylonian captivity, and has continued to this day as Judaism.

With the fulfillment of the 490-year prophecy in AD 34, in God's word we find no further purpose for the Jewish nation.[12] Their final probation came to an end with the stoning of Stephen. The destruction of Jerusalem and Herod's temple in AD 70 confirmed Jesus' denunciation of Judaism and its useless religious rituals. "Your house is left unto you desolate" and "there shall not be left here one stone upon another, that shall not be thrown down" (Matthew 23:38; 24:2).

They stumbled because they shut their spiritual eyes to truth. Jesus said: "Let them alone: they be blind leaders of the blind. And if the blind lead the blind, both shall fall into the ditch" (Matthew 15:14; see also Matthew chapter 23).The apostle Paul preached the same message to his fellow Jews. "They are not all Israel which are of Israel" (Romans 9:6). True Israel is a spiritual "nation" that believes in the Son of God, Jesus the Christ, the one and only "Lamb of God" who is the "Saviour of the world" (John 1:29; 4:42; 1 John 4:14).

> What then? Israel hath not obtained that which he seeketh for; but the election hath obtained it, and the rest were blinded (according as it is written, God hath given them the spirit of slumber, eyes that they should not see, and ears that they should not hear;) unto this day. ... because of unbelief they were broken off (Romans 11:7, 8, 20; cf. Hebrews 3:18, 19).

> But Israel, which followed after the law of righteousness, hath not attained to the law of righteousness. Wherefore? Because they sought it not by faith, but as it were by the works of the law. For they stumbled at that Stumblingstone (Romans 9:31, 32).

Individual Jews who receive the message of righteousness by faith in Christ will become part of the "remnant that shall be saved" (Romans 9:27). Acceptance of Jesus as the Saviour of the world is essential to salvation. Without Jesus there is no salvation from sin. "Neither is there salvation in any other: for there is none other name under heaven given among men, whereby we must be saved" (Acts 4:12).

---

12. For further study on what the Bible says about the rejection of Jews who refuse to accept Jesus as their Saviour, see also Matthew 21:42; Mark 12:10; Acts 4:12; 1 Peter 2:7, 8.

214

But the Lord has reserved unto Himself "branches" that will be grafted into the true Vine and be a part of the Israel of God "if they abide not still in unbelief" (Romans 11:23). Being a part of the true Israel has always depended upon a faith response to God's work in our life. When a person of Jewish descent accepts Christ as their Saviour and Lord, then they will be part of the true Vine, and bear much fruit for the Lord (John 15:1-5). Only those who walk with God by faith will be called Israel at the end of time when Christ comes to gather His people.

21

And Then There Was One

F or the love of Christ constraineth us; because we thus judge, that if One died for all, then were all dead: and that He died for all, that they which live should not henceforth live unto themselves, but unto Him which died for them, and rose again." 2 Corinthians 5:14-15.

Faith is more than a mental assent to some particular fact. Faith is described in the Bible as something "which works by love" (Galatians 5:6). Genuine faith is not self-centered, grasping for reward, but other-centered and especially God-centered. In other words, genuine faith is a heart appreciation for what it cost the Godhead to save us from our miserable sin-filled life. Faith realizes how much God gave, through His Son, in making the ultimate sacrifice on Calvary's cross, thus ratifying the everlasting covenant promise to redeem mankind from sin.

When Jesus walked this earth, He did many miracles of healing, both physical and spiritual. Multitudes flocked to hear Him preach and to be touched by His hand. All went away rejoicing over their healing, but few showed a true heart appreciation for what had been done for them. Some who witnessed these miracles would later be in the crowd in Pilate's courtyard screaming for the crucifixion of Jesus.

"And it came to pass, as He went to Jerusalem, that He passed through the midst of Samaria and Galilee." (Luke 17:11). Luke tells us that this "came to pass"—it literally happened; the event is a fact. The time frame for this narrative is Jesus' last journey to Jerusalem before He was crucified. He knew He was on His way to Calvary where, through the foreordained and immutable counsel of God, He would lay down His life to redeem the lost world.

During this final journey, Jesus passed through areas where He had previously preached and healed many people. Rather than take the more accepted, but longer route to Jerusalem which went down the east side of the Jordan River, Jesus "passed through the midst of Samaria." Samaria was generally avoided by most Jews, who thought the Samaritans were spiritually and ethnically unclean and therefore unredeemable.

"And as He entered into a certain village, there met Him ten men that were lepers, which stood afar off" (Luke 17:12). Leprosy was the most feared disease imaginable at the time. Persons who contracted it were condemned to the fringe of society, to live in deserted places and caves, never again to have contact with their family or friends. Persons who contracted the disease were considered by man as being cursed by God because of some personal transgression against Him. Leprosy is used in the Bible as a synonym for sin because it disfigured and maimed its victim, was incurable, and caused contagious lesions on the body that brought shame and misery to the individual.

The ten men mentioned by Luke acutely sensed the stigma of their disease, and following the dictates of society and Mosaic teaching, they "stood afar off" as Jesus passed by where they had secluded themselves. Unable to approach Him, they could only raise their voices crying, "Master, have mercy on us!"

These ten lepers illustrate that sin has separated us from God's original plan for us, which included face-to-face communication as Adam and Eve experienced in Eden before sin entered this world. Jesus repaired the breach caused by sin through His incarnation and death on the cross. He was "made to be sin for us" (2 Corinthians 5:21), and then corporately—as us—He took sin to the cross, thereby condemning sin itself, but not sinners.

We often quote John 3:16, but overlook the next two verses:

> For God sent not His Son into the world to condemn the world; but that the world through Him might be saved. He that believeth on Him is not condemned: but he that believeth not is condemned already, because he hath not believed in the name of the only begotten Son of God (John 3:17, 18).

Unbelief is the barrier to salvation. God does not condemn us, but is constantly seeking to transform our twisted lives; to make straight the crookedness, smoothing and refining our characters fitting us for eternal life among heavenly beings.

But let's return to the ten lepers. Jesus' response to these outcasts of society was immediate. "And when He saw them, He said unto them, Go, show yourselves unto the priests" (vs. 14). If a person was healed from some disease that excluded them from social contact, they were to present themselves to the priests to be declared healed from their illness before they could return to society (see Leviticus 14:1–3ff). The spiritual lesson for us is that when we realize our true condition, as those ten lepers did, and cry out for release from sin, God will never turn a deaf ear. Realizing that we are forgiven has an immediate, transforming effect. Fear of God vanishes and love bubbles to the surface.

The story does not tell us what the ten desperate men said in response to Jesus telling them to "go." We don't know who turned around first and began his journey to the Temple, but someone had to have moved first heading back toward Jerusalem, with the other nine following behind him. As he was walking, he noticed the change in his flesh, felt new life manifesting itself in his body. Fingers, toes and perhaps his nose that had been eaten away by the disease were suddenly restored whole. "And as they went, they were cleansed" (Luke 17:14).

Faith "worked" when, without questioning His command or waiting to see evidence before acting in faith, they obeyed Jesus' voice. They believed the "word only," and they were transformed from unclean lepers to whole, healthy men.

Faith grew in response to the power of God working in their lives. They realized how active is the word of God toward sinful man. The word of God is the living Word and full of creative power. When it is allowed to work in the life, there will be marvelous work wrought in the individual to transform their character into the image of God.

In this case as in every other instance in the Bible, it was the spoken Word of God that did it all. This is the difference between the word of God and the word of men. God's word is creative and able to do what it says. Man's word alone has no power to accomplish what it claims to be able to produce. Man must work in order to accomplish what he claims to be able to produce. A man's word may express the easiest possible thing for him to accomplish, and you may thoroughly believe it, yet it is altogether dependent upon the man himself doing something to accomplish it apart from his spoken word. It is not the man's word alone which accomplishes anything at all.

However, the power which brings physical and spiritual healing—redemption from sin—is the same power that spoke the world, indeed, the entire universe, into existence. In the Bible the Word which God speaks saves and sanctifies the believing soul.

We are not to think that because we, like those lepers, are "far off" from God, separated from Him by our sin, that He cannot reach us with His powerful word. Another story found in John 4:46-53 relates just how powerful and far-reaching is the word of God. Again, Jesus was traveling through Samaria, where He spent two days teaching the people that He was "the Christ, the Saviour of the world" (John 4:42). As He departed on His way back to Galilee, He met a nobleman from Capernaum who came to plead for the healing of his son. After making his petition, the man "believed the word that Jesus had spoken unto him, and he went his way" (John 4:50).

When the nobleman arrived home the next day, he found his son had been healed at the same hour that Jesus had spoken to him (vv. 51 and 52). The word of God is unlimited in its power. The ten lepers were within shouting distance of Jesus when they cried out for mercy. The son of the nobleman of Capernaum was at least a day's journey away from where the father encountered Jesus in Cana. Yet, both the son and the lepers were healed at the very moment when the word of God was spoken. God's word has in it the power to instantaneously accomplish what it says.

Many people are ready to admit, in a general way, that what the Lord says is true, as concerning other people (like the people in the Bible we just mentioned). But as it applies to themselves, right now in their present situation, they will not admit it is, or can be, true. They hesitate and doubt the power of God's word to save them from their sin. Doubt is not faith. If you doubt that the word of God is true to you personally, right now, in your present situation as you struggle with sin, then you do not have true living faith.

There is no limiting factor on the power of the Word of God except our unbelief. If we refuse to believe in His power to accomplish His will for us, which is that "sin shall not have dominion over you" (Romans 6:14), then we are choosing to *remain* in our sin, when we could be free. We are choosing to allow Satan to continue his control over our lives. If we continue in a life of sin, we have not believed just how good the good news is, nor have we learned to appreciate of the cost of our salvation.

The Bible proves most people do not appreciate the gift of salvation. Most take the gift of life and fritter away the time given during which God wishes to transform our characters. Inordinate amounts of time and energy is expended on things that do us no heavenly good. There is a lack of respect and love for the One who surrendered all things to woo and win back to His side.

Only one of the ten lepers returned to his Saviour.

And one of them, when he saw that he was healed, turned back, and with a loud voice glorified God, and fell down on his face at His feet, giving thanks: and he was a Samaritan (Luke 17:15, 16).

Only one of those ten men returned to thank Jesus for the gift of healing—and he was a Samaritan! The man was one of the hated race of people who were condemned by the Jews as unforgivable. He was the only one who showed a heart appreciation for the gift of salvation.

This one man not only received the word of God into his mind as a fact, but he received it with thankfulness into his heart. He recognized the full wretchedness of his miserable existence and how it separated him from all he longed to once again hold close to his heart. Standing "afar off," isolated on the side of the road, he saw his nakedness, and he was ashamed.

When he looked down and saw that the terrible lesions on his hands were healed, felt his face and nose and found them whole again, he was filled with joy. His heart was ready to burst with appreciation for what was restored to him. It was this heart-response that Jesus commended when He said: "Arise, go thy way: thy faith hath made thee whole" (Luke 17:19). "Whole," not just healed from the physical malady of leprosy, but spiritually whole. His unbelief was also cured and he received what his sin-sick heart needed most: the blessed assurance of salvation from sin and its destructive effects.

Are you sick of sin and its control over your life? Would you rather have the righteousness of God in your life than all the pleasures Satan promises you? Are you willing to let the sins go now, this moment, and believe with all your heart that God has ordained righteousness for you at this moment and for eternity?

Then, there is no reason why you can't have it now, right this very moment. This is justification by faith gladly receiving the forgiveness already given to you through the sacrifice of Christ. It is righteousness by faith, and it is a living, heart transforming faith which "works by love." And it is the simplest thing in the world.

22

Divine Appointment at the Well

The encounter between Jesus and the Samaritan woman at Jacob's well has an interesting background. By New Testament times, animosity and outright hatred had existed between the Samaritans and Jews for more than four hundred years. Jews considered the Samaritans as ethnically impure and religiously unsound. By Jewish standards, they were "unclean" and were to be shunned like lepers. It was considered spiritually prudent to avoid even walking through the territory where they lived.

The Samaritans of Jesus' day were a mixed group of remnant Israelites who were left behind when Assyrian King Shalmaneser destroyed the northern kingdom in 722 BC. King Hoshea of Samaria violated the conditions of the suzerain contract Assyria made with him by failing to pay his annual tribute taxes and seeking an alliance with the king of Egypt. We have this faithful report of the facts:—

> And the king of Assyria found conspiracy in Hoshea: for he had sent messengers to So king of Egypt,[1] and brought no present to the king of Assyria, as he had done year by year: therefore the king of Assyria shut him up, and bound him in prison (2 Kings 17:4).

In 975 BC, when the ten northern tribes chose to rebel against Rehoboam's harsh governance, the children of Israel began their downward spiral to complete apostasy. God sent prophets to guide them back to the right path, but the people refused to listen.

---

1. The Egyptian king was also called Piye.

Turn ye from your evil ways, and keep My commandments and My statutes, according to all the law which I commanded your fathers, and which I sent to you by My servants the prophets. Notwithstanding they would not hear, but hardened their necks, like to the neck of their fathers, that did not believe in the LORD their God (2 Kings 17:13, 14).

Continually, the people profaned the solemn contract they made with God at Sinai when they "signed on the dotted line" by promising, "All the LORD has said, we will do!" (Exodus 19:8; 24:3-8).[2] Over the ensuing centuries they compromised and confused their worship with the abominable practices of Baal and Molech. Their behavior and attitudes violated the clear stipulations contained in Israel's covenant agreement with God (see Deuteronomy chapter 28).

God's design when He brought them to Sinai was to write His laws on their heart, not tables of stone (see Hebrews 8:8-10). As a nation, the descendants of faithful Abraham, Isaac, and Jacob (Israel) could not comprehend God's intentions when He delivered them from Egyptian bondage. They lacked spiritual maturity, and could not appreciate God's love for them. They had not lived by faith while in Egypt and had lost experiential knowledge of their ancestors' devotion to God.

Their time under Pharaoh's dictatorship taught them strict obedience to his demands would avoid painful consequences. At Sinai, they assumed they were trading an earthly dictator for an immaterial one. Their slave mentality hindered their spiritual discernment; therefore, they could not serve God from a heart response to His love for them.

As a result, seven hundred years after Sinai, their probation expired and God did as He promised: the Creator God of heaven and earth allowed Assyria to inflict the covenant punishments upon the ten northern tribes.[3] The Israelites became an astonishment to the surrounding nations.

---

2. The children of Israel created a suzerain contract with God at Sinai. It was never God's intention, but He allowed them to enter into a covenant He knew they could never keep. They failed miserably within forty days of making their self-assured boast (see Exodus 19:9; 24:3, 7; and chapter 32).

3. Before the Assyrians arrived, the northern tribes had already fallen into deep apostasy, but the transportation of the priests left the remnant people without spiritual guidance (cf. 2 Kings 17:25-29).

Even all nations shall say, Wherefore hath the LORD done thus unto this land? what meaneth the heat of this great anger? Then men shall say, Because they have forsaken the covenant of the LORD God of their fathers, which he made with them when he brought them forth out of the land of Egypt: for they went and served other gods, and worshiped them, gods whom they knew not, and whom He had not given unto them: and the anger of the LORD was kindled against this land, to bring upon it all the curses that are written in this book [see Deuteronomy 28:15-48]: and the LORD rooted them out of their land in anger, and in wrath, and in great indignation, and cast them into another land, as it is this day (Deuteronomy 29:26-28). [4]

Archeological records reveal that King Shalmaneser carried away 27,290 persons living in the northern Israelite territories. These were the principal men of influence (and their families), men of wealth and political power, including all the priests, and many skilled tradesmen. The less educated classes were left to till the land, harvest crops, and tend the vineyards.

Conquering kings did not want to waste the productivity of the captured lands and, through forced migration, repopulated the area with people from other territories they controlled. After capturing and transporting most of the Israelites living in Samaria, Shalmaneser imported persons from Babylon and surrounding areas to repopulate Samaria. These immigrants soon intermarried with the remaining Israelites. Through the introduction of their pagan religions and influence within the marriage relationship, the remaining Israelites further compromised their knowledge of the true God of Israel. [5]

---

4. Please note this prophecy, written by Moses 720 years before it came to pass, was written in past tense, as though it had already happened.

5. "Do not be unequally yoked with unbelievers. For what partnership has righteousness with lawlessness? Or what fellowship has light with darkness?" (2 Corinthians 6:14, ESV). King Solomon's failure was due, in part, to his love of "strange women." "But king Solomon loved many strange women, together with the daughter of Pharaoh, women of the Moabites, Ammonites, Edomites, Zidonians, and Hittites; of the nations concerning which the LORD said unto the children of Israel, Ye shall not go in to them, neither shall they come in unto you: for surely they will turn away your heart after their gods: Solomon clave unto these in love." (1 Kings 11:1, 2).

Then the king of Assyria came up throughout all the land and besieged it three years … And the king of Assyria brought men from Babylon, and from Cuthah, and from Ava, and from Hamath, and from Sepharvaim, and placed them in the cities of Samaria instead of the children of Israel: and they possessed Samaria, and dwelt in the cities thereof (2 Kings 17:5, 24).

After these drastic political changes, the region had a series of catastrophes. The new settlers interpreted these disasters as a sign of displeasure from the local god, indicating that not enough attention was being given to him.

Wherefore they spake to the king of Assyria, saying the nations which thou hast removed and placed in cities of Samaria, know not the manner of the God of the land: therefore He hath sent lions among them, and, behold, they slay them, because they know not the manner of the God of the land. Then the king of Assyria commanded, saying, Carry thither one of the priests whom ye brought from thence; and let them go and dwell there, and let him teach them the manner of the God of the land. Then one of the priests whom they had carried away from Samaria came and dwelt in Bethel, and taught them how they should fear the LORD (2 Kings 17:26-28).

The result of this attempt to appease an "angry God" through half-truths and compromise with pagan ideas was that "they feared the LORD, and served their own gods, after the manner of the nations whom they carried away from there" (verse 33). Through these compromises, the remnant Samaritans were confused about who the true God was and about how to worship Him.

When the people of Judah returned from Babylonian captivity nearly 200 years later, the Samaritans considered themselves kin to the Jews. Extending brotherly friendship, they offered to help them rebuild the city of Jerusalem and the temple.

But Zerubbabel, Jeshua, and other leaders of the Jews rejected the offer unequivocally. They were convinced that the Samaritans had dangerously corrupted the worship of the LORD. After spending seventy years in Babylonian captivity for their own corruption of religion, they were suspicious and afraid of reverting to the errors of their unfaithful fathers.

As a result of this distrust of their neighbors, an increasingly hostile attitude developed between the two people groups. The Jews had a saying they used to show contempt: "Thou art a Samaritan, and hast a demon" (John 8:48). Jesus used the hatred of the Jews for Samaritans in His parable of the "good Samaritan" to show the Pharisees there was more worthiness in Samaritan mercy than in all their legalism (Luke 10:30-37).

Despite the open hatred between them, as evidence of their authenticity, the Samaritans pointed to their ancestor's association with the valley of Shechem that lies between the twin mountains, Ebal and Gerizim. When Jacob returned from his twenty-year exile, he first settled near the village of Shechem, which is between these two mountains (Genesis chapter 34). To avoid disputes over water rights with the local people, Jacob dug a deep well near where he made his encampment. The well is still in existence.

Another impediment to friendship between the Jews and Samaritans was disagreement concerning the place of worship. The Samaritans possessed an ancient copy of the Pentateuch, cherished by them for centuries. They claimed their copy was the only authentic manuscript available and was "the more sure word" than that brought back from Babylon by the Jews.

In their "five books of Moses" (Pentateuch means "five books"), there is a text that supports their idea that Mount Gerizim is the holy place for worshiping Jehovah.

> And it shall come to pass, when the LORD thy God hath brought thee in unto the land whither thou goest to possess it, that thou shalt put the blessing upon mount Gerizim, and the curse upon mount Ebal (Deuteronomy 11:29).

When Joshua and his army captured this area, he built an altar and performed the dedication ceremony on Mount Ebal, on the north side of the valley (Deuteronomy 27:1-4; and see Joshua chapter 8).

Because the Samaritans had evidence that their land was as sacred for worshiping the LORD as any place in Judah, conflict and animosity increased until the time of Jesus.

One day, Jesus journeyed into this region because He had a divine appointment to keep. Seating Himself on the stone border of Jacob's well, He waited. Soon He saw a woman of Samaria shuffling through the heat with her empty water jar on her head.

This particular woman always delayed until noon to come and fetch her daily water supply. Thus she avoided the venomous stares and whispers of the other women of the village. She was used to having the well to herself.

Everyone else went to the well in the early morning hours before the sun rose and the heat became unbearable. They came to socialize and catch up on the gossip, in addition to filling their water pots from the ancient well. This miserable, lonely woman was the frequent target of their gossip sessions. Everyone knew about her wild lifestyle. It made for some lively discussions.

Squinting into the shimmering heat as she approached the well, she saw a man sitting on the stones surrounding the pit. He was looking straight at her. Slowing her pace, she began to size up this stranger. She was used to being stared at, especially by men. The knowing looks, the glances of condemnation, the smiles of invitation, she knew them all.

The strong mutual resentment between the Jews living in the surrounding areas, and the Samaritans living under the shadow of Mount Gerizim, where they had established their worship center, caused the woman to pause in her walk. The natural response as she approached where Jesus was sitting on the rim of the well was: Why is this Jew sitting here on *our* well?

It was highly unusual for a Jew to be in the Samaritan territory. To avoid coming in contact with the hated Samaritans, the Jews usually took the longer route north by crossing just above the Dead Sea to the east side of the Jordan River. This way, travelers passed through the Roman districts of Perea and Decapolis until they came near the Sea of Galilee.

But Jesus had a divine appointment to keep with this woman. Her soul sickness and desperate longing had called Him from the usual path of His travels between Jerusalem and Galilee and placed Him at the well when she would be coming for her water.

As the woman drew nearer the well, Jesus said to her, "Give me some water" (John 4:7). Her haughty response was quick. "You're a Jew; why are you asking me for a drink? You know Jews don't have anything to do with us Samaritans." There was more than a little contempt in her voice.

In response to her comment, Jesus cut through the trivia, aiming straight at the woman's heart-need. "If you knew the gift of God, and Who it is that is speaking to you, you would have asked of Him, and He would have given you living water." The softness of His voice, the authority and boldness of His statement, turned away her anger and touched a chord in her heart. Feelings she had thought were long dead roused to life.

Jesus' attitude toward her softened her contempt. Perhaps she recalled Rachel's encounter with a stranger at a well and the great wealth and changed circumstances that came to her because of that man's kindness toward Rachel. But, more probably, it was that "a soft answer turneth away wrath" (Proverbs 15:1).

When the woman answered Jesus, she politely addressed Him as "Sir." Continuing, she pointed out the apparent obstacle to His delivering what He promised. She said: "You have nothing to draw with, and the well is deep: where are you going to get this living water?" Water from a well is considered "still," while water from a running stream is called "living water" because it moves. Here was a deep well, but there was no "living" stream nearby. Looking around and seeing no water jar at His side, she wondered where this "living water" was going to come from.

The woman questioned the Man's right to make any claim on the water from this well. "Are You greater than our father Jacob, who gave us this well, and drank from it himself, along with his children and livestock?" (John 4:12).

Jesus pressed on, knowing her need was spiritual, not physical. The Great Physician's knife cut expertly, dissecting the cancer of sin destroying her life. "If you continue to drink from the broken cisterns of the world, you will continue to be thirsty. What you need is water from the Spring of eternal life."

Still not understanding His meaning, she said, "Give me some of this water so that I don't have to come and draw from this well again." It would be a joy to never again trudge out in the heat of the day just to avoid the other women! One drink, and she would never be thirsty again. However, the spiritual meaning eluded her.

"Go get your husband and come back out here." Jesus' comment caused her rising emotions to chill suddenly. Quietly, nearly imperceptibly, she answered, "I don't have a husband." The Surgeon's knife was close to its objective. Jesus had touched the root of her pain.

"You speak the truth. You have been married five times, and the man you currently live with is not your husband." His words were not condemning, just an honest statement about the life she was living. She wondered: I've never seen this man around here before. How could this stranger know these things about me? Timidly she ventured her opinion, "Sir, you must be a prophet."

Then to escape His deep probing into her heart, she tried shifting the emphasis of the discussion away from her by returning to an accusatory and confrontational tone. "You Jews condemn us because we worship God on Mount Gerizim. You tell us that God can only be worshiped in the temple in Jerusalem."

Jesus did not answer her query concerning a prophet. He saw through her attempt to dodge His point, and instead answered the deeper question. "Woman, it is not where you worship, but how you worship. You don't really know what you are worshiping."

The prophecies concerning the coming Messiah were known among the Samaritans as well as the Jews. They all studied from the same Book, so the woman responded, "I know that when the Messiah comes, He will teach us all things." The Man's answer was much more than she expected, "I that speak unto thee am He" (John 4:26).

In just a few minutes of conversation, this Man went from being a Jewish stranger held in contempt to a man deserving respect whom she addressed as "sir," then she thought He was a prophet, and now He revealed Himself to her as "the Saviour of the world."

The woman was so excited by this good news that she left her water pot and ran back to the village. Exclaiming to the first group of men she encountered, "Come, see a man, which told me all things that ever I did: is not this the Christ?" (John 4:28, 29). This stranger must be "that Prophet" foretold by Moses, who would come from the "midst of thy brethren." If this was true, God commanded them to "hearken unto Him" (Deuteronomy 18:15).

A crowd ran out of the village to the well, where they found Jesus and his disciples, who had returned from the village with victuals for their lunch. The disciples had passed by the woman as they entered the village and were now concerned because their Master refused to eat the food they brought to Him. What had transpired while they were in the village? The disciples urged Him, "Master, eat!" but He replied, "I have meat to eat that ye do not know about."

For Jesus, seeking the lost and bringing them the good news of salvation from sin filled Him to the brim and satisfied the physical longing of His merciful heart. The "food" that sustained Him was shedding God's love abroad.

"My meat is to do the will of Him that sent Me, and to finish His work." The "work" did not consist of preaching salvation exclusively to the Jewish people living in Judea but included seeking all the "lost sheep" wherever they might be found.

When the Jews returned from Babylonian captivity, they isolated themselves to avoid religious contamination. They erected a "middle wall of partition" between themselves and the surrounding peoples, but in doing this, they failed in their commission to preach the good news of the coming Messiah. However, Jesus considered the Samaritans a part of the scattered "lost sheep" that He came to save and knew they should have received better consideration from their Jewish brethren.

By then, the men from Samaria had reached the well. Instead of eating what the disciples had purchased for Him, Jesus arose from the well and went with the Samaritans back to their village. There He revealed to them the gospel of salvation from sin. They gladly received the message.

> Many more believed because of what He said. And they told the woman, "We no longer believe because of what you said, for we have heard for ourselves and know that this really is the Savior of the world" (John 4:41, 42, HCSB).

How quickly Gospel truth can pierce the receptive heart, bringing contrition and repentance to a sin-sick soul—if that truth is not rejected or compromised by clinging to preconceived opinions. Like the Jews, the Samaritans had been waiting for the Messiah, and when Jesus came to their village, they were overjoyed to receive His message.

The love of Jesus did not condemn these people because they were Samaritans; God condemns no one. Jesus spent two days in the village. Gently, He took those "lost sheep" under His wing, patiently teaching them the truth, removing the rubbish accumulated from centuries of religious tradition and false ideas. By opening the Scriptures to them, Jesus gave overwhelming evidence of Who He is and revealed His mission as "Saviour of the world."

After two days of study with the Samaritans, Jesus converted most of the village. They believed His word because they were searching for truth and were willing to give up their preconceived ideas when the facts were presented. The people of that town knew by the message He shared with them that He was indeed "the Lamb of God" sent to save even the hated Samaritans (John 4:42).

23

Vacillating Extremist
Part 1

B y nature, Simon Peter was rash, erratic, impertinent, impulsive, and overconfident. He was also physically strong, kindhearted, forgiving, and loving. In short, Peter was a complex man who didn't know himself. But Jesus read his character from the first moment He laid eyes on him.

When Andrew excitedly brought his brother to Jesus, saying: "Come on—we have found the Messiah" (see John 1:40-41), Jesus looked at the man and said: Simon, you are like a pebble, rolled here and there by the storm waves of indecision. It is from this character assessment that Jesus added to Simon's Hebrew name the descriptive nickname "Peter," which means "pebble" or "tumbling stone" (vs. 42).

"Peter" comes from the Greek word "petros" and means a shifting, rolling, or unsecured stone or pebble anchored nowhere. The Greek word for a more substantial rock is "petra" and is used to describe a large rock not easily moved.[1] Another Greek word for a solid, immovable rock used as a monument is "lithos." But Jesus did not choose either of those words meaning a "solid, firmly embedded rock." He nicknamed Simon something more descriptive of his true character—an unstable pebble.[2]

---

1. "Petra" is the name for the ancient ruins of a city carved from solid rock, discovered in 1812 by a Swiss traveler named Johann Ludwig Burckhardt. The city is located in southwest Jordan. In the Bible, Petra is called by its Hebrew name, Sela in Isaiah 16:1 and 2 Kings 14:7.
2. Peter is not the "rock" Jesus referred to in Matthew 16:18. Jesus asked His disciples who people were saying He was. Peter answered, "Thou art the Christ, the Son of the living God." This immutable truth is the foundation Rock for the Christian church: Jesus Christ, the Son of God, is the Saviour of the world.

Simon, now called Peter, was to learn the most valuable lessons of his life over the next three and a half years while following Jesus. Through the lessons taught by experience, failure, and humble repentance, he would have his character permanently molded into the likeness of his Saviour until he was finally able to say, "Not I, but Christ in every way."

Sometime soon after their first encounter, Jesus came to the place where Simon Peter and his partners had pulled their boats onto the beach after a fruitless night of fishing. He stepped into Simon and Andrew's boat and sat down to preach to the crowd gathered on the beach to hear Him.

When He finished preaching, Jesus turned to Simon Peter and instructed him to push out into the middle of the lake and cast out his nets. Jesus' comment seemed incredulous to Peter, and he answered: "But, Master, we have toiled all night and caught nothing!" (Luke 5:4, 5).

Why would Simon argue with Jesus? Simon Peter was a professional fisherman. He knew the waters, the fish, and the appropriate times for catching fish. The clear waters of the Sea of Galilee drove the fish deep during the hot daylight hours. At night, when the surface waters cooled off, the fish rose to the top to feed and were easy to snare in the cast and drag nets used by the fishermen.

In essence, Peter's answer to Jesus' command was a gentle rebuke that, in effect, meant: "Master, you might be a great rabbi, but please, leave the fishing to us who know about such things!" But as Jesus continued to gaze at him without wavering from His command, Peter wisely responded: "Nevertheless, at Thy word, I will let down the net" (Luke 5:5).

True faith concludes that it is always right to obey the Word of God even when it seems unreasonable or, in fact, impossible for the Word to accomplish what it says. Faith believes the Word of God is true even when everything else seems to support the contrary.

Simon Peter knew intellectually that Jesus had power, but faith was yet to develop in his proud heart. He had already witnessed the power of Jesus' spoken word in his own home with the healing of his mother-in-law, and had seen multitudes of others healed (Mark 1:16-34). When Jesus spoke, "it was so."

As in those previous situations, doing what Jesus told them brought an immediate and amazing result. The net enclosed so many fish that the nets began to break. Excitedly, Simon called to his partners, and when they hauled the fish into the boats, the weight of such an enormous catch began to sink them.

At this point, Simon Peter saw himself as the unbelieving sinner he was. How could he have doubted what Jesus told him to do? How could he have been so arrogant as to speak to the Master as he did? Falling at the Saviour's feet, he cried: "Depart from me; for I am a sinful man, O Lord" (Luke 5:8-9). This experience gave Simon Peter a new vision of Christ and brought the proud fisherman to his knees in submission and surrender. When he saw himself in the light of the beauty and power of the character of Christ, Peter's ego was deflated, and his pride collapsed.

If not blocked by persistent unbelief, a single ray of the glory of God shining through the character of Christ can penetrate the most hardened heart. Rightly appreciated, it will expose every defilement in our character. Christ's perfect character, when viewed with the eyes of faith, boldly reveals all our unholy desires, the corruption of our hearts, and the impurity of our lips.

The more we come to Jesus through Bible study and prayer, the more faulty we will appear in our own eyes. Our sins and imperfections will be seen in broad and shameful contrast to His perfect character of love. Pride and self-promotion have no place in the heart of the truly converted Christian.

Simon Peter's impetuous and self-confident character was demonstrated on a number of occasions throughout the four Gospels. All were recorded for our learning, that we may put aside all the "sins which so easily beset us" and follow in the Master's footsteps.

> Wherefore seeing we also are compassed about with so great a cloud of witnesses, let us lay aside every weight, and the sin which doth so easily beset us, and let us run with patience the race that is set before us, looking unto Jesus the Author and Finisher of our faith (Hebrews 12:1, 2).

Some months after Jesus called His first disciples, He was preaching to a great multitude of people on a hillside beside the sea. It had been a long day and the people were growing hungry. Jesus would not send them home with their basic need unsatisfied. One of His disciples brought to Jesus five small loaves of bread and two dried fish. With them, Jesus fed more than five thousand men, in addition to many women and children who were among the crowd (Matthew 14:13-21).

Jesus then blessed and dismissed the people, sent His disciples away, and went up onto the mountain to pray (Matthew 14:22, 23). Jesus had preached all day to this large group and needed some private time in prayerful communion with His heavenly Father. With the crowd dispersed, alone at last, He sat down and opened His heart in supplication to the Source of all power. He was ready to receive from His Father's throne renewed blessings to dispense to the world.

While Jesus was praying, "in the fourth watch of the night," between three and six in the morning, a storm arose on the Sea of Galilee. Jesus' disciples were toiling in their boat, endeavoring to cross the lake in the midst of the tempest (Mark 6:48). From His position on the hill above the lake, Jesus saw their predicament and, as He often does, He allowed them to "toil" awhile at the problem before He came to their rescue.

Why does God often wait before intervening to solve our problems? Delay serves to show us our utter inability to save ourselves. When we have exhausted all our self-reliant means and, by human estimations, everything seems hopeless, then we are ready to receive blessings from the LORD. Then God's intervening power will be recognized for its ability to rescue us, not just from the present predicament, but from the drudgery of slavery to sin. This was a lesson the disciples needed to learn. Their self-reliant pride must be laid in the dust.

Heavy waves poured over the sides of the boat. The disciples' bodies strained at the oars attempting to keep the storm-tossed vessel from sinking. All their energy was concentrated on saving themselves. Then, suddenly, illuminated by the flashes of lightning, there appeared beside the boat a figure shrouded in sea mist and rain striding on the tops of the turbulent water.

"For fear," they let out an agonized scream because "they supposed it had been a spirit" (Mark 6:49 and Matthew 14:26). At that terrifying moment, unfounded superstition was stronger than their faith. Immediately the Saviour responded to their distress. Calling above the storm's roar, He declared: "Be not afraid!"

Jesus spoke with the same commanding voice that will one day call the dead from their graves—the same voice that spoke all things into existence. It was easily heard above the raging of the wind and waves. When the disciples recognized Him, they were beside themselves with joy. Their best Friend had not abandoned them!

The next verse is almost unbelievable in exposing Peter's childish impetuosity. "Lord, if it be Thou, bid me come unto Thee on the water" (Matthew 14:28).

What an outrageous request! Why did Peter ask for an invitation to go to Jesus on the water? Did he want to show off in front of the other disciples? Perhaps Peter was so afraid that all he wanted was to be cuddled in his Saviour's arms?

Peter was a man of pronounced extremes. He was preeminently a man of action and enthusiasm. However, his strong personality was marked by both virtues and serious defects. Because of his abrasive self-assertiveness, Peter's impulsiveness often led him to be boastful, unstable, undependable, and even offensive to others. But in a moment of crisis, he was likely to be weak and cowardly. No one could predict which side of his personality would prevail at any given time.

One thing was certain. He always wanted to be close to his Master.

Simon Peter's comment: "If it be Thou" was not an expression of doubt about who was walking beside the boat. And when he said: "Bid me," he showed that he would only act at the Master's will and command. Peter was not asking for power to duplicate the miracle of walking on water. Instead, he was demonstrating an impulsive love for the Saviour in this most trying hour of need. He knew he would be safe from the raging storm if he could get to the Saviour's side.

Satan had stirred up the storm attempting to destroy Jesus' disciples, physically and spiritually. They were fishermen, physically strong and knowledgeable of the power of the wind and sea. But their strength was nothing compared to Satan's determination to destroy them. Toiling with all their might, they could not save themselves. The truth they needed to learn was that Jesus is more powerful than anything Satan can devise to hurt or discourage us.

Peter's fledgling faith was learning that if he depended upon the word of God only, all things were possible. And so he said, "Lord bid me to come unto Thee." It would have been a fatal presumption for Peter to have jumped out of the boat and into those treacherous waves in an attempt to walk to Jesus in his own power. But his faith in the power of Christ to uphold him allowed him to make his request and then act in the strength of that faith in Christ's authority over all creation.

Peter's request was answered with only one word: "Come."

We cannot help but marvel at Peter's response. What would we have done under the same circumstances? With the shriek of the wind in his ears, the pelting rain stinging his face, and the crashing, boisterous waves soaking his body, with complete confidence, Peter stepped over the side of the boat.

In this one act, he exhibited not only great courage but even greater faith in the power of the Word to sustain him. At that moment, all Peter wanted was to be closer to his Master, like a frightened child wants to be cuddled in his father's strong, secure embrace.

While gazing intently into the face of his Lord, Peter walked securely on the surface of that storm-ravaged sea. But as he glanced back to his companions remaining in the boat, his vacillating personality released the hand of faith and twisted into self-satisfaction. His eyes diverted from the Saviour, even for this brief moment, and his faith crumbled. He "saw the wind was boisterous." Fear gripped his heart, and the angry waters began to engulf him.

Here is the chief cause of all our failures and defeats at the hand of God's enemy. We take our eyes off the Master who bids us to come and follow Him in safety. We must not, in pride and self-satisfaction, think that we have "arrived" in our Christian experience and that we have no further need of the Master's power to save us. Those who fail to realize their constant dependence upon God will be overcome by temptation.

Peter's next words are the most important anyone could ever utter: "Lord, save me!" Peter looked again to Jesus and prayed one of the shortest but most effectual prayers of all time. It was sincere and fervent and prayed in complete confidence that it would be answered. "And immediately Jesus stretched forth His hand, and caught him."

Jesus' gentle rebuke brought Peter to his senses. "O thou of little faith, why did you doubt?"

With his trembling hand clasped firmly in the Saviour's, and now humbled and speechless, Peter walked side by side with the Master back to the boat. Superficial readers usually overlook this vital experience. He walked again with Jesus. The Lord completely forgives our unfaithfulness and restores us to walk with Him again. But we are restored only by realizing our own weakness and by looking steadfastly unto Jesus for power to overcome the obstacles Satan places in our path.

Once again among his companions, Peter saw no reason to comment about his shameful behavior. He realized he nearly lost his life through his unbelief and self-exaltation. His footing was lost when he looked away from Jesus, and he immediately began to sink beneath the waves. Through his experience that night, Peter learned the lesson Jesus intended for him. This incident revealed to Peter his weakness and showed him that his only safety was in constant dependence upon divine mercy and power.

When trouble comes, how like Peter we all are! We look with fear at the crashing, drowning waves of trouble, trials, and temptation instead of keeping our eyes fixed upon the Saviour. Jesus did not tell Peter to step out of the boat so that he would perish in the waves. He does not ask us to follow Him and then forsake us to fight the enemy of our souls in our own feebleness.

We are Jesus' most precious treasure; our dear Saviour gave His life for us! He will protect every repentant, believing soul who sincerely calls upon His name. The heartfelt cry, "Lord, save me!" will be answered every time. Heaven's mighty angel army awaits the command from the throne of grace: Send forth the rescue squad and snatch the precious branch from the burning!

Fear not: for I have redeemed thee, I have called thee by thy name; thou art Mine. When thou passest through the waters, I will be with thee; and through the rivers, they shall not overflow thee: when thou walkest through the fire, thou shalt not be burned; neither shall the flame kindle upon thee. For I am the LORD thy God, the Holy One of Israel, thy Saviour. ... I, even I, am the LORD; and beside Me there is no saviour (Isaiah 43:1-3, 11).

One characteristic demonstrated during that stormy night which set Peter apart from the other disciples was his willingness to "speak up"—to put himself forward. This he did on most occasions without hesitation. He often spoke rashly from the impulse of the moment, and it frequently got him into trouble. Being naturally forward and impulsive, Satan had an opportunity to use these characteristics to overthrow Peter.

Before his conversion, the instability of Peter's character was plainly outlined in the Scriptures. Hidden in Peter's heart were his evil temper, self-assurance, and boastful pride that circumstances would fan into life. In addition, an underlying aggression and compulsion to always be foremost often flared into angry words.

He was destined for eternal ruin unless he became conscious of the danger he was in if these sinful characteristics went uncorrected. The Saviour saw in Peter a self-love and prideful assurance that would override his boastfully declared love for his Master. Jesus loved Peter and constantly brought him to situations where he could see himself as he truly was—a sinner in constant need of his Saviour.

Wait—"before his conversion"? How can that be right? Peter was one of Jesus' closest companions for three and a half years, yet Jesus said he was "unconverted." Yes, that is what Jesus said of His devoted and boisterous disciple. Jesus was sitting at the Passover feast table the night of His arrest when He said: "Simon, I have prayed for you, that your faith will not fail you. And when you are converted, strengthen your fellow workers" (see Luke 22:32).

Even after all the declarations from Peter about his love for his Saviour, Jesus could look Peter straight in the eye and tell him he was unconverted. Poor Peter. The sting of Jesus' gentle rebuke and warning must have caused a cold chill to run down Peter's spine as he quickly searched his thoughts and past actions. What was the Master seeing in him that brought forth such a comment about His devoted disciple?

True to his nature, Peter immediately came up with an answer to contradict Jesus' statement. Jesus was wrong, and Peter intended to let Him and everyone else know it. After all, Peter didn't want the other disciples to get the wrong impression of him. Loudly he proclaimed: "Lord, I am ready to go with Thee, both into prison, and to death."

But Jesus, knowing the extent of Peter's sinful self-centeredness, told him: "Peter, the cock shall not crow this day, before that thou shalt thrice deny that thou knowest Me." Christ's solemn words were a warning to Peter that he needed to prayerfully search the depths of his heart. Peter needed to distrust himself and have a deeper faith in Christ as his only means of overcoming sin.

After the Passover meal finished and the last hymn was sung, Jesus led His disciples to the olive grove on the mountain east of the city. The full moon was rising over them as they silently walked up the slope to an area where Jesus often went to pray. Here He chose Peter and the brothers, James and John, and went deeper into a secluded section of the grove. These three disciples were Jesus' most trusted companions,[3] and now, in His greatest struggle, He desired their close physical presence and emotional support. As Jesus left them to go even deeper into the gloom under the ancient trees, He admonished them, "sit ye here" and "pray that ye enter not into temptation" (Mark 14:32; Luke 22:40).

Because of his self-confidence, Peter had promptly forgotten Jesus' words of caution concerning his coming denial of his Lord. Even after three and a half years of personal tutoring by the Master, he had yet to learn many lessons about his character. Had Peter, in humility, received the warning and been watchful in prayer, he would have been spared a night of bitter anguish and remorse. It would be only a few short hours before Jesus' words to Peter would be fulfilled.

The disciples had often been with Jesus in this garden retreat, praying with Him and listening to Him teach the beautiful realities of the Gospel of salvation from sin. Now, as never before, Jesus wanted them to spend time with Him in earnest prayer for their own souls. He appealed to them, "Tarry ye here, and watch with Me" (Mark 14:34). It was an earnest invitation extended for them to participate with Jesus in much-needed preparation. Jesus was giving Peter, and all the disciples, an opportunity to gain the strength they needed to endure the rapidly approaching trials that would test their confidence in Jesus to the breaking point.

The privilege went neglected. Paralyzed by a stupor that enshrouded them like a heavy drape, they lay down and were soon in a deep sleep. They might have shaken off the oppressive lethargy if they had remained vigilant in prayer, pleading for strength to endure the coming trial. Instead, they slept and wasted their opportunity. They did not realize the great necessity of watchfulness and fervent prayer that would enable them to withstand temptation. Trusting in themselves, they failed to look to the mighty Helper for strength as Christ had counseled them.

---

3. James and John were first cousins of Jesus, sons of His mother's sister, Salome, who was married to Zebedee. See Matthew 27:56, Matt. 10:2; and Mark 15:40.

Just as the angry mob exited the eastern gate of the city and crossed the Brook Kidron, Jesus woke the disciples and led them out of the garden to meet His betrayer. Calmly, Christ faced the murderous throng and asked: "Whom seek ye?" When they identified Jesus of Nazareth as the man they were after, Jesus replied: "I am He." Jesus intended that His disciples would not be arrested with Him as co-conspirators.

But quickly sizing up the situation, Peter stepped forward to protect his beloved Master. Disappointed and indignant at seeing Jesus so rudely manhandled and bound with ropes, Peter angrily raised his fishing knife[4] and cut off an ear of one of the men. Had his aim been a little less hasty, Peter would have murdered the man as he intended.

What does this aggressive and hotheaded action reveal was residing deep in Peter's heart? Anger, resentment, and murder were buried there. Jesus had seen it, but for Peter, they were unrecognized sins lurking beneath his self-assured external character.

When Jesus saw what was done, He released His hands from the rope, though the Temple guards had firmly tied them, and touched the wounded ear, instantly making it whole again. He would not leave injury or illness unhealed, even in His enemies. His demonstration of mercy and power frightened the mob but did not turn them away from their appointed task. Through this swift action, Jesus proved he had complete control over the situation before Him. Never at any time during His arrest, conviction, and crucifixion did Jesus lose control.

Turning to Peter, Jesus answered, "Put up thy sword into his place: for all that take the sword shall perish with the sword. Thinkest thou that I cannot now pray to My Father, and He shall presently give Me more than twelve legions of angels?" (Matthew 26:53).

A legion was 6000 in number, thus twelve legions would amount to 72,000 mighty warriors sent from the throne of God to defend Jesus from this murderous mob. Christ needed no man's assistance, for He had the power of all heaven behind His work in the salvation of mankind. But calling down the army of heaven in His defense was not part of the plan of salvation for the human race. Jesus must go to the cross, take the bitter cup and drink it to the dregs.

---

4. Greek: *machaira*—a large knife used for killing animals and cutting up flesh; similar in shape to a machete.

The disciples were terrified when they saw their Master permit Himself to be taken, bound, and led away by the angry mob. They were offended that He should suffer this humiliation to Himself and them. In their indignation and fear, they were unable to fathom Jesus' conduct. When Peter suggested they save themselves, "they all forsook Him, and fled" (Mark 14:50).

How accurate were Christ's words. "Behold," He had said, "the hour cometh, yea, is now come, that ye shall be scattered, every man to his own, and shall leave Me alone" (John 16:32). How little Peter knew his own heart when, just a few short hours before, he had said: "Though I should die with Thee, yet will I not deny Thee" (Matthew 26:35).

How little we know of our own sinful hearts. When the pressure is on, when temptation is strong, do we flee to the Lord for power to overcome? Or do we rely upon our own imagined strength to do battle with Satan? Do we consider our own selfish interests, or do we yearn to vindicate God no matter what may happen to our mortal bodies?

That our faith might gain strength to overcome every temptation, let us continually pray: "Search me, O God, and know my heart: try me, and know my thoughts: and see if there be any wicked way in me, and lead me in the way everlasting" (Psalm 139:23, 24).

Notes

24

Vacillating Extremist
Part 2

After deserting their Master, Peter and John had second thoughts about their rash action. Both of them loved their Lord supremely and could not tolerate the idea that their Friend had been unjustly arrested and physically abused. They knew Jesus had committed no crime. Staying at a distance, they followed as the mob left the olive grove, watching for an opportunity to intervene on His behalf.

It was after midnight when the group of Temple guards, Pharisees, and scribes arrived at the high priest's palace[1] where the tribunal of specially chosen members was already assembled. Some of the Sanhedrin recognized John as being "known to the high priest," and they spoke in his favor at the gate (John 18:15). They also knew John was one of Jesus' disciples. Thinking that John might be of the same character as Judas, who had betrayed Jesus to them, they let John follow along into the main hall.

They assumed when John witnessed Jesus' withering humiliation under their intense interrogation, he would reject the questionable idea that this Man was the Son of God. If they could dissuade John's allegiance, they hoped to use him as an informant against their prisoner to gain a conviction of blasphemy against God and insurrection against the Roman government. Once inside, John realized that Peter had not

---

1. The ruling religious party were the Sadducees who controlled the high priest's position. Both Pharisees and Sadducees were members of the Jewish supreme court called the Sanhedrin, but the Sadducees dominated the council. There was a bitter religious division between the two parties. The apostle Paul later used this division to his advantage when he was on trial (Acts 23:6-10), but Jesus did not try to excite their prejudices, or thwart their purpose in condemning Him.

followed him. He returned to the gate, spoke in favor of Peter, and gained entrance for him also into the palace of Caiaphas (vs. 16).

A fire was burning in the palace courtyard, around which gathered a group of guards and servants. The cowardice Peter showed in Gethsemane was here again demonstrated. Instead of openly following John into the main hall, Peter stopped beside the fire and assumed a disinterested attitude.

He did not wish to be recognized as a disciple of Jesus. By mingling nonchalantly with the crowd and remaining in the shadows, he hoped his identity would be concealed. His design was to appear as one of the rabble crowd that arrested Jesus.

Peter's thoughts centered upon keeping himself out of trouble. Therefore, he took a position of indifference by standing near enough to hear but not too close to the activities to appear involved or overly interested. In this way, he rationalized that he would be available for his Master if there were an opportunity to free Him from the mob, while avoiding being implicated in the night's previous events.

As the firelight flickered on Peter, one of the women took a good look at him. She was the gatekeeper and gave him entrance on John's recommendation. She now noticed the troubled look on his face. Out of curiosity, she asked, "Art not thou also one of this Man's disciples?" (vs. 17). The query startled and confused Peter. He had hoped that by keeping his distance from the group, no one would speak directly to him, but now he had been brought to the fore by this simple question.

The eyes of the whole group instantly focused on this stranger among them. Peter pretended not to understand what was said to him, but the woman persisted in her inquiry. As others around the fire also began to press him, Peter felt compelled to answer and angrily blurted out, "Woman, I know Him not!" (Luke 22:55-57; Mark 14:66-68).

This was the first denial.

Drawing his cloak tighter around his shoulders, Peter moved farther away from the fire into the shadows near the porch of the great hall. Here, closer to the activities of the trial taking place inside, Peter continued his air of indifference.

But the sounds of physical and emotional abuse he overheard from the courtroom wrung his heart. Peter was amazed and angry that Jesus would submit to such humiliating treatment without saying a single word in His own defense. Peter was torn between his natural impulse to fight and his fear of condemnation from the court if he rushed to defend his Lord.

Having assumed a false role, Peter laid himself wide open to suspicion. His actions were unnatural; his comments and casual jesting were out of place with the seriousness of the events in the courtroom. The more he denied and tried to look unconcerned, the more guilty he appeared to the group by the fire. All this called attention to him a second time, and he was again accused of being a follower of Jesus. This time with cursing, he declared, "I do not know the Man!" (Matthew 26:72).

Peter let another opportunity to repent slip through his fingers. Now he was really in tough straits. Guilt flooded his conscience, fear gripped his heart, and the predawn chill added to his misery. He huddled closer to the ground, trying to be less visible to the group around the fire.

After about an hour, one of the men in the group spoke up. "Did not I see thee in the garden with Him?" (John 18:26). This man had been an eyewitness to Peter's presence with Jesus in the garden at the time of the arrest. His cousin was the man whose ear Peter had cut off. As a servant of Caiaphas, he was part of the company sent to arrest Jesus. The midnight gloom under the trees did not obscure Peter's face or form. He, without doubt, witnessed Peter's violent assault upon his cousin and the miracle Jesus performed to restore the severed ear.

Others were beginning to remark that his Galilean accent gave him away as one of Jesus' followers. No longer able to deny the facts, Peter flew into a rage. With increased cursing and swearing, he yelled, "I don't know what you are talking about! I tell you, I don't know the Man!"

And the cock crowed.

With the degrading oaths barely out of his mouth and the cock's crowing still ringing in his ears, Peter turned and looked into the hall where Jesus stood before His accusers. The Saviour had also heard the cock crowing. "And the Lord turned, and looked upon Peter. And Peter remembered how He had said unto him, 'Before the cock crow, thou shalt deny Me thrice.'" (Luke 22:61).

The sight of his Master's pale, bruised, and suffering face and the gentle expression of compassion and forgiveness which fell from Jesus' eyes, pierced Peter's heart like a barbed arrow. There was no condemnation, no anger in Jesus' expression, only deep pity and sorrow for this weak and vacillating disciple.

"For he that wavereth is like a wave of the sea driven with the wind and tossed." (James 1:6). The lesson Jesus attempted to teach His disciples on the storm-tossed sea was forgotten by Peter. In the courtyard, he depended on his own ingenuity to avoid appearing associated with the Man on trial. His faith wavered like the sea waves, depending on the circumstances, being up one moment and down the next.

Oh, how well the Saviour knew him and how little Peter understood about himself. How much sin was still embedded in his heart!

Recalling his bold assertion during the Passover meal that he would defend Jesus, even if it meant his death, the Saviour's words rang in his ears: "Satan hath desired to have you, that he may sift you as wheat: but I have prayed for thee, that thy faith fail not" (Luke 22:31-33). Peter reflected with horror upon his ingratitude, his lying, and his denial of his dearest Friend. Heartbroken, he ran from the scene, rushing headlong into the darkness, not caring where he went so long as it was away from the piercing gaze of his Lord.

The tide of three years' memories flooded over him, drowning him in sorrow and despair. Lessons he had failed to comprehend were now manifested before him. The night's events exposed the full depth of wickedness residing in Peter's heart. He realized how fully his Lord knew his true character, how accurately He had read his sinful soul. It was torture to his crushed heart to know that his verbal denials and actions had added to the Saviour's burden of humiliation and grief.

Peter was horrified when he fully realized what he had done in denying his Lord and Saviour. It was betrayal as surely as was Judas' action in selling his Lord for thirty pieces of silver.

Peter's statements in the upper room were earnest and sincere; at the time, he confidently believed every word he spoke. But he did not know his heart and the depth of sin that lay there waiting to flame to life.

"I am ready to go with Thee, Lord, both to prison and to death!" (Luke 22:33). "Though all men shall be offended because of Thee, yet will I never be offended" (Matthew 26:33). He recalled the vehemence with which he declared, "If I should die with Thee, I will not deny Thee in any wise!" (Mark 14:31).

His shame was almost unbearable. After denying the Son of God, how could he stand before God in his pride and self-assurance, offering prayers and useless sacrifices? He was no different from the self-righteous Pharisees who thought themselves pious beyond question. How could he ever face the other disciples? In their record of these events, both Matthew and Luke say Peter fled Caiaphas's palace, weeping bitterly. He was heartbroken and thoroughly ashamed.

In his agony, he ran blindly out of the city into the early morning gloom. Finding himself once more in the olive grove, he threw himself on the ground near where Jesus had lain in His agony only hours before. All Peter could think was how much he wanted to die rather than face those before whom he had presented so much bravado.

What a deceitful braggart he was! Pretending humility, Peter always had a ready answer to everything. Desiring to prove how much more he knew than his fellow disciples, he was the first to speak up in a conversation and often spoke imprudently (see, for example, Mark 8:31-33; Matthew 16:21-23; 17:4-6; John 13:6-8).

From this revelation of his true character, Peter felt unworthy to work for the cause of God. His self-confidence was shattered.

When Judas realized what he had done by selling Jesus to His enemies, he also wished that he might die. And he did—at his own hand that same night. The Bible tells us Judas "repented himself" (Matthew 27:3), but it was a sorrow for the awful consequences of his deed, not a heartbroken abhorrence of his sin. Judas' sorrow and "repentance" were generated by fear and the torture of his foolish guilty conscience—a "worldly sorrow that worketh death" (see 2 Corinthians 7:10).

After Jesus' arrest, Judas ran to the Temple in an effort to assuage his guilt by returning the money he had been paid, "saying, I have sinned in that I have betrayed the innocent blood. And they said, What is that to us? see thou to that. And he cast down the pieces of silver in the Temple, and departed, and went and hanged himself" (Matthew 27:4, 5).

Peter came within a hair's breadth of committing the same sin as Judas. His wounded conscience forced him to recognize the traitorous recantations of his earlier declarations of undying allegiance to his Lord. However, unlike Judas, Peter's true heart-sorrow for his sin resulted in a character-transforming repentance.

Jesus' compassionate look, at the moment Peter denied Him, was burned into his memory. As he lay on the ground crying his heart out, that sweet, forgiving expression rose before him. And so did the memory of Jesus' self-sacrificing love, demonstrated to everyone during the three and a half years of His public ministry. In his agony, Peter recognized now what Mary Magdalene learned at the feet of her Saviour—"God is love." A heart-response to this divine love drew Peter to a true repentance.

In the stillness of the early morning, Peter heard a commotion from inside the city and realized he needed to return. Exiting the olive grove, he knew he could no longer trust himself. He was a liar and a traitor and had presented wicked self-righteousness to the world.

But the profound question is: Why did Peter fail so miserably? Can we know what his real problem was? He repeatedly claimed to love his Lord and, at times, showed a certain amount of faith and knowledge of the Scriptures. So, what went wrong?

We need to understand Peter's behavior, or we also will fail in our own time of severe testing. The apostle Paul counseled us that the experiences of God's people are to be an education for us.

The story of Peter's tragic fall is closely linked to the attitude and behavior of the children of Israel as recorded in Exodus 19:8. At Sinai, God attempted to bring the children of Israel into a committed and loving fellowship with Him. God gave a message to Moses for him to deliver to the Israelites camped at the foot of the fiery mountain.

> And Moses went up unto God, and the LORD called unto him out of the mountain, saying, Thus shalt thou say to the house of Jacob, and tell the children of Israel; Ye have seen what I did unto the Egyptians, and how I bare you on eagles' wings, and brought you unto Myself. Now therefore, if ye will obey My voice indeed, and keep My covenant, then ye shall be a peculiar treasure unto Me above all people: for all the earth is Mine: and ye shall be unto Me a kingdom of priests, and an holy nation. These are the words which thou shalt speak unto the children of Israel. (Exodus 19:3-6).

The covenant God referred to in these verses was the promise He had already made to Abraham. If the family of Jacob, who was newly delivered from Egyptian bondage, would exhibit the faith of their forefathers, Abraham, Isaac, and Jacob (also called Israel, see Genesis 32:28 and 1 Kings 18:36), then God would be able to declare of them: "Here they are!—My peculiar treasure, My kingdom of righteous servants and My holy nation!" That's what God intended to take place there at Sinai.

However, the people knew not their true heart condition, and in response to God's invitation, they pridefully "answered together, and said, All that the LORD hath spoken *we will do*" (verse 8, emphasis supplied). Forty days later, having completely forgotten their pledge of allegiance to their Redeemer and King, they were dancing naked around a golden calf idol (Exodus 32:1-6).

In promising to obey, the people assumed they could meet the requirements of the Law through their own works, and, as demonstrated in the golden calf incident, they miserably failed. Working to keep the law only moves one farther from true obedience, which only happens as a faith response to God's unbounded love. "For in Christ Jesus neither circumcision[2] nor uncircumcision accomplishes anything; what matters is faith working through love" (Galatians 5:6, HCSB).

Peter, too, had all of his life depended upon his own skills and physical power to accomplish what he willed. He knew he was capable. That pride of self-sufficiency brought Peter to abject humiliation and shame. He was in the same trap that the children of Jacob had fallen into—the trap of old covenant thinking.

The years spent in Egyptian slavery had educated the children of Jacob wrongly about obedience and about God's character. They were bound to a merciless master who claimed to be God on earth. No matter what burden Pharaoh placed on them, they learned to bear it and accomplish the task before them.

This seemingly unshakable slave mentality caused them to misunderstand God's intentions for them as He led them through the desert to Sinai, and then on to Canaan. Their hearts were so hardened against comprehension of God's love that He conceded to their mind-set and allowed them to place themselves under an old covenant promise He knew they could never keep.

---

2. The Jews taught that circumcision was necessary for salvation. They made circumcision a "work" that the apostle Paul called "works of the law."

Repeatedly they "with one voice, said, 'All the words which the LORD hath said will we do.' ... And he [Moses] took the book of the covenant, and read it in the audience of the people: and they said, 'All that the LORD hath said will we do, and be obedient.'" (Exodus 24:3, 7).

At Sinai, Israel made the same sort of boastful promise that Peter made when he proclaimed, "I will never deny You!" As they were finishing the Passover meal, Jesus warned His disciples, "All of you will run away, because it is written: I will strike the shepherd, and the sheep will be scattered. But after I have been resurrected, I will go ahead of you to Galilee." Peter arrogantly responded, "Even if everyone runs away, I will certainly not!" (Mark 14:27-29, HCSB).

At Sinai, ancient Israel created an old covenant commitment for themselves when they made their vain promise, "All that the LORD has spoken, *we will do*," thinking they had the strength within themselves to fulfill any conditions their new Master might lay upon them. They had built pyramids and palaces for Pharaoh, and they could certainly do whatever this new Master required of them.

For nearly fifteen centuries, their old covenant ideas crippled them as a nation, causing them to hold misconceptions about God's character of love. Because they misunderstood God, the people were soon unable to distinguish between the pagan gods and Jehovah. They thought they could worship Him as the pagan nations around them worshiped their gods made of wood and stone and metal. Continual compromise blurred the distinction between truth and error.

Just like Peter, Israel's lack of self-knowledge and refusal to repent resulted in their rejection of the promised Messiah when He walked in their presence. The accumulated corporate guilt came full circle in Peter's vain promise that he would never deny his Lord.

It was a tough lesson for Peter to learn: our salvation does not depend on our making promises to God. It depends on our believing His promises to us. That's the "new covenant" in a nutshell.

How do you feel when you read the story of Peter's denials when the teenage girl taunted, ridiculed, and humiliated the proud fisherman? Does it strike a chord in your conscience; can you see something of yourself? Or does the story send you into a self-righteous condemnation of Peter's dreadful behavior?—"I would never do such a thing!"

But, wait … consider how like Peter we all are. We have read how self-centered and selfishly motivated he was. If we're honest with ourselves we must admit we are no different. Oh, how much we need a cleansing experience to purge us to the depths of our being.

The Holy Spirit constantly works with us, gently calling us to repentance. When the Lord brings up something that we never knew was in our heart and gives us the opportunity to repent of that thing, we must be willing to fall on the Rock and be broken. When the Holy Spirit has finally brought forth our most cherished sin, and we tell Him, "I'd rather have the Lord Jesus than that thing," when He will have reached the bottom at last, then God will place His seal of righteousness upon our forehead and declare: "Here are they that keep the Commandments of God, and faith of Jesus."

Notes

25

Vacillating Extremist
Part 3

Sunrise revealed a different character in Peter; his ego was completely deflated. Humbled with bitter remorse and shame after denying his Lord, he arose from his resting place a changed man. Had the disciple heeded his Lord's urging and spent the evening in earnest, heart-searching prayer, the way would have been closed to the commission of his great sin. Peter would not have been left to depend upon his own feeble strength, and he would not have denied his Lord.

When he joined the crowd in Pilate's courtyard, confusion and anguish were tormenting Peter's mind as he heard the charges against Jesus. He heard Pilate's refusal to condemn the innocent Man, and marveled at the satanic hostility demonstrated by the people who chanted, "Crucify Him, crucify Him!"

When the trial was ended, Peter went with the other disciples as they followed the group of condemned men to Calvary. All along the way, he heard the railing rebukes and vicious condemnations from the Pharisees, priests, and bystanders. He saw their irrational hatred for the One who had shown kindness and gentleness to everyone, even His implacable enemies.

They stood in amazement at the foot of the cross. Peter, the other ten disciples, and the women who followed Jesus were stunned by the events of the last twenty-four hours. It had all happened so fast! Soon some of the disciples and women could not bear to look upon the terrible scene and drifted back into the city. Jesus' mother was there, but John took her away, shielding her from the torment of witnessing her Son's agonizing death. Mary, called Magdalene, was also at the foot of the cross, drawn there because of her devotion to her Saviour.

None of them could believe Jesus was dying. It was over. All their dreams of overthrowing the Roman oppression, of holding positions of priority and power in Christ's new earthly kingdom, were smashed on the rocks of despair. Questions flew through their minds in rapid succession. Was this Man the Messiah, as they had been led to believe? Was He truly God's Son as He repeatedly had claimed? Were the words of the Pharisees valid: "Search, and look: for out of Galilee ariseth no prophet"? (John 7:52). What would become of their little group now? Would the Pharisees and Temple guards, or the Romans search them out and convict them of apostasy and treason?

While the few disciples remaining at the foot of the cross stood paralyzed by their confusion and grief, two men came forward to claim the body of their Master. Gently these men lowered the lifeless form onto a linen cloth, wrapped Him, and carried Him away. To see where the body of Jesus was going to be placed, the women followed closely behind. A newly-hewn tomb was not too far from the hill upon which He had been crucified. Into this cave, the two Pharisees, Joseph of Arimathea and Nicodemus, carried the body, laid it on a rock ledge, and rolled the huge stone into place to close the tomb's entrance.

As darkness brought on the sacred Sabbath, the disciples retired to the same upper chamber where they had taken the Passover meal the evening before. It was in the house owned by John Mark's mother, and there they felt secure. In this quiet room, they discussed the events of the last twenty-four hours and sought counsel from one another as to how they might proceed without their Master.

Yes, He did send them on a missionary trip, and during that time, they were able to heal the sick and tell the good news of the arrival of the long-awaited Messiah. The information was received by most people with a certain amount of apathy.

There had been other times when a man came to town claiming to be Israel's promised deliverer. Their claims had all come to nothing when the Roman army arrested, imprisoned or executed each one, and his followers were scattered. Now, along comes this Jesus who claimed to be the Messiah, and He, too, had gotten Himself arrested and crucified.

Between the two men, Jesus of Nazareth and Barabbas, it seemed Barabbas was the more likely man to lead a political insurrection. He had already proven his willingness to fight the enemy and, by it, gotten himself arrested. If the people were left to choose the man they wanted, it was a proven fighter. Pilate let the people have their way and released Barabbas while sending Jesus to Golgotha's hill.

Facts concerning Barabbas are scant, but reliable commentaries state that the people viewed him as a sort of "guerrilla resistance fighter" who had been captured by the Romans and was being held for execution at the time Jesus had been arrested. To the restless people of Judea, Barabbas was looked upon as a champion willing to fight to free Israel from Roman oppression. He was someone in whom they could place their confidence.

In the upper room, the disciples replayed the trial in their discussion, remembering the satanic hatred demonstrated by the mob in Pilate's courtyard. The memory brought fear of a backlash from the Temple leaders, Pharisees, and the people. All of the men were well known to be Jesus' disciples, which meant they could not go to the Temple for Sabbath worship.[1] If they walked the streets of Jerusalem, they would quickly be recognized. For the time being, they remained behind closed and fastened doors and awaited their fate.

Many times during that night and the following Sabbath day, they moaned, "We had trusted that it had been He which should have redeemed Israel" (Luke 24:21; cf. Isaiah 41:14; 49:7). Even blind men had declared Jesus to be the promised son of King David (Matthew 20:30; cf. Isaiah 9:6, 7; 11:1, 2). What had gone wrong?

Their expectations had evaporated, and as they awaited the Sabbath dawn, the disciples were almost overwhelmed by their despair

---

1. On that extraordinary Passover Sabbath, there would have been confusion and uncertainty concerning how the priests were to carry out the sacrifices of the day. At the time Jesus died on the cross, the heavy wool curtain that separated between the holy and most holy apartments had been torn from top to bottom by an unseen hand (Matthew 27:51). Before the priest could enter the holy place to refresh the oil in the lampstand, make the morning incense offering, and sprinkle the blood of the sin offering on the curtain, the curtain must be replaced. Replacing the curtain was forbidden work on the sacred Sabbath day. The priests were in a quandary and had no answers for the people about what happened, or how their worship service was to proceed.

and disillusionment. Without a leader and without direction, they were like lost children. All that Sabbath day, much discussion took place between the disciples, but no one had an answer to their dilemma.

The Sabbath was ended. The darkness of the first day of the week brought gloom to the upper room, but the disciples dared not to venture out among the large crowds of worshippers that remained in the streets. How thankful they were for their refuge, where they spent another night in wonder and worry.

The next morning just as it became light enough to see, Mary Magdalene and a few of the other women set out for the tomb. They needed to anoint the body of their Lord with the spices and ointment Nicodemus had purchased for them on Preparation Day (John 19:39).

The words of Christ which foretold of His resurrection were forgotten. All He had shown them of His power over death was far from their minds as they trudged along the garden path down to the tomb. Mary Magdalene and her sister, Martha, did not remember the words of their Lord spoken to them before He raised their brother from his grave: "I am the resurrection and the life!" (John 11:25). Jesus had already proven His power over death, more than once.

As they approached the tomb, the women noticed that the stone had been removed and saw a light shining through the opening. Startled, the women cautiously edged closer. With the stone rolled back from the entrance, they could look straight down to where Jesus' body had been laid three days before by Nicodemus and Joseph. But … He wasn't there! Jesus wasn't in the grave! Immediately they assumed that someone had come in the night and stolen His body.

Looking closer, the women saw a shining angel sitting on the rock ledge where Jesus' body had been, with the grave wrappings folded neatly by his side. He spoke to them, saying, "Fear not, ye, for I know that ye seek Jesus, which was crucified. He is not here: for He is risen, as He said." The angel added: "Go your way, and tell His disciples—and Peter—that He goeth before you into Galilee" (Mark 16:6, 7).

Risen! Their Lord wasn't dead! Quickly the women hurried back to the upper room to tell the disciples what they had seen and been told by the angel, and to give Peter the angel's special message.

"And Peter." Don't overlook these two little words; they are loaded with meaning. The angel specifically mentioned Peter. He was to receive a special message from his risen Saviour that he was not rejected. His Lord loved him and would meet him again in Galilee. Even though Peter had shown himself a coward and shamefully denied his Master, forgiveness was his, full and free.

The next few weeks were a busy time for the disciples. There was so much Jesus wanted to teach them to prepare them for the work that lay ahead of them as His messengers to the world. To the disciples, everything seemed to have returned to normal. Their Lord was back with them; life was again a happy routine. They could not comprehend the coming separation from their Saviour or the enormous task that lay in their future.

And there was one final lesson for Peter.

Peter's denial of his Lord had been contemptible in contrast to his former profession of loyalty. He had dishonored Christ and had earned the distrust of the other disciples. Before he was fit to take up his apostolic work, he must give evidence of his repentance. Lovingly, the Saviour gave him the chance to remove the reproach he had brought upon the Gospel and regain his brethren's confidence.

One morning after a fruitless night of fishing, the disciples saw Jesus on the beach as they returned to shore. As soon as Peter recognized who was sitting by the fire preparing a simple breakfast, true to his impulsive nature, he jumped overboard and swam ashore, so eager was he to be with his Lord.

Jesus finished preparing the morning meal for them, and as they sat around the fire eating, Jesus looked gently at Peter. Quietly He asked, "Simon, son of Jonas, lovest thou Me more than these?" referring to the other disciples sitting around them (John 21:15).

Jesus did not call him "Peter" but Simon, a name which means "listen" or "hear." Purposely and to draw attention to the lesson He was about to teach him, Jesus did not call him by his nickname meaning a "tumbling, unstable pebble"; He asked him to "listen."

Humbled and contrite, remembering his arrogant professions of constant allegiance and his subsequent shameful denials, Peter could now make no boastful claim. With his head bowed, he softly answered: "Yea, Lord; Thou knowest that I love Thee."

There was no prideful assurance that his love was greater than any of the others. He did not now exclaim that his devotion would never fail, no matter the circumstances. His sinful arrogance was conquered through repentance and faith.

Two more times, Jesus tested Peter, repeating the same question. Three times Peter had denied his Lord, and three times Jesus gave Peter the opportunity to assert or deny his love and loyalty. But pressing the question on him in the hearing of all the other disciples pierced like a sword into Peter's wounded heart. Finally, grieved by the apparent distrust Jesus had of him, looking up at the Saviour's face he softly replied, "Lord, thou knowest all things; Thou knowest that I love Thee." (John 21:17).

What more could he say? Peter had finally learned that in him was "no good thing." His life was turned upside down by the denial of his Lord. He saw how sinful his heart really was. No matter how good and faithful he wanted to be, without the power of Christ in his life, he would fall again and again.

That morning on the beach before the assembled disciples, Jesus revealed the depth of Peter's repentance and showed how thoroughly humbled this once proud and boasting man had become. The other disciples witnessed the change of Peter's character, and were humbled to admit to themselves how like him they were in attitude. Jesus called His cousins "sons of thunder" because they rashly wanted to call fire down from heaven and destroy a city (Luke 9:53-57; cf. Mark 3:17). Thomas was a doubter, and when confronted by the angry mob, they had all deserted their Friend.

With Peter's final confession and recognition of his unworthiness, he was prepared to act as a shepherd to Jesus' flock, so He instructed him, "Feed My sheep."

Jesus never intended that Peter should be cast aside. On the contrary, he knew Peter's potential and strengths, and these were needed in the early work of Christ's church. But his impetuous outspokenness and rash behavior had to be whittled away before he was ready to accomplish what Jesus needed him to do. Peter had to learn that he was nothing without his Lord's guidance. He had to learn "not I, but Christ" in everything.

Peter, along with the other disciples, received the outpouring of the early rain at Pentecost. The in-filling of the Holy Spirit's power would enable each of them to maximize their individual strengths and talents for the promotion of the kingdom of God (Acts 2:1-4).

Peter went on to be one of the foremost leaders of the New Testament church. His first sermon was a powerful, Holy Spirit-inspired call to the Jews to repent of their rejection of the Messiah (Acts 2:14-36). Many Jews were baptized as a result of his preaching (vs. 41). He helped organize the first "general conference" of the early church at Jerusalem, which settled several major points of doctrine (Acts 15:1-35), and later wrote two epistles which became part of the New Testament canon.

For all discouraged, backsliding people, Peter is the example of what we may become if we surrender ourselves entirely to the will of God through the power of Jesus Christ. Then, it will be found that "I can do all things through Christ which strengtheneth me" (Philippians 4:13) as we work to promote the glory of God in this evil world.

Notes

26

The Model Christian

The Bible tells us of an individual whose life was a total wreck—no, not the Gadarene demoniac. Always, day and night, that man roamed the tombs on the mountainside, roaring for deliverance from the devils that tormented him. Though the man from Gadara was inhabited by "a legion" of demons,[1] uncontrollable, physically violent, self-abusive, and completely insane, when the man first saw Jesus, he ran to Him seeking deliverance. When Jesus asked the man his name, the demons answered, "My name is Legion: for we are many." (Mark 5:9). Perhaps the demon army inhabiting the insane man thought they could intimidate Jesus by announcing boldly that He was vastly outnumbered. But when the Saviour spoke: "Come out of the man," the demons were powerless to disobey the voice of their Creator.

We are not informed how this man heard about the Saviour, but the demoniac recognized Him as soon as Jesus set His feet on the beach. We are compelled to believe that the Holy Spirit still had access to some portion of the man's mind and urged him forward. He hastened down the hillside to meet Jesus and bowed at His feet. "When he saw Jesus afar off, he ran and worshiped Him" (Mark 5:6). Thousands of powerful evil angels could not restrain the man who longed for deliverance.

There was a young woman who, in many ways, was more pitiful even than this man's miserable condition. Her demons controlled her mind and heart, convincing her that she was worthless, unlovable, and beyond redemption, so it didn't matter how she lived her life of misery. No one cared what happened to her.

---

1. In the Roman army, a legion was composed of between 4500 and 6000 men.

Her story is encouraging to anyone suffering from depression and self-abusive behaviors and is an important demonstration of how the Gospel works to change a sinner's life. It reveals something vital about Christ's mission to this earth. Her story bears out the glorious truth that "while we were yet sinners, Christ died for us" (Romans 5:8). What we see in this woman's story will encourage us and, at the same time, humble our pride in the dust.

This young woman had suffered sexual and emotional abuse at the hands of a family member. She grew up with the burden and associated fears of being a "ruined woman." Due to social and religious stigma, she knew no man in his right mind would marry a woman who could not prove her virginity.[2] By strict religious law, she was a condemned woman without hope. According to the Mosaic law, anyone caught in the act of adultery or fornication was sentenced to be stoned.

> And the man that committeth adultery with another man's wife, even he that committeth adultery with his neighbour's wife, the adulterer and the adulteress shall surely be put to death. (Leviticus 20:10).

All of her life, this young woman carried in her heart the burden of guilt thrust upon her by another person, along with the fear of condemnation and its death penalty. She knew no freedom from it and always walked in its shadow. In her torn emotional state, she considered herself a hopeless case, knowing she was worthy of death. Her guilt and shame overwhelmed her.

After her assault, crushed and humiliated, she ran away from her home, assuming a life of reckless abandonment. Licentiousness ruled her. At the same time, she learned to protect and defend herself and to provide for her own needs; she relied on no one and trusted no man.

Scars from the abuse she suffered ran deep, influencing everything she did. What difference would it make who she was with or what she did? She was already consigned to hell by her past. With no support from family or friends, she ended up making her living as a prostitute

---

2. "But if this thing be true, and the tokens of virginity be not found for the damsel: then they shall bring out the damsel to the door of her father's house, and the men of her city shall stone her with stones that she die: because she hath wrought folly in Israel, to play the whore in her father's house: so shalt thou put evil away from among you." (Deuteronomy 22:20, 21).

in a distant city. She lost all sense of self-control and fell into a self-destructive frame of mind. She was definitely "nothin' goin' nowhere."

Abuse and a life of sin taught this woman to distrust "love." When a person is told that they are "loved" while she is being abused by the person claiming to love them, the definition of "love" takes on a sinister meaning. "Love" is equated with pain, suffering, shame, and guilt. That kind of "love" causes deep wounds and scars in the heart and mind.

The man who set this young woman's feet on a path of sin and degradation was an "upright" man in the community, a teacher of God's holy word. He was a well-regarded religious leader. Growing up in his home with her sister and brother, this young woman learned from him a perverted view of God's character of love and mercy. God's intention that His self-sacrificing love would be manifested through His earthly clergymen was destroyed through the actions of this "pious" man's salacious lust for his beautiful and innocent young niece.

From the beginning of time, humanity's enemy has done a thorough job of misrepresenting God's character to the world. Satan often uses persons who claim to be God's followers, who present a façade of "righteousness" to the world while living like the devil himself. Thus they misrepresent God's character of holiness to the watching world. And so this young woman's perception of God and His character of love was confused by those who most influenced her life.

But one day, she chanced to meet the Man named Jesus. When He was preaching near where she lived, out of curiosity and the desire for some entertainment, she joined the group gathered around Him. As she listened to His tender voice, something awakened in her sorrowful and burdened heart.

She began to follow along with the mass of people who crowded Him every day. But because people knew her and the life she was leading, to avert any confrontation and embarrassment, she kept her face veiled and hugged the perimeter of the crowd to avoid recognition.

Occasionally while intently focused on this Man's words, if she glanced directly at His face, she felt He was speaking to her personally. His steady gaze bound her to Him, yet it bore no lustful desire. Instead, His eyes demonstrated deep compassion and empathy for her. She was mysteriously attracted to Him in a way she had never experienced. It was as if He knew and understood the terrible trauma and suffering she had endured that drove her to abuse herself with men.

When she listened to this man's words regarding the heavenly Father's love for sinners, she began to wonder: Could it be true that there is hope for me? But the remembrance of her deep-seated sin would sweep over her like a dark, engulfing wave, filling her with guilt. *No!*—no, she told herself. She was too far gone to even think of being free from her life of sin. How could she change the course of her life? There was nowhere for her to go for help. No man would accept her after the life she had lived, and so she retreated into the shadows of self-recrimination and social ostracism.

But still, she followed and listened to this fascinating Man. Gradually she began to respond. She sensed genuine love flowing from Him, not the kind she was exposed to by the men she knew every day, not the kind of "love" that wanted to use her and then cast her aside. No, this Man was not like the men who used her. As she intently watched His face, letting His soft voice flow over her heart like cleansing water, she could see that this Man was very different. His love was pure and holy; it seemed to elevate her mind when she heard Him speak.

Each time she had another opportunity to hear Him teach, she found herself strangely drawn into His presence. She began to move forward in the crowd, desiring to be closer to Him. She could feel His love reaching out to her heart and mind, inviting her to come to Him. There was something extraordinary about Him, but she would not let herself trust what she was hearing from Him—she knew too much about men to trust anything a man said to her. Never could she give her heart to a man! And so, again and again, she would walk away, returning to her wicked ways, unable to say no to the men who bought her. She seemed hopelessly entangled in her unhappy and confused life.

As she struggled to believe the good news she heard this Man preach, she unwittingly became the pawn in a plot to destroy Jesus devised by a group of conniving Sadducees and Pharisees. One morning as dawn was breaking over the city, suddenly, everything was confusion in the room where she lay in the arms of yet another man. Intruders invaded the room, and rough hands dragged her naked from her bed. She was pulled and shoved toward the door by grunting and laughing men.

She recognized some of the men. She had seen them coming and going the Temple; some of them had even used her. Their self-righteous piety exuded from them as they dragged this depraved woman down the street, yelling for the way to be cleared so they could pass through the crowds. Just outside the Temple, they found Jesus sitting and teaching a group of early-morning worshipers. There they stopped before Him and threw Mary down at His feet. Oh! the humility of it, to be so violently exposed and degraded before this wonderful Man who had always shown her kindness.

She crouched in the dirt to make her naked body as small and insignificant as possible. With her head bowed in abject shame, her long dark hair tumbling around her shoulders, she covered her face with trembling hands. She knew what was coming and expected condemnation and the death sentence. She hoped her death would come quickly.

Her sordid story was loudly proclaimed before every listening ear and watching eye. Anticipating the stones about to rain upon her head, she found she didn't care. Death would release her from a life of despair and emotional suffering.

Suddenly, there was only silence after the noisy accusations from the religious leaders. Then one of the Pharisees insisted, "Master, this woman was taken in adultery, caught in the *very act*!" He went on, his voice frigid with pretended moral outrage. "Moses in the law commanded us, that such should be stoned: but what do you say?" She held her breath, waiting for the first stone. Instead, she heard scratching and shuffling of feet. She dared not to raise her head as the men continued to demand an answer from Jesus. His response surprised her: "He that is without sin among you, let him cast the first stone."

Remembering the men who had dragged her from her bed—some of whom had been in her bed and were guilty of adultery with her—she wondered where this line of reasoning would end. Would all those men suffer with her? Again she heard scratching and more shuffling of feet. Were they reaching for stones?

Reading what Jesus was writing in the dust with His finger, those hypocrites who condemned the woman were stunned by Jesus' silent yet piercing revelation of the depth of sin in their own hearts, and "being convicted by their own conscience, they went out one by one, beginning at the eldest, even unto the last, and Jesus was left alone with the woman still in front of Him." (John 8:9).

Jesus stood up and quietly asked her, "Woman, where are your accusers?" (John 8:10). Timidly, Mary raised her head. Where was everyone? Even the people who generally assembled at the Temple seemed to have dispersed. Jesus asked her, "Where are the ones who can charge you with sin?" Quivering with fear and the strain of her exposure, Mary whispered, "There is no one here."

Having dealt with the despicable hypocrites who charged her with guilt, Jesus bent down, covered her with His own outer garment, then gently lifted her by the hand, saying, "Neither do I condemn you; go and sin no more." (John 8:11).

Gazing directly into the face of her Saviour, Mary breathed the one word that transformed her life: "Master!" Now, out of a genuine heart appreciation for His divine love for her, she fully surrendered to Him. Jesus finally won her heart completely. What a release! Her heart fluttered with the sweet freedom and joy that flooded through her, healing her tortured soul.

Instead of condemnation and death, she received a full pardon. While fully expecting to die for the burden of her sins, she was lifted up from her former sexual filth and emotional misery, and her feet were set on a new path to eternal life.

Mary learned her lesson. She was not a "worthless piece of trash"! She had real value in the eyes of this Man. No matter what she had done in her past, by faith in her Saviour, she could walk "in newness of life." Encouraged by her experience and complete sense of forgiveness, she returned to her home in Bethany, where her sister and brother resided.[3]

Jesus had a persistent and prolonged struggle to save this woman. Each time she was on the verge of responding to His call, she would fall back into her old ways. Casting out the legion of devils who controlled the Gadarene demoniac seemed effortless compared to His struggle with Mary.

Jesus raised His voice in prayer seven times for this seemingly worthless woman. Why did He continue with her? What did He see

---

3. "Now a certain man was sick, named Lazarus, of Bethany, the town of Mary and her sister Martha. (It was that Mary which anointed the Lord with ointment, and wiped His feet with her hair, whose brother Lazarus was sick)" (John 11:1, 2).

that kept Him reaching out to this one woman who clung so tenaciously to her old sinful ways? Why? Because He knew her heart much better than she knew herself.

But Mary still had to face the last obstacle to her complete recovery—Simon the Pharisee, who was her abusive uncle. This man had deeply wronged her, and his guilt had brought upon himself the most dreaded of diseases—leprosy. Early in Jesus' ministry, Simon sought healing from Jesus and was cured.[4]

> And there came a leper to Him, beseeching Him, and kneeling down to Him, and saying unto Him, If thou wilt, thou canst make me clean. And Jesus, moved with compassion, put forth His hand, and touched him, and saith unto him, I will; be thou clean. And as soon as He had spoken, immediately the leprosy departed from him, and he was cleansed. (Mark 1:40-42).

Three and a half years later, Simon desired to make a self-righteous demonstration of his respect for the itinerant Preacher. To impress some of his highly esteemed political and religious friends, he invited them, along with Jesus and His twelve closest disciples, to a feast at his home in Bethany.

Of course, Mary also wanted to say "Thank You" to the Man who had given her freedom from sin. But how? She feared any display that would bring attention to her, drawing her out of her shadowy existence. And she was reluctant to make a scene in her uncle's home, especially during such an important feast.

Jesus often visited in the home of His friends, Martha and Lazarus. The atmosphere of their home was peaceful and quiet. When she was also there, Mary, completely enthralled through her love for her Saviour, sat continually at His feet, listening intently to all He taught His disciples.[5]

As she listened to Jesus talk with His disciples, earnestly instructing them about what would transpire in the coming weeks, Mary discerned something they were too spiritually blind to comprehend. Jesus'

---

4. "And being in Bethany in the house of Simon the leper." (Mark 14:3).
5. "Now it came to pass, as they went, that He entered into a certain village: and a certain woman named Martha received Him into her house. And she had a sister called Mary, which also sat at Jesus' feet, and heard His word." (Luke 1:38, 39).

disciples operated under the baleful influence of their own preconceived opinions concerning the Messiah and His work, and missed vital points their Master was attempting to teach them.

However, Mary was sure about what she heard—Jesus said He was going to die! And soon. She had heard Him speak of it on more than a few occasions, especially during the last few months. His instructions were more intense as He sought to prepare His closest followers for what they would soon witness and experience.

Grasping His words' real meaning, she suddenly knew what she could do. She decided to give Him her all. He already had her heart; He could have her worldly possessions, too. She would spend her life's earnings, money she had gained from her work as a prostitute, and purchase an expensive bottle of perfume, something only the very wealthy could afford. It was worth three hundred denari,[6] more than a year's wage for a laboring man. Stashing it away, she would save it until Jesus' burial time, when she would anoint His lifeless body with the fragrant perfume.

When she heard Simon was planning a feast to honor Jesus, Mary changed her mind. Why wait until Jesus was dead? He couldn't enjoy it then; it would be a wasted expression of her love for Him. Facing the possibility of public condemnation and humiliation by the man who initially wronged her, Mary was nonetheless irresistibly drawn to the Man who had restored her. Jesus' forgiveness erased her shame and doubt about her worth. His love gave her life value.[7] Nothing could stop her from emptying her heart in appreciation for what Jesus did for her. No amount of verbal abuse, harassment, or rejection would turn her away from honoring her Saviour and Lord.

On the evening of Simon's party, Mary was with Martha preparing things for the feast. When the meal was nearing its end, it was time for her to carry out her plan before the opportune moment passed forever.

---

6. See John 12:1-6 in which a price is put on the ointment. A "pence" or denarius was a Roman silver coin, the value of which was about 20 cents. It was the ordinary daily wage for a laborer, (see Matthew 20:1, 2). The Greek word is uniformly rendered "penny" or "pence" in the King James Version of the Bible.

7. God's love is *agapé*—self-sacrificing love. *Agapé* creates value in the person it loves. Jesus values us so much He was willing to lay down His own life for the lost sheep (John 15:13; Romans 5:6-10).

Taking her precious bottle, she eased into the room where the men were assembled around the table, absorbed in their conversations. There she found Jesus surrounded by His disciples and Simon's wealthy, influential friends. Her heart was so overflowing with love and appreciation that, at first, Mary was oblivious to the commotion caused by her presence. Whispers flew around the table, some not so hushed. Like arrows sent to kill, the men's stares of astonishment and disgust were accusingly aimed at her.

Hoping to remain out of sight, she quickly knelt behind where Jesus reclined on His couch and began pouring the ointment on His head and feet. She intended to get her deed done and rapidly exit the room, hurrying back into the shadows of the gathering twilight. But instead, the tantalizingly intense fragrance of the perfume permeated the room. There was no hiding what was taking place before them. Every eye was drawn toward Mary as her extravagant gift flowed onto the head and feet of her Saviour.

To the proud, self-righteous men gathered in the room, what Mary did was beyond their comprehension. Aghast that a woman was even in their dining hall and further insulted by the fact that she was touching a man she was not related to, their mouths gaped wide in horror at the scene unfolding before them. Glancing from Jesus to their host, their stares and whispers demanded an answer.

Precisely what Mary hoped to avoid was drowning her unstable emotions. She huddled behind her Friend and prayed for a way of escape. The excoriating looks burned into her exposed and fragile soul.

Unexpectedly, her heart burst open with a flood of tears she never knew were there. Mary's tears shed uncontrollably before the stunned roomful of arrogant men rained down on Jesus' feet. Exasperated by attracting even more attention to herself, she reached for what was nearest and began drying Jesus' feet with her long, flowing hair.

When Mary intruded on his party, Simon looked at her with scorn. He knew about Mary's former life, knew "what manner of woman" she was and knew her weakness and inability to resist manipulation. He knew because he had been the one who led her into sin. And now he continued to condemn her as a "sinner" and unworthy of a place, even as a servant, at his festive table. He had no compassion for this woman he had destroyed through his lust.

Disgusted by Mary's unabashed display of emotion, Simon reversed his opinion of his guest of honor. Sneering, he thought to himself, "This Man can't be the Prophet I assumed He was, for if He were, then He would know that the woman at His feet is a *sinner*"[8] (Luke 7:39). And no pious man would ever publicly acknowledge that he knew such a woman, or allow himself to be touched by her!

Mary ignored Simon. Her love for her Saviour shielded her from her uncle's excoriating glare.[9] She had been the recipient of the lavish outpouring of Jesus' love, and for this reason, from her heart flowed forgiveness toward the one who ruined her.

By forgiving her and setting her free that awful morning in the Temple, Jesus freed her from guilt, condemnation, and the fear of death that all her life had hounded her into the ground.[10]

He was fully conscious of how it felt to be innocent yet rejected, belittled, scorned, and ridiculed. "I am a worm, and no man; a reproach of men, and despised of the people. All they that see Me laugh Me to scorn: they shoot out the lip, they shake the head" (Psalm 22:6, 7). "Though He were a Son, yet learned He obedience by the things which He suffered; and being made perfect, He became the author of eternal salvation unto all them that obey Him." (Hebrews 5:8, 9).

Looking into the future, Jesus knew that some of the honorable men He was dining with that evening would be howling for His death on a cross in just six more days (John 12:1-3). He was to be "despised and rejected of men; a man of sorrows, and acquainted with grief." So disgusting would He appear that even those who knew Him best would hide their "faces from Him," and the people would "esteem Him not" (Isaiah 53:3). All this Jesus knew and anticipated for Himself.

Mary had followed her Saviour thus far, but she must take the final step in restoration. She must face and forgive the person who caused

---

8. The Greek word translated "sinner" means an especially wicked person who committed certain detestable vices and crimes.

9. This relationship is verified by reading the Bible texts pertaining to Mary, Martha, Lazarus, and Simon the leper. See Mark 1:40-45 where "Simon the leper" is mentioned; and Matthew 26:6-13; Mark 14:1-9; Luke 7:36-50; John 11:1, 2; John 12:1-3 for the identification of the other peoples' relationships.

10. Through His own experience in overcoming the propensities and inclinations of fallen flesh, Jesus knows how to "deliver them who through fear of death were all their lifetime subject to [the] bondage" of sin. (Hebrews 2:15).

her life of misery. Only by sincerely forgiving him, by exhibiting toward him an undeserved love, could she bring an end to her misery. Forgiving the one who hurt her so deeply brought Mary complete release from her past life of sin-induced depression, self-recrimination, resentment, and hate. *Agapé* "bears all things, hopes all things, endures all things, and never fails" (1 Corinthians 13:7).

When she rose from the floor at Jesus' feet, she was free of the "seventh devil" that had controlled her life. That "seventh devil" was her deep-seated hatred for Simon, who abused her, drove her from her home, and condemned her to a life of shame and hopelessness.

Still sitting at Simon's table, Jesus now sought to redeem the actual guilty party. As He often did, Jesus told a parable in an effort to teach Simon the simple but profound lesson that he was more in need of a Saviour than the poor wretched woman at His feet that Simon so quickly scorned and condemned. While still facing Mary, Jesus said, "Simon, let Me tell a short story," and Simon permitted Him (Luke 7:40). Looking at the woman still bowed at His feet, Jesus continued.

> There was a certain banker who had two persons owing him money. One owed him five hundred dollars, and the other owed him fifty dollars. When it was found that neither of them had any means to pay back their debt to him, this man, out of compassion, forgave both of them their debts.

Then, turning toward Simon, Jesus said, "Now, tell me, Simon, which of those two persons do you think loved that man the most?" (Luke 7:41, 42).

With the question, Jesus turned toward Simon with a penetrating look. Simon responded without much thought, giving the logical answer. "I suppose the one who had been forgiven the most would love most." Turning away from Simon to again face Mary, Jesus gently said: "You have answered correctly" (vs. 43).

> Now, look at this woman bowed at My feet. You invited me to this feast, Simon, but you didn't offer to give Me a basin of water so I could wash My tired and dirty feet, one of the most common courtesies for a host to perform for his guest. Yet, this woman has washed My feet with her tears and dried them with her beautiful long hair.

Again, Simon, you did not greet Me at the door with a simple kiss of fellowship on My cheeks, but this woman whom you scorn has not stopped kissing My dusty feet since she came into this room.

And last, Simon, you did not offer to anoint My head with common cooking oil, but this precious woman has poured out on My head and feet an entire bottle of the most expensive perfume anyone could purchase.

Therefore I say unto you, her sins which are many, are forgiven; for she loved much: but to whom little is forgiven, the same loves little (see Luke 7:44-47).

Even though Simon had received healing from his degrading affliction of leprosy, he stunted his spiritual growth by not fully yielding his sin-filled life to his Saviour, therefore he was only able to "love little." He, too, had freely received from Jesus not only healing from the leprosy but forgiveness for his sins. However, his self-righteous attitude made Simon unwilling to confess and repent of all his sins or forgive others. Therefore, he remained a self-centered, proud, and unloving Pharisee who found no fault in himself but many faults in everyone else.

As Mary was about to leave, another condemning voice was heard as Judas Iscariot spoke. He knew this woman because she had been in the crowds following Jesus. In his self-righteous mind, she was an idiot. Her waste of this expensive ointment was proof of her utter lack of good sense. Speaking to those closest to him, he murmured, "Why was not this ointment sold for three hundred pence, and given to the poor?"

Judas's comment was not spoken out of compassion for the poor but "because he was a thief and held the purse" of the disciples (John 12:5, 6). Early in Jesus' ministry, Judas had joined himself to Jesus' group of disciples and assumed the role of treasurer. But he only did so to enable him to embezzle from the purse which contained all the money donated to provide for the group's needs. Some of the money in that bag had come from Mary.

Soon afterward He was traveling from one town and village to another, preaching and telling the good news of the kingdom of God. The Twelve were with Him, and also some women who had been healed of evil spirits and sicknesses: Mary, called Magdalene (seven demons had come out of her); Joanna the wife of Chuza, Herod's steward; Susanna; and many others who were supporting them from their possessions."(Luke 8:1-3, HCSB).

Once again, Jesus rescued Mary from her tormentors. Looking Judas straight in the eye, the Son of God said: "Let her alone; why do you trouble her? She has done a most precious work for Me. She has done what she could." (John 12:7; Matthew 26:10). Before that assembly of self-righteous and indignant men, Jesus publicly expressed the most enthusiastic endorsement He ever uttered about anyone.

This that she has done will be talked about every where the Gospel is preached. Throughout the whole world, it will be known that this one person appreciated what I came to do for the human race (see Matthew 26:13).

All the men assembled around that table assumed Mary was the most unlikely candidate imaginable to receive such an honor as was expressed concerning her character. Jesus by-passed all the "righteous" Pharisees, law-keeping scribes, the church do-gooders, and even His hand-selected disciples, reaching down into the abysmal slime pit of shameful sin to pull out the one He knew truly appreciated Him. Though so far gone in sin that it was said of her that her mind was inhabited by "seven devils," nonetheless, Mary was the one person who grasped what Jesus' work was all about, and she fully appreciated it.

Six days after Simon's party, Jesus was arrested by some of the same men who exposed Mary in the Temple and demanded that she be stoned. These men hauled Jesus before an illegal tribunal, where they succeeded in getting Him condemned as a heretic and political malefactor and sentenced to the horrific death of a Roman cross.

When Mary witnessed the suffering and pain her Saviour endured, her heart seemed about to explode from the horribleness of the scene unfolding before her. Shamelessly standing at the foot of the cross, engulfed in pity and love for the suffering her Saviour was enduring, and feeling intense remorse for her sin that put Him there, Mary endeavored to fathom what was transpiring before her eyes.

This righteous, gentle, and kindly Man was being tortured to death for crimes He never committed. How was it possible for such an injustice to take place? Though repulsed by it all, she could not leave His side; she was compelled to stay in hopes that she could give Him some form of comfort, even if it were only her presence on that hill of pain and death. Mary remained by her Lord to the bitter end.

Jesus prayed aloud to His heavenly Father, and Mary heard His words clearly when He spoke. "Forgive them, Father, for they do not know what they are doing" (Luke 23:34). Before her complete conversion and release from her hatred for Simon, Mary would never have understood how Jesus could forgive those who were abusing Him so violently.

But now she more fully comprehended the depth of self-sacrificing love openly displayed before the world. She could look with compassion upon the men who surrounded Jesus and scoffed at His misery. They did not know what they were doing, and she prayed their hatred would be conquered and they would understand His love for them, and come to repentance.

And from her personal experience, she could comprehend in a small way some of what Jesus felt, so exposed and degraded, hanging there naked before the watching world. He had saved her and covered her nakedness with His own robe, but no one could save Jesus from His shame and abuse.

Learning from all she witnessed during those last weeks of Jesus' life, Mary was transformed, never returning to her former sinful and degraded life. How could she, when Jesus had suffered so much to save her from sin? Nothing was more precious to Mary than her Saviour; all earthly possessions and honor were less than worthless to her.

When she fully surrendered to Jesus, He freed Mary of her seventh devil—her deep-seated resentment against the man who had ruined her. She learned to forgive Simon because she had been the recipient of the lavish outpouring of Jesus' love. When Mary comprehended the fullness of the beautiful truth of God's redeeming love (agapé), she was able to turn her back forever on her old life of sin. Her world was turned upside down by God's unconditional love. Through this experience, she was able to forgive and pray for the man who had ruined her and condemned her to a degrading existence. She was then free; her conversion was complete; never again would she slide back down into the pit of sin.

Giving everything to Jesus is the key. Holding back nothing from Him, we can receive the full transforming power of His forgiveness into our life. We can forgive our abusers only after we appreciate how much we have been forgiven. As we receive, we are able to give to others freely (Matthew 6:12; 10:8b).

This is the lesson Mary learned, and it gave her a new life:—

Therefore if any man be in Christ, he is a new creature: old things are passed away; behold, all things are become new (2 Corinthians 5:17).

There is therefore now no condemnation to them which are in Christ Jesus, who walk not after the flesh, but after the Spirit (Romans 8:1).

And you, that were sometime alienated and enemies in your mind by wicked works, yet now hath He reconciled (Colossians 1:21).

Therefore being justified by faith, we have peace with God through our Lord Jesus Christ (Romans 5:1).

Overflowing with the love she received from Jesus, she found she could forgive others, even those who made her a miserable wreck. Nothing could steal the peace that flowed into her heart from the throne of grace. To everyone she met, she found it impossible to dam up its outflow. Mary's faith comprehended that "it is God which worketh in you both to will and to do of His good pleasure" (Philippians 2:13).

Christ paid an incomprehensible price through His life and death to save humanity, even dying the equivalent of the second death so that we don't have to die eternally. He "tasted death for every man" (Hebrews 2:9), including all who, in the past and will in the future, reject His gift of eternal life.[11] On the cross, Jesus experienced the black hopelessness of

---

11. "And I saw a great white throne, and Him that sat on it, from whose face the earth and the heaven fled away; and there was found no place for them. And I saw the dead, small and great, stand before God; and the books were opened: and another book was opened, which is the book of life: and the dead were judged out of those things which were written in the books, according to their works. And the sea gave up the dead which were in it; and death and hell delivered up the dead which were in them: and they were judged every man according to their works. And death and hell were cast into the lake of fire. This is the second death. And whosoever was not found written in the book of life was cast into the lake of fire" (Revelation 20:11-15).

total separation from the Father, the only source of life. For the eternally lost, separation from the Source of life will result in their annihilation in the lake of fire.

Jesus toiled among sinful humanity for three and a half years, telling everyone of His Father's love for the lost. At times, He must have felt discouraged and wondered if the whole project was hopeless, so few understood what He was saying. Even His closest associates did not comprehend the real meaning of His mission to earth; their self-centered motivations blocked their minds. Surely, before He must die, He ought to be able to find at least one person who could comprehend His message, one person of whom He could say, "Here, this one knows Me and appreciates Me. Here is the model Christian."

Before He died, Jesus *did* have a visible prototype of the 144,000 who will vindicate Him at the end of the world—the redeemed sinner, Mary Magdalene. And for this reason, "Wheresoever this gospel shall be preached throughout the whole world, this also that she hath done shall be spoken of for a memorial of her" (Mark 14:9).

Who is the model Christian? Not the self-righteous and pious leaders and members of the church who loudly proclaim their "faith" in God while standing in the marketplace and on street corners pounding their Bibles. Not the proud Pharisee who quibbles over every "jot and tittle" of the Law in hopes of finding merit through his punctiliousness. Not even the humble-appearing pew-warmer who nods his head in agreement when listening to sermons on righteousness by faith.

No! The "model Christian" is a humbled sinner who saw herself fully exposed for what she was—"miserable, poor, blind, and naked" (Revelation 3:17), and completely dependent upon her Saviour for everything. Her heart overflowed with love because she knew she had "been forgiven much" when she truly deserved nothing but eternal destruction.

From her deep appreciation for the cost of her salvation from sin and eternal death, Mary was willing to give everything to the One who came and surrendered His life to satisfy the just demands of the broken Law that condemned her. Only through appreciating the depths of this profound gift could she find freedom from sin in this life and gain eternal life through faith in His power.

Can this demonstration of profound faith be duplicated? Yes, in all who are willing to believe in Jesus' power over sin. He is able to "save to the uttermost" anyone who will believe the good news.

It follows, then, that His power to save those who come to God through Him is absolute, since He lives for ever to intercede for them (Hebrews 7:25, NJB).

Do you have "seven devils" controlling your life? Give your life to Jesus; "present your bodies a living sacrifice, holy, acceptable unto God, which is your reasonable service" (Romans 12:2). He is more than willing to lift you up from the pit of sin, cover you with His robe of righteousness, and place your feet on the solid Rock of salvation.

He brought me up also out of an horrible pit, out of the miry clay, and set my feet upon a Rock, and established my goings (Psalm 40:2)

O come, let us sing unto the LORD: let us make a joyful noise to the Rock of our salvation. Let us come before His presence with thanksgiving, and make a joyful noise unto Him with psalms. For the LORD is a great God, and a great King above all gods (Psalm 95:1-3).

Notes

27

A Wasted Life

He was found unconscious, lying along side the highway. When the ambulance arrived on the scene, he was semi-responsive, but would not communicate with anyone. He was evaluated and loaded for transport to the hospital. The assessment revealed that he was under serious chemical impairment.

Upon arrival in the emergency room, the man was talking, but would only say that he wanted to die. He stated that he was HIV and hepatitis positive; that he was an alcoholic and heavy illegal narcotics user. He begged for a lethal injection, so that he would never wake up again. This forty-five year old man had wasted his life with drugs and alcohol. He was a curse and a drain to welfare's resources. No matter how much money and time were spent on him in health care, as soon as he was released, he fell back into the same self-abusive lifestyle. He contributed nothing positive to society. By society's standards, he was indeed a "worthless piece of trash."

We define a "wasted life" by saying the person has not lived up to their potential, or that they are non-contributing to society's goals. They may have had great opportunities to be successful, but something happened and they fell by the wayside. The Bible is full of stories about people who may have thought they had wasted their lives.

Abraham was a wealthy man when he was living in Ur, which was one of the most advanced cities of the time, having running water and indoor plumbing in its finer houses. Abraham left it all behind to wander 100 years in a strange country, dwelling in a goatskin tent, never again owning any property except the grave he purchased.

Moses was raised by the princess of Egypt. She gave him the finest education available and trained him in advanced military tactics expecting that, one day, he would lead Egypt's army as defender of her realm. His adoptive mother planned for him to rule all Egypt as pharaoh. Then one day, he blew it by killing an Egyptian to save a Hebrew slave. He spent the rest of his life (eighty years) wandering in exile in the Sinai desert.

Joseph was the favored son of his father. He was destined to inherit a double portion of his father's goods and live the rest of his life in luxury. His own dreams seemed to foretell of his preeminence over the rest of his family. His youthful confidence was shattered when he found himself tied in line with a group of other captives headed for Egypt and a life of misery as a slave.

Young David was hunted like a wild beast by the king of Israel. Saul chased David all over Judah, trying to kill him. He was called from the sheepfold and anointed by the old prophet Samuel, was married to the king's daughter, and had been a faithful servant and honorable warrior for the king. Where had he gone wrong? It was easy for David to question if his life was being wasted away hiding in rocks and caves, and it was reasonable to think God had forsaken him. How could God be with him when his anointed king was against him?

As a prince of the Hebrews, Daniel would one day have been in a position of authority in the society in which he was raised. The invasion of a foreign nation quickly changed all that and he never saw his home again, living more than seventy years in exile.

At the beginning of their adventures, each of these men may have wondered if their lives had been wasted. They all had so much potential, so much they could contribute to the society in which they originally lived. In each case, their lives took a drastic turn, placing them where they never dreamed they would be.

There is another man in the Bible who once possessed unimaginable wealth. He had a vast, unconquerable army and ruled the greatest territory ever known. He had the admiration and love of everyone who knew Him. Incredibly, He laid it all down and became a slave (Philippians 2:6-8). This Man "thought it not robbery to be equal with God" because He was God. He controlled and upheld the entire universe through His infinite power, had the ability to create anything He wanted just by speaking a word, but He laid it all aside to become a finite human being.

Why would He do such a thing? Because of His love for fallen humanity. He looked down though the ages and saw the tragedy that was to come to His creation. He could see pitiful men lying along the highways of life, drunk with self-indulgence and enslaved to sin. From the foundation of the world, He pledged Himself to rectify the crime should Adam fall into sin. And as soon as there was sin, He stepped forward with the good news that He would take the penalty upon Himself, and Adam, and the whole human race that was "in his loins" yet unborn, would have a second chance.

In due time and in fulfillment of His covenant promise, He "made Himself of no reputation, and took upon Him the form of a servant [literally, a slave], and was made in the likeness of men." He took upon Himself the very same humanity that needed redeeming. He could have chosen to be born into a wealthy family, or even the family of the high priest. If He had thus been born, He would have had social position and authority. Some may think if He had assumed a higher status, He might have accomplished more with less suffering and pain to Himself. But instead, "He humbled Himself" and was born into the family of a poor carpenter in the despised little village of Nazareth. The most precious thing He possessed was His life.

This innocent Man worked for three and a half years trying to teach people about their need of a Saviour. He never tired of responding to their physical and emotional needs. He fed them, healed them of their diseases and afflictions, continually showing them mercy and, through it all, He demonstrated how much God loved them. In the end, some of these same people stood in the Roman courtyard and screamed, "Crucify Him, crucify Him!"

After 33 years of daily toil and self-sacrifice, He was accused of trying to overthrow the religious institutions and government of Israel. The penalty called for by His self-appointed prosecutors was death, and not just any death, but crucifixion—hung suspended between heaven and earth, indicating that no one wanted Him. It was believed that death on a tree would show He was rejected by God and man.

> And if a man have committed a sin worthy of death, and he
> be to be put to death, and thou hang him on a tree: his body
> shall not remain all night upon the tree, but thou shalt in any

282

wise bury him that day; for he that is hanged is accursed of God (Deuteronomy 21:22, 23).

Christ hath redeemed us from the curse of the law, being made a curse for us: for it is written, Cursed is every one that hangeth on a tree (Galatians 3:13).

For He hath made Him to be sin for us, who knew no sin; that we might be made the righteousness of God in Him (2 Corinthians 5:21).

Was all of His work for nothing? It seemed no one understood Him or comprehended His mission. No one appreciated what He had done for them. On the night of His unjustified arrest, even His most trusted friends turned and fled from His side, afraid of facing the same condemnation. After a rapid and illegal trial He was handed over to the Romans for execution.

As He hung on the cross, His depression was so great He felt like the One who sent Him had also abandoned Him. "I am poured out like water, and all My bones are out of joint: My heart is like wax; it is melted in the midst of My bowels. ... My God, My God, why hast Thou forsaken Me? why art Thou so far from helping Me?" (Psalm 22:14, 1; see also Matthew 27:46).

As He hung there, He may well have wondered if His life had been wasted. He had given His utmost, surrendered to every abuse without complaint, but there was no one who cared—"while we were yet sinners, Christ died for us" (Romans 5:8). No one seemed to appreciate what He was doing for them. "God was in Christ, reconciling the world unto Himself, not imputing their trespasses unto them" (2 Corinthians 5:19). Was His precious blood poured out for nothing? Would no one appreciate this wonderful gift of eternal life secured through His death?

He gave up the splendor and majesty of heaven to come to this sin darkened corner of His universe. After living a perfect life, in every word and deed showing how much He loved the rebellious people He came to save, He willingly laid down His life for His enemies (Romans 5:8-10). "Greater love hath no man than this!" (John 15:13). He freed all mankind from Satan's chains. "Because the LORD hath anointed Me to preach good tidings unto the meek; He hath sent Me to bind up the brokenhearted, to proclaim liberty to the captives, and the opening of the prison to them that are bound" (Isaiah 61:1; Luke 4:18).

By His death, Jesus Christ paid the full penalty for every sin that has been, or will ever be committed on this earth. Even for the sins of the man EMS picked up by the side of the highway in a drunken stupor. Though he had never heard the "good news" of salvation from sin, maybe never attended church in his life, that drunken man was already loved and forgiven by our merciful and loving God, the Creator of heaven and earth. The very fact that the drunkard *had* a life to abuse proved there was a God who wanted him saved from his wretched condition. "For God sent not His Son into the world to condemn the world; but that the world through Him might be saved" (John 3:17).

If God had already cast him off, he would have died before his night of crisis on the roadside. God patiently waits and calls us to Himself. He is not willing that any should be lost, but that all should come to repentance (2 Peter 3:9). Like all of us, the life the drunkard was abusing was probationary to see what he would do with the gift. How he managed his existence was proof of his appreciation for, or rejection of, what God gave him. No man, saint or sinner, takes his next breath, or eats his next meal but that he is blessed by the blood of Jesus poured out for him on Calvary.

As you look upon the cross and recognize the fact that your sins put Jesus there, you begin to comprehend the awfulness of the power of sin. It took the life of the Son of God to free you from its grip, and spare you from the fires of hell. But the wonderful good news is—you *have been freed!* Believe it and act like it! Walk out of your prison house into the sunshine of your Saviour's love. Believe the good news that you are the precious child and co-heir of the King of the Universe and learn to live the life you have been called to experience (see Revelation 3:21).

Can you begin to appreciate what you have been saved *from*? Not just a life of debauchery, but eternal destruction in the lake of fire. The Saviour stands with His arms outstretched barring the way to that horrible end. We must fight against the saving grace in order to be lost. Only by casting away our gift of salvation, and barging headlong over the top of our Saviour can we end up in hell.

The drunkard said he wanted to die, begged for us to let him die, but that night he was not ready to face the judgment. God gave him another chance to hear the good news and to believe he had already been reconciled to his loving Heavenly Father. God never ceases trying to save the lost (see Luke 15; 19:10; Matthew 18:11).

In the imagery of that famous hymn, the cross stands between you and the chasm "that gapes both deep and wide." The eternal grave is that deep chasm which brings total separation from the Source of life. But Christ is the bridge that saves us from its fearsome blackness.

When we are able to appreciate what we have been saved *from*, then we will joyfully turn from our wicked ways. By looking at the life of Jesus, we can see our path marked out clearly. He has gone on before us through every temptation Satan can possibly think to use against us. He tells us, "This is the way, walk ye in it" (Isaiah 30:21). If we will listen to His calling, follow Him only, we will be overcomers just as He was an overcomer.

> To him that overcometh will I grant to sit with Me in My throne, even as I also overcame, and am set down with My Father in His throne (Revelation 3:21).

Living a life of victory over sin is possible, and *not only possible but a certainty,* through faith in His power to save us from sin (Matthew 1:21).

> Wherefore seeing we also are compassed about with so great a cloud of witnesses, let us lay aside every weight, and the sin which doth so easily beset us, and let us run with patience the race that is set before us, looking unto Jesus the Author and Finisher of our faith; who for the joy that was set before Him endured the cross, despising the shame, and is set down at the right hand of the throne of God (Hebrews 12:1, 2).

If you are continuing to live a life of sinning and repenting, then sinning and repenting again, you are not living up to your high calling in Christ (Philippians 3:13, 14). Like the man found lying beside the highway, you are wasting your potential and the resources of heaven. You are crucifying the Son of God afresh with each continued sin.

> For it is impossible for those who were once enlightened, and have tasted of the heavenly gift, and were made partakers of the Holy Ghost, and have tasted the good word of God, and the powers of the world to come, if they shall fall away, to

renew them again unto repentance; seeing they crucify to themselves the Son of God afresh, and put Him to an open shame (Hebrews 6:4-6).

Jesus' righteous life and death were accomplished to redeem you *from* your sins and to give you power to be a Commandment-keeper through a heart-appreciation for the gift of salvation. If this is not a reality in your life, then His precious blood was wasted. This is the greatest crime of all eternity—to trample upon the crucified Redeemer in your determination to throw away your birthright possession in exchange for satisfying your temporary earthly lusts.

Beneath the Cross of Jesus

Elizabeth Cecilia Clephane
(1830-1869)

Beneath the cross of Jesus
　　I fain would [choose to] take my stand,
The shadow of a mighty Rock
　　Within a weary land;
A home within the wilderness,
　　A rest upon the way,
From the burning of the noontide heat,
　　And the burden of the day.

Oh, safe and happy shelter!
　　Oh, refuge tried and sweet!
Oh, trysting place where heaven's love
　　And heaven's justice meet.
As to the holy patriarch
　　That wondrous dream was given,
So is my Savior by the cross
　　A ladder up to heaven.

There lies beneath its shadow,
　　But on the farther side,
The darkness of an awful grave
　　That gapes both deep and wide;
And there between us stands the cross,
　　Two arms outstretched to save,
Like a watchman set to guard the way
　　From that eternal grave.

Upon that cross of Jesus
   Mine eye at times can see
The very dying form of One,
   Who suffered there for me;
And from my smitten heart, with tears,
   Two wonders I confess,
The wonders of His glorious love,
   And my own worthlessness.

I take, O cross, thy shadow
   For my abiding place;
I ask no other sunshine than
   The sunshine of His face;
Content to let the world go by,
   To know no gain nor loss,
My sinful self my only shame,
   My glory all the cross.